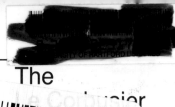

The  Corbusier

D0932647

Deborah Gans

Princeton
Architectural
Press

d by
ı Architectural Press
rch Way
n, NJ 08540
-2424
910413-23-1

d in England by
ıitectural Press Ltd
ı Anne's Gate
London SW1H 9BY England
(ISBN 0-85139-155-9)

To Bill

Printed and bound in the United States

The following correspondents provided
invaluable assistance in preparing these
entries:
Lynne Breslin (Tokyo and Moscow)
Mark Dulaney Glen (India)
Elizabeth Harris (Rio de Janiero)
James Wallace (India)
Diego Wainer (La Plata)

Special thanks to Ken Botnick, Ann
Urban, Melissa Dawson, Elizabeth
Short, and Thomas and Shari
Johnston-O'Neill

Library of Congress
Cataloging-in-Publication Data

Gans, Deborah,
  The Le Corbusier guide / Deborah Gans
      p.   cm.
  Includes index.
  Bibliography: p.
  ISBN 0-910413-23-1 (pbk.: alk. paper)
  1. Le Corbusier, 1887-1965—Catalogs.
2. Architecture, Modern—20th century—
Catalogs. I. Title.
NA1053.J4G25   1987   87-22301
720   é.92é4—dc19   CIP

Contents

Acknowledgements

I would like to thank Kevin Lippert, the publisher, for the opportunity to take on this project and his unflagging support throughout. Robert Wechsler, the editor, also deserves many thanks. Alan Plattus offered guidance as well as the fine introduction. Francesco Passanti provided valuable source material and also many insights. Carol Willis, Thomas Schumacher, Liz Moule, and Stefanos Polyzoides gave careful readings of the text. Bill Considine was a tireless sounding board and critic. Thanks as well as credit must go to the foreign correspondents (Lynne Breslin, Mark Dulaney Glen, Elizabeth Harris, James Wallace, and Diego Wainer) who answered questionnaires, wrote descriptions, edited texts, and provided photographs of Le Corbusier's far-flung work. M. Jean-Jacques Duval was a gracious guide to his own Manufacture Duval. Finally, I would like to thank the Fondation Le Corbusier and Madame Frey of the Bibliothèque de la Ville, La Chaux-de-Fonds for their kind cooperation and provision of materials from their archives.

Deborah Gans
New York City, August 1987

Using The Le Corbusier Guide

PARIS WILL BE THE FOCUS OF MOST ITINeraries devoted to the architecture of Le Corbusier. It is his adopted city and the place where he came of age. Within its environs is a representative sample of his built work. It contains most of his purist houses, and an early foray away from the crisp surfaces of Purism. It has his first buildings at a scale larger than the individual dwelling and an example of his post-World War II style. A traveller with limited time to spend might begin and end the journey here.

For those with more time or ambition, there is a logic and a pleasure in an itinerary that follows the outlines of Le Corbusier's life's work. Beginning at his birthplace in La Chaux-de-Fonds, Switzerland, the route continues to Paris, to the perimeter of France, and finally to the international scene. The one path not retraced is Le Corbusier's own youthful journeys, first to the monuments of Renaissance Italy, then to the capitals of Europe as an apprentice to architects of the Modern age. Escaping from the machine of the present, he traveled through the folk cultures of Eastern Europe and was drawn inexorably to the Acropolis. Although we do not follow this map, Le Corbusier recapitulates it for us many times in his own architecture. If, after Paris, our itinerary must for practical reasons mix chronology, that has some parallel in Le Corbusier's thinking. Even as he completed his Parisian villas in "the new spirit," he began to question his own categories of history, culture, and technology and to call up others simultaneously: atavistic folklore, the utopian future, the modern and the antique.

The pleasures of this itinerary include not only the buildings (which are generally farther away than one expects and no longer in the pristine condition shown in the *Œuvre Complète*) but also the process of getting from one to the next. On the "open road" it is a pleasure to remember Le Corbusier's own joy of self-propulsion in the automobile, efficiency and speed in the train, and the thrill of flight as he experienced it with the poet of flight, Antoine de Saint Exupéry.

All these mimetic pleasures are ancillary to the experience of the buildings *in situ* in their complex relationship to local landscape, national spirit, and international vision. There is a tension in Le Corbusier's architecture between the response to local character and the formulation of an international modern style. The villas of La-Chaux-de-Fonds illustrate the dominance of a national romantic impulse; the Parisian villas show the international modern one. But the houses of Paris contain (almost secretly) the tradition of the French *hôtel,* and the Swiss villas incorporate the lessons of Peter Behrens and Auguste Perret. Related to this is the play between *genius loci* and the formulation of general types. Extreme examples of the two points of view are the chapel at Ronchamp, born of its hillside, and the Unité d'habitation, fixed in all its aspects. Yet, as is typical in Le Corbusier's dualistic thinking, each view contains the other; the site of Ronchamp is not simply a single hillside, it expresses all mountain tops, which in turn refer to the one, archetypal mountain of the Acropolis. The Unité, while frozen out of place, postures toward distant vistas and evokes a ship at sea, to such an extent that it transforms each site into a particular one. Le Corbusier explains this phenomena : ". . . . the key to aesthetic emotion is a function of space. *Effect* of a work of art (architecture, statue, or painting) on its surroundings: waves, outcries, turmoil (the Parthenon on the Acropolis at Athens), lines spurting,

radiating out as if produced by an explosion: the surroundings: both immediate and more distant, are stirred and shaken, dominated or carressed by it. *Reaction* of the surroundings: the walls of a room and its dimensions, the city square . . . yes even the bare horizons of the plain and the twisted outlines of the mountains, the whole environment brings its weight to bear upon the place where there is a work of art, the expression of the will of man . . . ." The experience, and perhaps the unravelling, of the site's complexities, belong only to the traveler.

In visiting the sites there are a few simple guidelines. Many of the works are occupied houses where privacy should be respected. Where the buildings are public institutions, with listed phone numbers, it is advisable to call first to confirm visiting hours. Public transportation and its limitations are listed for each building, but always check local schedules. In the same township as the site, the residents (and tourist office) can generally supply directions to the "Le Corbusier" and are glad to do so.

Le Corbusier: A Dialectical Itinerary

Alan Plattus

LE CORBUSIER IS THE NAME OF a phenomenon: the *deus ex machina* of twentieth-century architecture, but of a peculiar kind. This machine both resolves and, just as frequently, provokes many of the crises in the extended plot of the drama of modern architecture. In the history and interpretation of that architecture it seems to be so often the case that all roads lead either to or from Le Corbusier—and occasionally both—that even at twenty years' remove one feels a certain sympathy with Alison Smithson's characterization of life in the shadow: *When you open a new volume of the Œuvre* Complète *you find that he has had all your best ideas already, has done what you were about to do next.*[1]

And while the twenty years in question are precisely those years since the death of the man, years of radical reconsideration of the architecture he produced and promoted, the phenomenon most certainly persists. It survives, and in fact continues to grow, not only through the ongoing work of archival excavation, the publication of which often provides an explicit reminder of what Smithson and her generation experienced, but also—and arguably most importantly—through our inevitable self-fashioning in terms of that phenomenon. That is to say, we construct ourselves as architects or, more generally and grandly, as Modern, post-Modern, or even anti-Modern individuals, partly by means of, or at least in relation to, the manifestations of the Corbusian phenomenon.

More than a few of the most significant works of architectural theory and criticism of the post-war years take as one of their central tasks (acknowledged or unacknowledged) the interpretation, analysis, and criticism of some aspect of Le Corbusier's performance.[2] It is not simply that Le Corbusier supplied several of the ubiquitous iconic images of modernity, but that those images, far from exhausting their significance at the iconic level, like so many of their neighbors in the textbooks, turned out to support, indeed required a critical and historiographic sophistication and inventiveness that has permanently altered the rules of the game and raised the stakes for architectural theory and practice. Even for the most general surveys, Le Corbusier's work, with its virtuoso manipulation of multiple and often apparently contradictory themes, and its unpredictable and seemingly inexhaustible transformations, has provided the most challenging—if rarely the limiting or climactic—case.

All of which is to say that Le Corbusier is unavoidable. This is nowhere more clear than when it is the evaluation of his controversial performance that is at issue, whether in revisionist historiography, which pivots on what it would eventually repress, or in anti-Modern polemics, which use the polemical tactics, and even the graphics, originally deployed by the object of their attack.[3] Those who would bury him most thoroughly end up confirming his fundamental contribution, albeit transposed into a new key. Furthermore, until very recently, and still more often than not, to challenge, reevaluate, or reject Modern architecture was to wrestle with its original Proteus in one or more of his many guises. This suggests that the effect of half a century of commentary, criticism, research, and design has not been so much to situate Le Corbusier as to dissolve him into the collective bloodstream of the century in a way done only to a few other characters become phenomena, such as Freud, Marx, and Picasso. Like them, Le Corbusier has become not so much an object for our discourse as part of the very ground upon which that discourse must be founded.

How impossible then, but how absolutely necessary, to pursue an unmediated encounter with the works that have inspired, provoked, and precipitated such a large part of our critical and monumental heritage. To undertake a Corbusian grand tour is simultaneously to reinforce and to discredit the mythology that the architect himself helped to construct. Going either as friend or foe, it is something of a pilgrimage and, like most pilgrimages, the quest for revelation, novelty, or experience will be a pretext for a more desperate mission: the confirmation of what we believe ourselves to have already found. And yet, the fundamental heterogeneity of the work seen *in situ* somehow never loses its capacity to surprise and to defy the various unifying fictions proposed and imposed willy-nilly by its critics.

In our age of single-issue architecture, when even the most faithful revivals of Le Corbusier's work engage one—or at most a very narrow band—of the issues that preoccupied the subject in question, his richly multivalent production may be somewhat difficult to digest, like some exotic dish or subtle wine which demands the attention of *all* our faculties and is an amalgam of an alarming range of flavors.[4] Indeed, most of the buildings, after an initial moment of recognition, tend to slip out of the focus provided by various versions of Corbusian orthodoxy: contrary to the neat classroom analyses, they are not really fully resolved compositions; contrary to the loudest criticism, they are not really disastrous in their contexts; and contrary to their author's polemics and touched-up photographic representations, they are not sleek, seamless, timeless *machines à habiter*. Insofar as all of these questions and many others ought to remain open and on the agenda, the role of an introduction is not to provide yet another definitive account, however clever or comprehensive. One should try, rather, to delineate the rudimentary outlines and mechanisms of the Corbusian discourse in its mediating role, not as an absolute structure or set of rules, as Le Corbusier himself unfortunately often suggested, but as a set of available interpretive strategies, as he actually deployed them.[5] These strategies may hold the specimen in focus long enough to allow one to begin to appreciate its spatial and thematic density, and then, like Wittgenstein's ladder, they may be thrown away.

To describe these strategies, as I will, in terms of the dialectical possibilities sponsored by apparently opposing, but complementary, categories, is to indulge in a habit of mind that is both Corbusian and structuralist. Many of the most powerful recent descriptions have exploited that convergence and have found in the ostensibly dualistic character of Le Corbusier's thought and work an interpretive principle of considerable utility.[6] We shall be tempted more than once to invoke an amended version of Clifford Geertz's observation that "societies, like lives [and, I would add, like architectural projects], contain their own interpretations. One has only to learn how to gain access to them."[7] In this instance it is, more often than not, the architect who indicates and even opens the door, supplying us with the means to decipher his code. And if that is increasingly the case with modern art in general, culminating perhaps with "conceptual art" in the sixties and its architectural correlatives, then Le Corbusier is exemplary and precocious in this respect. The *promenade architecturale* is only the most dramatic example of how, with didactic intent, he "teaches us to gain access" (here, quite literally) to the interpretive experience of architectural space. At the same time, this space is presented as the intersection—but not

necessarily the resolution—of the extraordinarily complex, although provisionally binary, formal, and iconographic thematics of his projects. And so it is not simply that we have constructed a fair amount of our culture from the *disjecta membra* of the Corbusian phenomenon, but that Le Corbusier remains, in our metatheoretical elaborations of his characteristic strategies, his own best critical guide.[8] The hermeneutic circle has become a figure eight; our problem is less one of closure and more one of maintaining some degree of equilibrium as we execute the loops and turns.

The more we seek to classify Le Corbusier, the more the phenomenon seems to deconstruct itself in a potentially infinite number of variations on whatever theme we have chosen. Le Corbusier's sketches abound with illustrations of the sort of analogical thinking that supports this conceptual promiscuity.[9] Seeing the buildings only intensifies their propensity to ramify, rather than stabilize, interpretation. Just as one cannot not know Le Corbusier, it is moderately difficult to know him. There is, after all, no *œuvre complète*, only the ongoing work of interpretation, to which Le Corbusier himself knowingly and brilliantly contributed and in which we are inextricably implicated.[10]

Romantic And Classical: Cultural Dialectics

Of all the possible dichotomies that might be useful for the characterization of Le Corbusier's attitude and his crucial position vis-à-vis the twentieth-century avant-gardes, the thoroughly slippery opposition of romantic and classical seems the most comprehensive. This is due not only to the ambiguities of those terms, but also to their emphasis on the extent to which Le Corbusier's work is embedded in, and cuts across, the principal strata of

Western culture since the Renaissance. As a card-carrying member of the Parisian avant-garde of the twenties and a corresponding member of any number of other European movements, he responded to, and exploited, a view of history, and of the role of the artist/intellectual in relation to history, that was grounded in the romantic challenge to the discourses of the Enlightenment. But as an unregenerate idealist and a believer in, if not always a practitioner of, the philosophical tradition of French rationalism that culminated in the Enlightenment, he balanced—or juggled—the relativism of that evolutionary view of history with the absolutist spirit of the classical tradition, especially in its French version. [11]

The specifically romantic roots of Le Corbusier's early reading and training in La Chaux-de-Fonds are now as well known as his alleged rejection—or, at least, suppression—of his juvenilia in later years. [12] What remained, and continued to be of fundamental significance for Corbusian polemics as for Modernism in general, was the essentially romantic search for a "style for the age" and the image of the modern artist as midwife to the birth of such a style. This was, after all, only a somewhat grander and internationalized version (in keeping with the universalizing tendencies romantically attributed to modern technology) of his youthful search for a Suisse-Romande regionalist style and his recurrent references to a Mediterranean style. All these formulations were predicated on the cultural relativism according to which romantic historiography assigned to each age, each country, or each climate its characteristic forms of expression. [13] For the often voluntarily (if artificially) deracinated intellectuals of the avant-garde it was the spirit of the age, the Zeitgeist, which tended to take precedence over other determinants. By the time Le Corbusier reached his intellectual maturity, evolutionary historicism had unequivocally identified the Zeitgeist with the progressive forces of modern science and technology.

The young Charles-Edouard Jeanneret had to adjust his evolutionary pace to that of the rapidly moving Zeitgeist—to bring himself up to speed. His early travels, especially those between 1907, when he first ventured forth from La Chaux-de-Fonds, and 1911, on the eve of his "Journey to the East," were designed to do precisely that. Travel was a quintessentially romantic form of experience. His version of the Grand Tour, reconfigured to point towards a progressive future rather than a moribund past, took him through the capitals of European Modernism—in a highly significant order: from Vienna to Paris to Berlin to Paris—and through the offices of several of the leading figures of what Henry-Russell Hitchcock so poignantly termed the New Tradition. The "constituent facts" of his life were, in effect, made to correspond to the constituent facts of the history of modern architecture and, in good Darwinian fashion, his ontogenesis as an architect could be seen to recapitulate the phylogenesis of Modernism itself. [14]

These facts, however, encompass more than the name-brand monuments of emergent Modernism. More importantly, they include the anonymous monuments and artifacts of industrial modernity. As Le Corbusier described it more than a decade later, it was as if he had already anticipated the limits of any critique based upon the Ruskinian romanticism of his youth as well as of any reform based solely in the decorative arts, with their romantic image of the artist/craftsman, such as he found persisting in the Wiener Werkstatte (already under prophetic attack by Adolf Loos). [15] His sense of the Zeitgeist pointed to the need to inform himself of—and architecture with—the exigencies and possibilities of both industrial production and new techniques of construction, and in both cases he was able to find and appropriate formulations in which the new futurist romanticism of the machine was sublimated in the fundamental idealism shared both by the romantic tradition as descended from Hegel and by its apparent opposite, the classical tradition as descended from Renaissance aesthetic theory.[16]

In the case of industrial production, Jeanneret learned from the practical example set by the Deutsche Werkbund during his employment with Peter Behrens in Berlin in 1910, but ultimately he absorbed the rationalism of Werkbund practice through the idealism of Herman Muthesius's theory of types. In the same way, the significance of his employment with Auguste Perret in Paris in 1908, far from being limited to his introduction to the practical discipline of reinforced concrete construction, was magnified through association with French structural rationalism and the French tradition of academic classicism.[17] The dialectical possibilities inherent in both lessons, but suppressed in the relatively stable compositions of both Behrens and Perret, adumbrate the creative tension implicit in the polemical juxtapositions that frame Le Corbusier's arguments in the twenties. The romantic search for a "style for the age" becomes identified with the classical transcendence of styles, just as the search for a "new architecture" turns out to have been a search for architecture *tout court*.

The operative term here remains "search," for in spite of what seems like an argument tending towards resolution, one continues to find the themes and figures associated with the romantic-classical polarity in a state of suspension. Apparently blended, or confused,

at one moment, at the next they have separated into distinct strands to be recombined in some new, equally unstable substance. In the seminal years of the magazine *l'Esprit Nouveau*, which Le Corbusier edited with the painter Amédée Ozenfant and the poet Paul Dermé from 1920 to 1925, the critical potential of these recombinant themes is especially apparent. Just as romantic ideas of progress and of the immanence of the new had been employed throughout the nineteenth century as cudgels to belabor the forces of academic reaction, so now, at a crucial juncture, classical ideas of reason, natural law, and the timeless and transcendent autonomy of the work of art were invoked to redirect the energies of the avant-garde. In the "age of mechanical reproduction," in the face of the socially and formally entropic forces unleashed by the modern metropolis, the classical could be genuinely radical. This is the point of the purist revision of Cubism put forward by Ozenfant and Le Corbusier in 1918, with its emphasis on the classical invariance of the *objet-type* set against and stabilizing the dynamic decompositions of Futurism and analytic Cubism.[18]

In Le Corbusier's four books of the mid-twenties, based on articles published in *l'Esprit Nouveau,* this dialectic is transmitted through the medium of photographs providing a comprehensive iconography of modernity, in both its rational and romantic aspects, and sketches illustrating the "lesson of Rome" and universal classicism. The source of most of the sketches that depict architecture as the "pure creation of the mind"—and a continuing source throughout his literary and architectural career—was Le Corbusier's "Journey to the East."[19] And if the first part of young Jeanneret's Grand Tour may be identified with his recapitulation, and projected extrapolation, of the inexorable progressive emergence of the spirit of the age, then the 1911 trip should be understood as a voyage of discovery, of the collection of evidence for the countervailing values associated with classicism. The distinction is articulated by Le Corbusier's depiction of northern Europe as clusters of sites associated with culture and industry— with the historical emergence of modern Western civilization—while eastern Europe and the Mediterranean are characterized by sites associated with culture and folklore, with the ahistorical continuity and universal "spirit of order" shared by both classicism and the vernacular.[20] Le Corbusier's own description of the significance of these travels is unequivocal:

I saw the grand and eternal monuments, glories of the human spirit.

Above all, I succumbed to the irresistible attraction of the Mediterranean....

The Turkey of Adrianople, Byzantium, of Santa Sophia or Salonica, the Persia of Bursa, the Parthenon, Pompeii, then the Colosseum. Architecture was revealed to me. Architecture is the magnificent play of forms under light. Architecture is the coherent construct of the mind. Architecture has nothing to do with decoration. Architecture is in the great buildings, the difficult and high-flown works bequeathed by time, but it is also in the smallest hovel, in an enclosure-wall, in everything sublime or modest which contains sufficient geometry to establish a mathematical relationship.[21]

And yet for all the apparent decisiveness of this comfortably neoplatonic theoretical position, once it is set in a context broader than the polemical moment in which it was posed, it, like the examples it cites, tends to blur around the edges. Even classicism, it turns out, is a plural and dialectically constructed

phenomenon. One can find abundant evidence, in the Corbusian scripture and in projects from throughout his career, to suggest that the "lesson of Rome" included not only the purity of the Phileban solids, but also the sophisticated strategies of elemental analysis and composition, and the subtle equilibration of primary and secondary axes learned from Rome, but by way of the hated Ecole des Beaux-Arts.[22] By the same token, the possibilities of Le Corbusier's ultimate architectural epiphany, his pilgrimage to the Acropolis, are hardly exhausted, or even limited, by his appreciation of the Parthenon as a classically static and absolute type. Rather, his comprehensive and highly romantic experience of the Acropolis from a moving point of view, as a dynamically balanced and even picturesque site plan, anticipates the way in which purist painting and architecture oscillate between the figurative identification of elemental forms and artifacts and the experience of those forms within a dynamic spatial matrix. The closure of a finite composition, and its status as a canonical type, is always balanced by the open-ended potential for addition, replication, or reinterpretation within the larger field of the landscape or the city.[23]

Thus, in spite of what has so often been claimed concerning modern architecture's relation to cultural traditions, one might argue that few critics before Le Corbusier had been capable or willing to find in a single monument the occasion for such a wide range of cultural and interpretive response. One thinks, perhaps, of Goethe, similarly suspended between classicism and romanticism, creating from the dialectical possibilities something that, in its context, can only be called modern. In any case, what seems certain is the sense that, since Le Corbusier, we cannot return to a simplistic view of any culture and its monuments, including our own.[24]

Individual And Collective: Utopian Dialectics

For an architect who seemed, at least to an overanxious public, to transform himself and modern architecture with breathtaking flights of invention, Le Corbusier returned with stubborn regularity to monuments, images, and themes experienced and recorded during his early travels. The only rival to the Acropolis in terms of persistence and fecundity was the Carthusian Monastery at Ema, near Florence, which he visited in September 1907 and again in 1911 on the return leg of his "Journey to the East." While there was considerable romantic potential in the siting and character of Ema— Jeanneret's guide to medieval Tuscany was Ruskin—the most profound impression was derived, even at that early date, not from the particularity of the building but from the generic typology of the Carthusian monastic plan. This scheme—highly standardized and reproducible, the product of a strict "rule"—was identified by Le Corbusier as a diagram for an ideal communal structure, balancing "individual freedom and collective organization."[25] This was, of course, a fairly romantic conception of a possible social order. Indeed, a certain level of naïveté about social and political program would remain a characteristic feature—often a shortcoming—of even Le Corbusier's most architecturally ambitious and sophisticated projects.

The idea and image of the collective community represented by Ema was overlaid with other preoccupations, such as the utopian socialist speculations of Charles Fourier and the proposals of his followers, to which Jeanneret was probably first introduced in 1908 when, soon after his visit to Italy, he paid a call on Tony Garnier in Lyon. Somewhat later, Le Corbusier's ongoing transformation of communal typology absorbed the modern image of the ocean liner, so powerfully evident in projects from the Cité de Refuge in Paris to the Marseille Unité. As for the individual cell of the Carthusian monk, he made this the ideal dwelling unit of the modern man. Transformed by way of the Maison Citrohan projects, with their appropriation of the vernacular Parisian studio-residence type in the interest of a prototype mass-production house, a thoroughly recognizable version of the monk's cell reemerges in the *immeuble-villa* unit. Both of these crucial prototypes were built only once as demonstration models, the Citrohan at the 1927 Weissenhof Exhibition in Stuttgart and the *immeuble-villa* as the Pavillon de l'Esprit Nouveau at the 1925 Exposition des Arts Décoratifs, but they served as the typological basis—or at least the kernel—not only for most of Le Corbusier's mass housing schemes, but for most of the major houses and villas of the twenties.[26] As such they usually carry with them the implication, and often the rules, of reproducibility in the service of an idea of the collective whole, as well as the explicit spatial image of the modern individual.

This individual turns out to be as complex as the spatial and typological transformations from which his image was constructed. Le Corbusier's "hero of modern life," the *homme-type* who will occupy the *maison-type* and ultimately be the citizen of the Contemporary or Radiant or whatever city, is an extraordinary composite: part monk, part steamship captain and airplane pilot; part worker, part intellectual captain of industry; part artist, part athlete. Le Corbusier has supplied us with many scenes from the life of this individual, and his brilliant typological and formal dialectics, for all that they tend to emphasize the opacity of the object and the autonomy of the language, are in the service of the explicit delineation of a modern lifestyle. As Colin Rowe has proposed, in discussing the formal logic of the free plan, "a building by Le Corbusier, whether successful or not, is always a statement about the world and never simply a statement about itself." [27] The fact that this individual turns out to be less like Everyman and more like Le Corbusier's carefully cultivated self-image, or like many of his clients in the twenties, no doubt has a great deal to do with the problems inherent in the collective entities he proposed.

Le Corbusier was, of course, devoted to the image of the modern man he created, replying, when asked to design a house for an architect: "Why an architect's house? My house is everyone's, anyone's house; it is the house of a gentleman living in our times." [28] Thus the double-height studio space, with its distinctive factory glazing expressing the principal volume, was asymmetrically central not only to houses actually built for artists, but to the house of the worker and the villa of the enlightened bourgeois. Le Corbusier proselytized at length for the virtues of this lifestyle. We still recognize that muscular gentleman of our times in the heroic figure of the Modulor Man, an updated version of the Renaissance Vitruvian Man through which, in characteristic Corbusian fashion, the universal validation of mathematics conspired with other arguments to guarantee his demonstration [Fig. 1].

The Modulor Man, emblazoned on the side of projects such as the Marseille Unité, became the sign of the limits of Le Corbusier's utopian vision. For whatever the legitimacy of neoplatonic anthropometrics, not everyone would find themselves comfortable on the rather spartan and procrustean bed made for the heroic artist-monk whose identity still provided the spatial theme, if no longer the poetics, of the Unité. Furthermore, the rule according to which these individuals were assembled to form a community was, more often than not, that of simple addition. Peter Serenyi's critique of the *immeuble-villas* project as "nothing but a collection of single figures put on top or next to one another by the architect," could be applied equally well to the bottle-rack principle of the Unité. [29] This is, in large measure, the disappointment of Le Corbusier's urban proposals as well: that the promised dialectics of individual and collective, public and private, city and landscape, chaos and order, which are identified as the proper concerns at the scale of urbanism, fail to rise above the level of mere additive or juxtapositional assertion. Indeed, diagrams that illustrate claims to "synthesize" individual liberty and collective forces "with the help of Ford" point to the roots, not to the solution, of the problem. Those occasions when the communal or urbanistic whole was more than the sum of its Corbusian

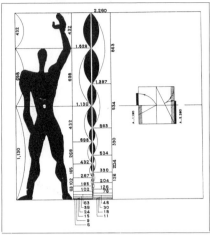

1 Modulor Man

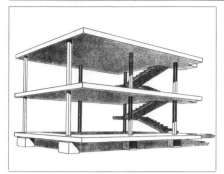

2 Maison Dom-ino

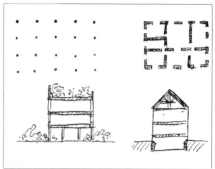

3 The Five Points

parts —Cité de Refuge, La Tourette, Plan Obus—were those instances when Le Corbusier relied, for his *modus operandi,* not on the rhetoric associated with Fordism, Taylorism, or Syndicalism, but on transformational and architectonic strategies grounded in his own discipline, of which he was a master.[30] The genuinely critical possibilities of Le Corbusier's "utopia of forms" emerges when he was being most the architect, and least the ideologue, of modern life, when he was not offering architecture as a surrogate for revolution.

Structure And Enclosure: Spatial Dialectics

As one places Le Corbusier "in context" and traces the historical genealogies of the themes and images he inherited, it is easy to lose sight of the fact that he, along with a handful of others, is responsible for the invention of a genuinely *modern* architectural space, within which those themes could be clearly and simultaneously articulated. That Le Corbusier could, as early as 1915, identify the generic conditions of modern construction, subject them to the typological analysis required by his classicizing predilections, and summarize the results in an icon so potent and concise that it would rival Laugier's primitive hut as a constructive emblem of its era, is remarkable

enough [Fig. 2].[31] He then proceeded, over the following decade, to extrapolate from the hypothesis of the Dom-ino not only a set of house types that challenged as they transformed the received domestic repertoire, but also and even more importantly, he formulated the basic rule structure of an architectural language predicated upon both modern construction and the revolutionary spatial experiments of cubist painting. The fact that, with respect to both space and technique, Le Corbusier's contribution turns out to have been fundamentally rhetorical, does not diminish the significance of the achievement announced in 1926 by the "five points of a new architecture" [Fig. 3].

Each of the Five Points, in their literal manifestations, can be traced in the history of the recent past. By the same token, each Point was connected with a particular, and sometimes idiosyncratic, polemic which might place it in apparent conflict with another Point considered in terms of its ancestry. For example, the free plan is derived in part from Auguste Perret's use of the concrete frame in his Rue Franklin building of 1903. However, the ribbon window, which was for Le Corbusier the index of a new mode of vision as well as the sign of his transgression of the expressive limits of trabeated construction, was a particular point of contention between him and

Perret.[32] The argument is not simply one of anthropomorphism (the vertical window) versus abstraction, but also of a taste for finite resolution versus the dialectical possibilities opened up by the confrontation of free plan *and* free facade. These possibilities may all be inherent in the free plan, but it was Le Corbusier's peculiar contribution, with a little help from his avant-garde contemporaries, to push all of them, simultaneously, to their logical limits.

From a logical point of view, the free plan has a certain priority among the Five Points, and it has, not surprisingly, been the principal target of recent attacks on the spatial characteristics of modern architecture and urbanism.[33] The positive critical value of the most perceptive of these attacks is their emphasis on the extent to which the free plan, like most of Le Corbusier's confrontations with architectural tradition, depends upon a conceptually symbiotic relationship with the spatial and representational systems constitutive of that tradition. Thus, the figural shaping, molding, or carving of space to create the particularized and defined "places" associated with traditional architecture and urbanism, is countered in the free plan by the displacement or interruption of continuous space by figural solids, the disposition of which serves to emphasize the freedom of modern architecture from the constraints of bearing-wall construction. As an important corollary, the fusion of a system of structural and spatial modulation and a representational vocabulary that was fundamental to the logic and meaning of the classical language is dissolved in the free plan, which juxtaposes an abstract and rational grid of columns against freely disposed objects that are figural in the sense of both formal gestalt and rhetorical expression.

Those objects represent function. They often conspicuously contain the functional equipment that in traditional planning had been hidden in the poché of walls that both support and enclose. Thus the real significance of the separation between structure and enclosure does not lie simply in the formal and architectonic play of column and wall, but in the delineation of the relationships between what they stand for: the generic and mathematically regular order of structure and the particular and contingent order of the program as articulated by enclosure and circulation. To say this is not by any means to succumb to the simplistic pragmatic arguments often advanced by Le Corbusier for the Five Points. We have already seen that when push came to shove, he was more interested in the typological and poetic potential of any architectural problem than in its merely utilitarian accommodation. Nevertheless, the famous Four Compositions, which summarize Le Corbusier's domestic work of the twenties, must be understood as the refinement of a proposed solution to the pragmatic and theoretical problem posed since the eighteenth century by the need to assimilate increasingly complex and specific programs generated from outside architecture per se to the properly architectural discourse of form [Fig. 4].

Le Corbusier's research into this problem must be understood in relation to two traditions. The first, the paradigm of which might be the French *hôtel,* particularly in its neoclassical phase, is articulated in a theoretical literature descended from Blondel, and treats the aforementioned problem as an exercise in hierarchical packing within the limits of a conventional, symmetrically massed and fenestrated building envelope.[34] The second is best represented by the picturesque English villa and is, at least with respect to the functional rationalization—as opposed to the earlier aesthetic formulation—of its massing, indebted to the arguments of Pugin, who ridiculed the absurdity of trying to stuff a modern program into the iconic container of a Greek temple. The first tradition was, of course, well known to Le Corbusier, who studied both the buildings and the texts in question, while the second passed to him via the German and Austrian appreciation of the free planning of English Arts and Crafts houses, which express rather than suppress the casual irregularities generated by the commodious distribution of the necessities of modern bourgeois life. Loos had already tried, in his *Raumplan,* to combine the two traditions, but it was Le Corbusier's development of the planning potential inherent in the Dom-ino that opened the way for a "transparently" modern—and dialectical—collage of the classically pure prism and the freely disposed functional "machinery" of programmatic rationality.[35] The Four Compositions illustrate the range of possible solutions, from the still *pittoresque* Maison La Roche to the literal wrapping of the L-shaped plan of La Roche in the taut skin of Villa Savoye.

Interestingly, the discretely revealing wrapper of the free facade that mediates the public presentation of Le Corbusier's domestic projects, holding the functional organs tightly if precariously in place, is generally absent in the large public projects of the twenties and thirties. In proposals such as the League of Nations and the Palace of the Soviets, and in buildings such as the Cité de Refuge, the Swiss Pavilion, and the Centrosoyus, Le Corbusier allowed the functionally expressive figural elements of the composition, representing, as they do, public functions such as assembly, to "appear" in public as part of a more or less monumental, classically grounded, and constructivist inspired ensemble. On closer inspection *in situ,* however, they too turn out to be

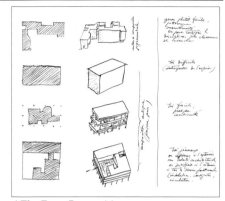

4 The Four Compositions

carefully framed purist compositions, circumscribed by the limits of their actual or implied sites. As in the case of the villas, the formal interest is less in the possibility of a fully resolved synthesis than in those areas of enormous spatial energy generated by the confrontation of systems operating according to apparently independent logics. Thus the autonomous centers of these systems compete with each other and with the abstract geometric center of the composition, as well as with the equally insistent perimeter of the entire field.

Center And Periphery: Dialectics of Place

It is tempting to assert that the thematics of center and periphery are crucial not only to the formal analysis of Le Corbusier's work, but to his entire world view and to the trajectory of his life as well. He provisionally identified Paris as the center of activity, but only, as we have seen, after comparison shopping among the available European cultural capitals. Even as early as the late twenties, Le Corbusier, with his keen and opportunistic sense of cultural geography, was looking beyond what had become his polycentric Mediterranean cultural homeland to the new worlds at the periphery of Western civilization: the Soviet Union, North

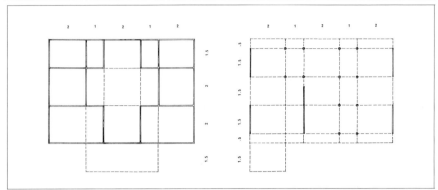

5 *Villa Foscari (left), Garches (right)*

and South America. Ultimately and ironically, the ideological and architectural burdens of a world capital in search of a site were laid upon the plains of the Punjab—upon a provincial capital at the edge of the Indian subcontinent—where grand ambitions are dissipated in a field so vast that the familiar, lively dialogue of center and periphery is lost altogether.

Again, the loss of genuinely dialectical energy seems characteristic of the problems of Le Corbusier's urban proposals. If the later urban schemes, from St-Dié to Chandigarh, chart the gradual dissolution of the field within which public centers and edges might meaningfully interact, then the early projects are perhaps all too clear about the schematically distinct formal and political identities of center and periphery. This is, as has often been noted, in dramatic contrast to the dynamics of virtually all of his individual projects, as Colin Rowe has pointed out in his influential comparison of Villa Stein at Garches and Palladio's Villa Foscari [Fig. 5]:
"*. . . at Garches central focus is consistently broken up, concentration at any one point is disintegrated, and the dismembered fragments of the center become a peripheral dispersion of inci-*

dent, a serial installation of interest around the extremeties of the plan." [36]

It is at this point—trapped in the layering between shallow and deep space, between center and edge, when one is inclined to think that such an account of Corbusian dialectics is mainly a product of staring until one goes cross-eyed at the two-dimensional images of plan and elevation as if they were cubist paintings—that Le Corbusier rescues us with an interpretive strategy based upon the actual experience of the space in which these suspicious events transpire. The *promenade architecturale* is more than a preferred route of circulation; it is a hermeneutics of modern space which provides a rigorously orchestrated tour through the themes, images, and ordering systems deployed in a given project.[37] Nor is it entirely far-fetched to suggest that one's own itinerary among the various outposts of the Corbusian phenomenon extends the interpretive role of the *promenade architecturale* at the level of the individual project—as it describes the powerful relationship between shifting centers and a periphery full of its own interest—while appealing to the model of experience preferred by Le Corbusier in his own heroically autodidactic quest for the elusive vantage point—whether at the center of things or outside, beyond the edge.

Nature And Culture: Dialectics of Myth

Vantage point, or point of view, is in fact a fundamental issue in all of Le Corbusier's work: built, drawn, painted, and written. In the case of the changing, but always crucial relationship proposed between an idea of nature and the constructed artifacts and monuments of human culture, point of view not only expresses but often determines the character of that relationship. Le Corbusier's projects frequently have as one of their principal purposes the provision of a specific view of nature as the means of establishing a dialogue with it. Indeed, the "captive" nature, or artificial terrain, provided by the roof garden or the *jardin suspendu,* has as much to do with the establishment of a foreground and a horizon against which a more or less distant nature is viewed, as it does with literally bringing a piece of nature into the building. This sense of nature framed by an architecture that carefully establishes its distance from it, is the dominant mode of the relationship in question in most of the Corbusian work associated with the "machine aesthetic." Whether nature is seen as subject to and manifesting the same rational principles of order as those which govern the world of man-made form, or whether it is seen as a benignly "wild," romantic other, the point of view tends to fix the limits of the relationship.

It is, however, nothing more or less than a changing point of view that eventually threatens to dissolve the distance between nature and culture, recalling Le Corbusier to his organicist roots in the *fin-de-siècle* culture of Art Nouveau, but now, on the far side of the Modern Movement, at a very different scale of concern than that of the ornamental motif. One should not underestimate the role of Le Corbusier's painting in the reformulation of his vocabulary with respect to the natural world. From the mid-twenties on, the *nature morte* of machine-made, Purist *objets-types* is joined, often within the same frame, by organic *objets à réaction poétique* with distinctly surrealist overtones. Eventually, both are subordinated to the ultimate organic form: the curve of the female body. But the fact remains that it was the neoclassical and Purist painter's framed view of a nature, against which the *objets-types* of classical or machine-age culture are set in sharp relief, that was challenged and opened up by what might be characterized as the aviator's view of nature. Le Corbusier's enthusiasm for flight privileged the aerial view as a supplement to earthbound modes of vision. From increasingly Olympian heights, he perceived the large-scale unity of nature and culture in which architecture can become a feature of the landscape and part of—rather than either master of or subject to—natural processes.

In the Contemporary City, nature, in the form of an English garden, is meant to be looked at as it flows continuously beneath the cruciform skyscrapers, which provide a rational and artificial modulation of, and counterpoint to, a tame landscape [Fig. 6]. Myth remains on the side of the machine, rushing through city and landscape, in its headlong flight into the future. In the Radiant City, however, the city has become another nature, designed to accord with natural processes and to allow for organic growth. In fact, the city has become quite literally a body, and the text that accompanies the project, while it still preserves the machine analogies of *l'Esprit Nouveau,* now abounds with biological analogies, in support of a plan with a head, heart, lungs, and guts. Unfortunately, it also articulates a rigid

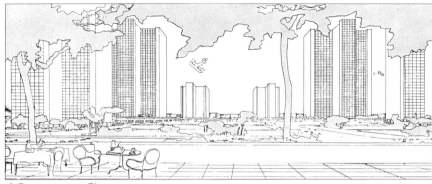

6 Contemporary City

scheme of zoning which, oversimplified in the Athens Charter of 1933, was to have disastrous consequences for post-war urbanism.

Increasingly, however, the poetics of nature and culture tend to overwhelm rational, pragmatic argument; nature, still viewed "scientifically" in the Radiant City, usurps the mythic role of the machine as a metaphor for architecture. In the Plan Obus for Algiers (1930), the familiar themes of a road-based, linear city, continuous terrace housing, separation of traffic, and zoning of functions, are fused and transcended in a breath-taking image of the city as topography: a man-made nature that mediates and transforms the *objets trouvées* of the traditional urban culture of the Casbah and the existing landscape of the sea and mountains as it gathers into itself the functions of both.[38] After the epic failure of his plans for Algiers, Le Corbusier seems to have invested less mythic energy in urbanism, while the responsibility for the elaboration of such themes as the engagement and embodiment of the landscape fell to individual projects such as Ronchamp, which has so frequently been taken as the sign of the abandonment of the Apollonian dialectics of high Modernism.

Ancient And Modern: Historical Dialectics

There have been any number of descriptions, and almost as many explanations, of the dramatic sea-change that was increasingly manifest in Le Corbusier's work from around 1930 on.[39] While it is important to understand the significance of these apparently new developments, one should also recognize that their importance tends to be exaggerated, especially by historians fixated on a linear account of something called a career, which must preserve a semblance of unity.[40] The "rupture" that announced the second style is also, perhaps inevitably, overrated by a younger generation of architects, such as the British Brutalists, for whom the developments became the basis, rather than the ongoing exploratory expression, of their own careers.[41] From our point of view, it should be suggested, first of all, that the "new" themes and preoccupations had been present all along either in latent form or in the context of different dialectical relationships—as in the case of the relationship between nature and culture discussed above—and, secondly, that the "old" themes were hardly relegated to some scrap heap of youthful folly, but continued to be explored and elaborated, in some cases quite persistently, alongside later lines of investigation.

Kenneth Frampton's apt characterization of the post-1930 Corbusian project as "the monumentalization of the vernacular" should alert us right away. After all, Le Corbusier had already recognized, in the course of his "Journey to the East," that the vernacular, like classicism in its astylistic interpretation, was inherently monumental and, in its abstract typological refinement, not unlike the products of industrial civilization. Indeed, in going beyond the abstract appreciation of the vernacular to an interest in the tactile and expressive possibilities of its materials and techniques, Le Corbusier, rather than rejecting modernity, may have been opening up another area of rapprochement between the timelessness of the vernacular and the evolutionary perfection of the new. In projects like the Maison de Weekend and the Maisons Jaoul, vernacular materials and construction are used side-by-side with reinforced concrete and other industrial materials in a way that suggests they are not fundamentally incompatible, especially to Le Corbusier's *bricoleur* sensibility. Just as Le Corbusier brought a classicizing sensibility to the romantic experience of the *Zeitgeist*, and a romantic sensiblity to the experience of the classical order of universal geometries and monuments, so he primitivized concrete and modernized the vernacular.

If anything is lost in this process, it is the sense of historical development. The more we are convinced by Le Corbusier's dialectics of primitivism and modernity, the more history tends to collapse in upon itself as the dialogue between ancient and modern becomes desperately direct, dispensing with the intervening evolutionary steps. Those themes and images that tend to recur with the greatest frequency in the late projects are, in fact, those that emphasize the face-to-face confrontation of ancient and modern man. Such an image is that of the tent, which can emerge directly from the troglodytic vault, as in the garden pavilion of the Maison de Weekend, or from the heavy concrete shell of Ronchamp, or from the light metal parasol of the Maison de l'Homme (Heidi Weber Pavilion). It can be used serially and in utilitarian constructions, or it may float as an isolated sign atop larger, more complex structures.[42] The tent is clearly related to Le Corbusier's abiding interest in primitive huts and other *ur*-architectures, but in certain respects it is both more primitive and more modern. The "primitive temple" that Le Corbusier illustrates in *Vers une architecture,* as a study in regulating lines, is actually the movable tabernacle of the Exodus—a demountable architecture from before the first permanent settlement—but it is already monumental. As Le Corbusier comments: "There is no such thing as primitive man; there are primitive resources. The idea is constant, in full sway from the beginning."[43]

Like the biblical Hebrews, modern man, in his variegated tents, is nomadic, wandering from place to place in search of law—but also of experience.

NOTES

[1] Alison Smithson, quoted in Reyner Banham, "The Last Formgiver," *The Architectural Review* (August 1966).

[2] See Colin Rowe's seminal essay, "The Mathematics of the Ideal Villa," *The Architectural Review* (March 1947).

[3] In the revisionist category, see Alan Greenberg, "Lutyens' Architecture Restudied," *Perspecta* 12 (1969), which helped initiate the spectacular reconstruction of Lutyens, in part by comparing his work to that of Le Corbusier and Wright.

[4] Some projects designed by practitioners of *le style Corbu* provide analytic demonstrations that have significantly increased the understanding and availability of the originals. See, for example, the texts and projects of *Five Architects* (New York, 1972).

[5] The best comprehensive monographic treatment remains Stanislaus von Moos, *Le Corbusier: Elements of a Synthesis* (Cambridge, 1979; W. Germany, 1968).

[6] The best recent dialectical treatments of Corbusian dialectics are two essays by Alan Colquhoun, "Architecture and Engineering: Le Corbusier and the Paradox of Reason," *Modulus* (1980-81), and "The Significance of Le Corbusier," *The Le Corbusier Archive, Vol. 1* (New York and Paris, 1982).

[7] Clifford Geertz, "Deep Play: Notes on the Balinese Cockfight," in *The Interpretation of Cultures* (New York, 1973), 453.

[8] For a treatment that allows Le Corbusier to function as the critic of his own urbanistic oversimplifications, see Manfredo Tafuri, "*Machine et mémoire*: The City in the Work of Le Corbusier," *The Le Corbusier Archive, Vol. 10*.

[9] On Le Corbusier's analogical thinking, see Alexander Tzonis and Liane Lefaivre, "Syncretism and the Critical Outlook in Le Corbusier's Work," *Architectural Design* 55 (1985).

[10] An itinerary through the primary and secondary sources starts with a look through the 32 volumes of *The Le Corbusier Archive* and the 4 volumes of the *Le Corbusier Sketchbooks*, recently published by the Architectural History Foundation. A visit to the Fondation Le Corbusier in Paris will provide some idea of the scope of the scholarly enterprise underway.

[11] This is essentially the interpretation proposed by Colquhoun in "The Significance of Le Corbusier."

[12] For Le Corbusier-Jeanneret in his larval stage, see Paul Turner, *The Education of Le Corbusier: A Study of the Development of Le Corbusier's Thought, 1900-1920* (New York: Garland, 1977), and Mary Patricia May Sekler, *The Early Drawings of Charles Edouard Jeanneret 1902-1908* (New York: Garland, 1977). Both authors also have important essays in Russell Walden, ed., *The Open Hand: Essays on Le Corbusier,* which contribute to the discussion of Le Corbusier's romanticism.

[13] For the role of historicism in Le Corbusier's thought, see Alan Colquhoun, "Three Kinds of Historicism," *Oppositions* 26 (Spring 1984), the Introduction to his *Essays in Architectural Criticism: Modern Architecture and Historical Change* (Cambridge, Mass., 1981), and the two essays cited above.

[14] On Jeanneret's early travels, see the studies by Paul Turner cited above and Le Corbusier's own accounts in his first book, a study commisioned by his school in La Chaux-de-Fonds, *Etude sur le mouvement d'art décoratif en Allemagne,* in Le Corbusier, *The Decorative Art of Today,* trans. James Dummet (Cambridge, Mass., 1987; translation of *L'Art décoratif d'aujourd'hui*); and in the Introduction to Vol. 1 of the *Œuvre Complète*.

[15] See the Loosian arguments in *The Decorative Art of Today.*

[16] For a more detailed discussion of the chronology and arguments relevant to Le Corbusier's development and use of the positions schematically outlined here, see Colquhoun, "Architecture and Engineering"; and Reyner Banham, *Theory and Design in the First Machine Age* (London, 1960), chaps. 15-17.

[17] On the interaction of these two traditions, see Robin Middleton, "The Abbé de Cordemoy and the Graeco Gothic Ideal," *Journal of the Warburg and Courtauld Institutes* XXV and XXVI (1962-1963).

[18] See Banham, *Theory and Design*, chap. 15; and Christopher Green, *Léger and the Avant-Garde* (New Haven, 1976).

[19] On the "Journey to the East," see Le Corbusier's account in *The Decorative Art of Today* (1925), and the posthumously published *Le Voyage d'Orient* (1966); Ivan Zaknic, "Of Le Corbusier's Eastern Journey," *Oppositions* 18 (Fall 1979); and Giuliano Gresleri and Italo Zannier, *Viaggio in Oriente, Gli Inediti di Charles Edouard Jeanneret* (Venice, 1983).

[20] Peter Serenyi has included Mediterranean and Northern in an interesting list of Corbusian polarities, in "Timeless But of Its Time: Le Corbusier's Architecture in India," *The Le Corbusier Archive, Vol. 26.*

[21] Le Corbusier, *The Decorative Art of Today,* 206-207.

[22] On Le Corbusier and the academic tradition of classical composition, see Banham, *Theory and Design,* chaps. 1-3; and with particular reference to

Rome, Kurt Forster, "Antiquity and Modernity in the La Roche-Jeanneret Houses of 1923," *Oppositions* 15/16 (Winter/Spring 1979).

[23]See Richard A. Etlin, "A Paradoxical Avant-Garde: Le Corbusier's Villas of the 1920's," *The Architectural Review* CLXXXI, no. 1079 (January 1987), and "Le Corbusier, Choisy, and French Hellenism: The Search for a New Architecture," *The Art Bulletin* LXIX, no. 2 (June 1987).

[24]On Le Corbusier's revision of the canon with respect to the Acropolis, see Stanford Anderson, "Critical Conventionalism in Architecture," *Assemblage* 1 (October 1986): 21.

[25]Le Corbusier, *The Modulor* (Cambridge, Mass., 1954), 28. See also Peter Serenyi, "Le Corbusier, Fourier, and the Monastery at Ema," *The Art Bulletin* XLIX (1967).

[26]For an analysis of the Villa Stein as "a set of overlapping Maisons Citrohans," see Thomas Schumacher, "Deep Space, Shallow Space," *The Architectural Review* CLXXXI, no. 1079 (January 1987): 37.

[27]Colin Rowe, "Neo-'Classicism' and Modern Architecture II," *Oppositions* 1 (1973): 25. For a critique of this position, see Peter Eisenman, "Aspects of Modernism: Maison Dom-ino and the Self-Referential Sign," *Oppositions* 15/16 (Winter/Spring 1979).

[28]Quoted in von Moos, *Le Corbusier*, 53.

[29]Serenyi, "Le Corbusier, Fourier," 278.

[30]For these isms in Le Corbusier's thought and practice, and the general problem of his politics, see Mary McLeod, "Le Corbusier and Algiers," *Oppositions* 19/20 (Winter/Spring 1980).

[31]On the development of the Dom-ino, see Eleanor Gregh, "The Dom- ino Idea," *Oppositions* 15/16 (Winter/Spring 1979), and, in the same issue, Peter Eisenman, "Aspects of Modernism," and Barry Maitland, "The Grid." See also Paul Turner, "Romanticism, Rationalism."

[32]This interesting debate is presented in Bruno Reichlin, "The Pros and Cons of the Horizontal Window: The Perret-Le Corbusier Controversy," *Daidalos* 13 (September 1984).

[33]See, for example, Steven Peterson, "Space and Anti-Space," *The Harvard Architectural Review* 1 (Spring 1980).

[34]See Michael Dennis, *Court & Garden: From the French Hôtel to the City of Modern Architecture* (Cambridge, Mass., 1986), chap. 6.

[35]The persistence of this dialectical theme in Le Corbusier's work is demonstrated in Alan Colquhoun, "Formal and Functional Interactions: A Study of Two Late Buildings by Le Corbusier," *Architectural Design* 36 (May 1966).

[36]Colin Rowe, "Mathematics of the Ideal Villa," 12.

[37]On the romantic roots of the *promenade* and its development in nineteenth-century theory and historiography, see the two articles by Richard Etlin cited above.

[38]The critical significance of Le Corbusier's projects for Algiers has been increasinlgy appreciated in recent years; see Manfredo Tafuri, *Architecture and Utopia* (Cambridge, Mass., 1976; original, Italian ed., 1973), ch. 6; Tafuri, "*Machine et mémoire*"; and Mary McLeod, "Le Corbusier and Algiers."

[39] See Kenneth Frampton, "Le Corbusier and the Monumentalization of the Vernacular, 1930-1960," in *Modern Architecture: A Critical History* (London, 1980).

[40]This sort of critique of the ideology of the career is associated with recent post-structuralist criticism, but for an interesting and important architectural parallel, see Robert Venturi, "Diversity, Relevance and Representation in Historicism, or *Plus ça change . . . ,*" *Architectural Record* (June 1982).

[41]See James Stirling, "Garches to Jaoul: Le Corbusier as Domestic Architect in 1927 and 1953," *The Architectural Review* CXVIII (September 1955).

[42]On Le Corbusier's roof forms, see von Moos, *Le Corbusier*, 95-98.

[43]*Towards a New Architecture*, trans. Frederick Etchells (London, 1927; translation of *Vers une architecture*), 66.

Le Corbusier: A Biographical Note

LE CORBUSIER WAS BORN
Charles Edouard Jeanneret on October
6, 1887, in La Chaux-de-Fonds, Switzerland. He was the second son of
Edouard Jeanneret, a dial painter in the
town's renowned watch industry, and
Madame Jeanneret-Perret, a musician
and piano teacher. The family proudly
traced its ancestry to the Cathars, who
fled to the Jura Mountains during the
Albigensian Wars of the twelfth century, and the French Huguenots, who
migrated to Switzerland following the
Edict of Nantes (1598). La Chaux-de-
Fonds' tradition of offering refuge includes both Rousseau and Bakunin.

His family's Calvinism, love of the
arts, and enthusiasm for the Jura Mountains, were all formative influences on
the young Le Corbusier; Charles
L'Eplattenier, a teacher at the local art
school, dominated his education.
L'Eplattenier, whom Le Corbusier
called "My Master," combined into a
National Romanticism many strains of
late-nineteenth-century thought, from
Ruskin to Hermann Muthesius. He involved his students in his search for a
new kind of ornament expressive of the
Jura landscape and able to sustain the
local craft industry. Apprenticed at thirteen to a watch engraver, Le Corbusier
abandoned watchmaking in part because of his delicate eyesight, and continued his studies in art and decoration,
with the intention of becoming a
painter. L'Eplattenier insisted that the
young man also study architecture and
arranged for his first commissions.

After completing his first house, Villa Fallet, in 1907, Le Corbusier set out on a series of travels that lasted until 1912, when he returned to La Chaux-de-Fonds to teach beside L'Eplattenier and to begin his own practice. These travels took him first to Italy, then to Vienna, Munich, and Paris. They included a period of apprenticeship to architects with philosophies at odds with L'Eplattenier's teachings, most significantly the structural rationalism of Auguste Perret, a father of reinforced concrete construction, and the Werkbund perspective of Peter Behrens. They concluded with a "Journey to the East" by way of the Balkans and Eastern Europe, culminating in a visit to the Acropolis.

Back in Switzerland, Le Corbusier designed a series of villas and embarked on a more theoretical study for a structural frame of reinforced concrete he called the Maison Dom-ino (a pun on the Latin word for house, *domus*, and on the playing pieces from the game). He envisaged it as an affordable, prefabricated system for the construction of new housing in the wake of World War I's destruction. Developed with the help of Max Dubois and Perret, the system differed from the then standard Hennibique frame in its idealization of floors as flat slabs without exposed beams. Its columns were perfectly straight posts without capitals, set in from the edge of the slab. This system freed both exterior and interior walls from all structural constraints.

At the end of the war Le Corbusier moved to Paris. There he worked on concrete structures under government contracts and ran a small brick manufacture, but he dedicated most of his efforts to the more influential, and lucrative, discipline of painting. First in a book entitled *Après le cubisme,* and subsequently in an art show at Galerie Thomas, he and Améedée Ozenfant began a movement called Purism, which called for the restoration of the integrity of the object in art. As their style developed, it drew closer to Synthetic Cubism's structure of overlapping planes, but retained a distinct attitude toward the mass-produced "tools" of industrial culture, from laboratory flasks to café chairs, which they called *objets-types.*

The emerging spirit of industrialized culture in all its aspects became the theme of the journal *l'Esprit Nouveau,* founded in 1919 by Le Corbusier, Ozenfant, and the poet Paul Dermée, and published until 1925. Le Corbusier collected essays from the journal in the book *Vers une architecture.* In the essays Le Corbusier proposed an architecture that would satisfy both the demands of industry and the timeless concerns of architectural form as defined in antiquity. His proposals included his first city plan, the Contemporary City. He also proposed two housing types, which were the basis for much of his architecture throughout his iife: the vaulted Maison Monol and the Maison Citrohan, a "shoebox" volume with a double-height salon (the salon was modeled on, among other sources, the bistro Legendre, rue Godot-de-Mauroy, where the architect lunched daily).

In order to distinguish their work as painters from their work as critics and theorists, Ozenfant and Jeanneret took pseudonyms. Ozenfant adopted his mother's family name, Saugnier. Jeanneret took the name of a cousin, Lecorbezier. Separating the Le out, the name sounded suitably like an *objet-type*; it also suggested the architect's profile, which resembled a crow's (*corbeau*). Le Corbusier's self-invention continued with the encouragement of the elder, more self-assured Ozenfant. Adopting a costume of bow-tie, starched collar, and bowler hat, and a rhetorical literary style combining discipline, enthùsiasm, ironic wit, and moral outrage, he became what he considered to be the perfect standard for the times.

Ozenfant and Le Corbusier parted in 1924, with much acrimony over who deserved credit for their joint efforts. In 1922, Le Corbusier formed an architectural partnership with his cousin Pierre Jeanneret; Jeanneret was to play the quieter role, developing plans and details and dealing with clients. They set up an office in the corridor of a former Jesuit monastery at 35, rue de Sèvres. It remained Le Corbusier's office for the rest of his life.

With mother and brother Albert Jeanneret

During the 1920s Le Corbusier realized his first mature architecture in a series of villas for artists, their patrons, and a few industrialists. The absence of a state program for public housing in France contributed to Le Corbusier's inability to realize his ideas on a larger scale and for a more varied clientele. The one exception was a complex of workers' housing in Pessac, built for an industrialist. For the 1927 Deutsches Werkbund exhibition in Stuttgart, Le Corbusier built the Citrohan prototype in a rather pure form. In a booklet for the exhibition he codified his principles as the Five Points of Modern Architecture, derived from the potentials of the concrete frame. They are the roof garden on top of the house, the consequence of a flat roof; the pilotis, or columns, that raise the house above the ground; the free plan, unencumbered by structural partitions; the similarly free facade; and the strip (continuous, horizontal) windows, which provide maximum illumination to the house. Eventually, he categorized the spatial organizations derived from these points as the Four Compositions, illustrating each one with a house built during the 1920s.

By the end of the decade, Le Corbusier and Jeanneret had achieved a status and skill that seemed about to earn them their first public commission: the League of Nations (1927). Their eventual elimination (ostensibly for the illegal use of China ink) after winning numerous rounds of the competition was seen as the triumph in the architectural world of academicism over the modern. It instigated the formation of CIAM (Congrès Internationaux d'Architecture Moderne), whose charter members included S. Giedion, W. Gropius, and Le Corbusier, and whose principal areas of concern were architecture's relation to economic and political spheres. Their 1933 meeting on a boat headed to the Acropolis produced the Athens Charter, a document on urbanism published by Le Corbusier in 1943; it served as bible for much city planning in the following two decades. Eventually, Le Corbusier and Jeanneret did obtain two large public commissions: the Soviet Centrosoyus (begun in 1929) and the Cité de Refuge for the Salvation Army (1930).

Even as Le Corbusier completed the ultimate purist house, Villa Savoye (1931), and implemented his first glass curtain walls at the Centrosoyus and Cité de Refuge, a shift in the direction of his work and life became apparent. The female figure and other natural forms emerged in his painting as *objets à réaction poétique* (objects of poetic reaction) to be distinguished from the *objets-types* of his earlier compositions. Natural materials in a rough state appeared in his rural dwellings, then, coupled with more sophisticated technology, in his urban works, such as the Pavillon Suisse (1932). This revived interest in the natural, from a new perspective, was a consequence of his experience with the real limits of modern construction technology and also of a set of inspiring travels to tropical landscapes: Brazil (1928) and Algiers (1929). His flights with Antoine de Saint-Exupéry over the coast of Rio instigated a series of plans for sinuous viaduct cities. Similarly, his journey to the Soviet Union was in part responsible for the revision of his first Contemporary City as the Radiant City (1931). Besides this second bout of travel, the event most significant to Le Corbusier's life in this period was his marriage in 1930 to Yvonne Gallis, a model and couturier from Monaco. He subsequently adopted French citizenship.

With the worsening economic situation throughout Europe and the strenuous opposition to his ideas evident in some circles, Le Corbusier failed to secure any further large commissions and turned increasingly to urban planning and writing. He produced plans for almost every city in which he lectured or built: Geneva, Antwerp, and Stockholm in 1933, Hellocourt, Zlin, and Paris in 1935. This ongoing investigation of urban form produced plans for a "linear city." In 1935, at the invitation of the Museum of Modern Art, he traveled to the United States for the first time. America, especially New York City, aroused both his enthusiasm and his disgust. There the skyscraper existed, but without the guidance of a plan, thus, without satisfying the "fundamental needs of the human heart."

Many of Le Corbusier's writings of the period stemmed from his involvement with the Syndicalists, a politically ambiguous group who held that the means of production should be owned and managed by independent groups of workers (*syndicats*). He became an active contributor to the syndicalist journals *Plan* and *Prélude*. Through the membership of its editorial board, *Prélude* had a connection to the Italian fascist movement. Le Corbusier's own connection with Italian fascism was fleeting, lasting only as long as Mussolini was interested in his ideas of the Radiant City

Despite his varying fortune, in the thirties Le Corbusier established a fulfilling pattern of life and work. Mornings he would paint in his studio at Porte Molitor. His wife, a gourmet cook, would prepare lunch for them. Afternoons he would spend in his office on rue de Sèvres, working with his young, international employees on architectural projects. At least one evening a week, he and Jeanneret would join a fierce game of basketball in the dance studio/gym of his brother Albert. Periodically he vacationed on the Mediterranean, near Cap Martin, where he would take olympian swims.

With the onset of World War II, Le Corbusier left with Jeanneret for Ozon, in the Pyrenees. Their partnership ended in 1940, when Jeanneret left for Switzerland and joined the Resistance, while Le Corbusier approached his Syndicalist friends in power at Vichy in hopes of finding there an authority to implement his ideas for reconstruction. For eighteen months he attempted to make his way in Vichy circles, first as part of a commission to study housing, and then as an increasingly annoying advocate of his own plan for Algiers. He left Vichy in 1943, after Algerian authorities had denounced him as a Bolshevik.

After Liberation, Le Corbusier was able to take part in the reconstruction of France. Under the auspices of the Ministry of Reconstruction, he began plans for the port of Marseille, which culminated in the construction of his first Unité d'habitation. He prepared plans for the towns of St-Dié and La Rochelle. He was selected as French delegate to the architectural commission of the United Nations. For a moment it seemed that many years of somewhat self-imposed martyrdom had borne fruit. He told an interviewer in New York, "For thirty years I'd been a consultant talking in a desert. Since 1945, I've led the architectural movement in France. I have arrived at a stage where things in my life flower, like a tree in season."

By 1950, this moment had passed; no city had accepted his plans. The U.N. disappointed him by making Wallace Harrison chief architect in the execution of a design he considered his own. The United States delegation to UNESCO refused to accept him on the design team. Despite this litany of official rejection and the bitterness it engendered, Le Corbusier entered on a productive period marked by the emergence of a well-defined aesthetic based on the plastic use of exposed concrete. Projects for several Unités, the chapel at Ronchamp (1954), the convent at La Tourette (1957), and the city plan and state architecture for Chandigarh, India, filled the decade.

Le Corbusier brought to bear on the Unité and all his subsequent architecture the research he had conducted during the war on the Modulor, a rule of proportion that applies the geometric properties of quadrature and the Golden Section to the measure of the human body. He had previously used these geometric properties, in the spirit of Auguste Choisy, as *tracés régulateurs*

(regulating lines) for proportioning designs. Now he developed a system of measure in relation to man. Through the ladder of Golden Sections called the Fibonacci Series, he extended his intial Modulor to infinitely large and small dimensions. He asserted both its aesthetic value and utility as a standardized scale. He understood the Modulor as part of a great tradition extending back to Renaissance anthropometrics, to Vitruvius and Pythagoras.

In his "Poem to the Right Angle" (1947-1953), Le Corbusier engaged in another exploration of man's relation to the cosmos, one belonging less to the rational humanist tradition of the Modulor and more to a personal spiritualism rooted in his attachment to nature and, perhaps, to the dualistic conceptions of spirit and matter from his Catharist heritage. The poem's images, such as the open hand and the bull, appear in the form of emblemata painted or engraved on his late buildings and in his dramatic use of natural elements, such as light, shadow, and water.

Toward the end of the 1950s, Le Corbusier withdrew more from social life and spent increasing periods of time at his cabin in Cap Martin. His wife had died in 1957, a blow from which some say he never totally recovered. Despite this partial retirement, he had as many architectural commissions as ever. Although these late works do not fall easily into a single category, many retreat from the primitivism of his Indian architecture toward a refined handling of materials, including steel; in them he reexamined his earlier vocabulary. He was at work on a project that promised to be of major significance in terms of his own development, the Venice Hospital, when, in 1965, he died of a heart attack while swimming in the Mediterranean.

Paris and environs

Maison Planex (Planeix) 1927

24, boulevard Masséna
75013 Paris

Le Corbusier and Pierre Jeanneret

VISITS: Private residence visible from street. Small alterations have been made in the studio door and the square studio window.

LOCALE: The boulevard leads east to a zone of warehouses along the Seine and west to a strip of large, modern apartment complexes. The Sudac Factory (1891) by J. Le Claire is located on Quai de la Gare, no. 13. Slightly to the north is Le Corbusier's Cité de Refuge. See the Cité entry for a more extended tour.

DIRECTIONS: Closest métro stops are Porte d'Ivry, line #7, and Blvd. Masséna, line RER-SNCF.

PLANEX IS PERHAPS THE MOST URBANE OF the houses that, in the 1920s, defined Le Corbusier's purist phase. Choosing as his models elite city dwellings of the past, Le Corbusier made Planex contextual, not as a good neighbor to the surrounding buildings but rather as a patrician critique.

In his placement of the artist's studio and main residence above two ground-level apartments, Le Corbusier adopted a classical palace structure and transformed it according to the modern principles of Purism and his Five Points. Pilotis and a glass wall replace the traditional solid and rusticated base. The roof terraces serve as the attic story and the roof garden handrail as a cornice line. Main residence and studios are combined as a symbolically elevated zone through the ambiguous central figure of a papal balcony above a projecting loggia window. At the suggestion of M. Planex, a sculptor of funerary monuments, Le Corbusier and Pierre Jeanneret organized the facade in Palladian fashion, with a central bay and symmetrical flanks, but undermined the traditional balance between window and wall, center and edge, through the placement of long vertical slots at the very periphery of the building.

Through this formal play, Le Corbusier engaged in a dialogue traditional to grand urban dwellings, between gracious gestures toward the city and protective measures against it. While the primary facade maintains the plane of the street wall, the vertical windows cleverly disengage it from its less distinguished neighbors. Though the entrance axis is royal

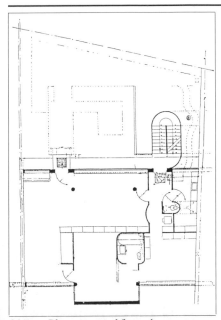

Maison Planex, second floor plan

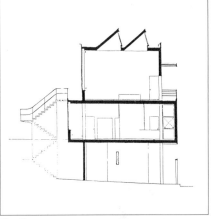

Section

as it leads below the balcony and between the columns, it arrives at a garage; no continuation to the main floor is visible. The four columns at the entrance recall the court of a Roman patrician house, but the glass wall divides the room in two parts, half inside, half out. The balcony projects out into the public realm but has a solid front with a small window of cyclopean demeanor, which surveys the city distrustfully. Von Moos has suggested that this closure is Le Corbusier's conscious reversal of the huge open loggia of Adolf Loos's house for Tristan Tzara in Montmartre.

Le Corbusier used symmetry and closure on the facade as a foil for the asymmetry and openness of the house within. Inside, Maison Planex turns its back on formality and the street, focusing instead on a two-story garden with picturesque paths inserted into an irregular site bordered by a railway spur. The rear facade steps down toward the terraces, becoming increasingly transparent. From the main floor, one door opens onto a bridge to the upper garden, the other onto an exterior stair. Both main rooms of the house, studio and salon, center not on the front loggia but on the garden bridge. The only access to either main or attic story is the exterior stair leading to the rear doors. As a miniature palace entered from an elaborate backyard, Maison Planex is a witty reformulation of the individual dwelling in the city.

Asile Flottant
1929

Quai d'Austerlitz
75013 Paris

Cité de Refuge (l'Armée du Salut)
1933

12, rue Cantagrel
75013 Paris

Le Corbusier and Pierre Jeanneret

Asile Flottant (above); Cité de Refuge (below)

VISITS: The entry sequence of the Cité de Refuge is visitable every day during working hours. Though the Asile Flottant, a barge, is permanently docked alongside the quai, it is closed during the winter. A third asylum of the Salvation Army, the Palais de Peuple, on rue des Cordelières, had a dormitory addition by Le Corbusier, but it has been destroyed.

LOCALE: The barge is located north of Pont de Bercy on the Seine. The Cité borders the warehouse district along the Seine to the south of the bridge. An itinerary starts at Gare d'Austerlitz and its adjoining structures by E. Freyssinet, descends to the barge, and goes south along the water to the exhibition hall at Quai de la Gare. Continue south to the neighborhood of the Cité, where there are many new housing projects off rue du Chevaleret. Behind the Cité de Refuge slab and connected to it is the Centre Espoir (1978) by G. Candilis and B. Verrey, 39-43, rue du Chevaleret. Le Corbusier's Maison Planex is located several blocks away, on blvd. Masséna. From here a more extended tour might travel by bus (line "Petite Ceinture") to the Swiss and Brazil Pavilions at Cité Universitaire.

DIRECTIONS: The closest métro stop to the barge is Gare d'Austerlitz. For the Cité, get off either at boulevard Masséna, RER-SNCF, or Porte d'Ivry on line #7.

IN THE SALVATION ARMY LE CORBUSIER found a client in sympathy with his social ideas. As Brian Brace Taylor has explained, Le Corbusier saw the need for paternalistic organizations, such as the Army, and their programs of social engineering. The Army's program to save the faltering by educating them in the fundamentals of daily existence harmonized with the architect's belief that to know how to dwell is to know how to live (*savoir d'habiter, savoir vivre*). The Army's structure of communal living and social services complemented Le Corbusier's own vision of community. Both believed in the moral effects of salubrious living conditions. Le Corbusier even dedicated a portion of the project to a devout Calvinist aunt and recommended to Minister Locheur that the Army be appointed as the people's commissariat of housing.

In the Asile Flottant, the combination of program and vessel to contain it coincided perfectly with Le Corbusier's personal language. The floating asylum is a barge intended as a shelter for vagrants and prostitutes during winter nights and as a playground for the poor children of Paris during the summer. For Le Corbusier the ship was a model community based on a balance of individual freedom and collective life. It provided individuals with cabins for meditation and communal facilities for shared recreation. While as a streamlined machine for sailing it was a product of the engineer's aesthetic, it also carried with it a mythic idea of primal shelter: the ark. In the Asile Flottant, Le Corbusier adapted his ocean liner model both to the needs of an underclass and to the reality of the old barge left over from World War I. He transformed its long hull into a communal dormitory with bunks for 160, a dining room, kitchen, bath, separate

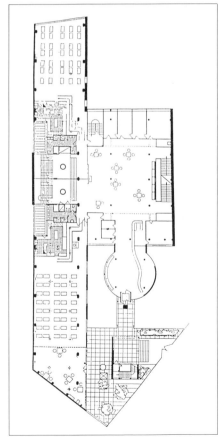

Cité de Refuge, plan at podium level

apartments for the sailors and the director, and a roof terrace.

The same year as the barge, the Salvation Army commissioned the Cité de Refuge as a headquarters and a large asylum with dormitories for men and women, single rooms for mothers with children, and communal facilities, including dining rooms and workshops. Here, for a complex community on a grand scale, Le Corbusier developed architecturally the social themes of the Salvation Army. Seeing the headquarters, like the Asile Flottant, as a temporary residence for the dispossessed, he designed it as a great ship. The building podium and entrance sequence of stack, bridge, and control cabin recall a ship's deck. With individual cabins on the top deck and a pointed prow, the massive hull of the dormitory slab glides above the "sea" of urban fabric.

More than simple refuge, Le Corbusier sought to provide an environment that would improve and guide its residents. The building format of a long dormitory slab with separate volumes below recalls the contemporary Soviet communal housing projects, which joined blocks of dwellings and social facilities in an attempt to encourage collective life. At the Cité, the transformation of the resident through a controlled sequence of events began even as he entered the gate, climbed the stair, and passed from the world of the street to the shifted internal geometry of the podium. Standing beneath the shelter of the canopy, the resident originally registered with a receptionist. After crossing the bridge to the cylindrical entrance, he passed through the columned forecourt and deposited his worldly possessions at the serpentine desk. Drawn by the bands of light in the ceiling through the layers of grey columns, he entered an office "like a confessional," where personnel would listen to his story. Relieved of all burdens, he could now enter the regulated environment of the refuge.

Le Corbusier extended the idea of human engineering to control over physical comfort in two environmental systems which were radical for the time: *la respiration exacte* (exact respiration), a form of air conditioning that circulates humidified and temperature-controlled air, and the *le mur*

Cité, entry sequence

neutralisant (neutralizing wall), continuous double glazing with a hermetically sealed cavity for the circulation of temperature-controlled air. Like the "life-support" systems proposed for his Centrosoyus, these would maintain a constant temperature of 18 degrees C., while providing maximum light. Unforeseen expenses, primarily the 35-meter-deep piles required by unstable soil, resulted in the elimination of both the double glazing and the central cooling plant. Despite severe overheating of the southern glass wall during the summer, Le Corbusier remained committed to the technology and its pure aesthetic formulation in sealed glass. Despite his protestations, windows were eventually installed and brise-soleil added by Jeanneret.

Throughout the building, from the entrance sequence to the environmental controls, Le Corbusier set up parallel metaphors of mechanical and human functioning. The glass wall is both a machine that breathes and a skin that processes light and air. The volumes of the entry sequence suggest an engine or a factory assembly line. In the entrance promenade, the spiritual purification implied by this mechanistic functioning is most clear. In total, the building is, as Le Corbusier called it, a "factory of good" (*usine de bien*) through which the resident achieves physical well-being and hence spiritual fulfillment.

In his search for a building form resonant with his institutional program, Le Corbusier discarded the envelope of the purist villa. In a sense he turned the villa inside out, placing the inventive, geometric episodes of the plan in front of the wall of the dormitory slab rather than inside the box. A collection of independent objects of disparate size is dropped onto a confined site in a chaotic urban fabric. No intermediate gesture connects the isolated volumes to the slab. Rather, the building is composed through the close spatial proximity of its parts and the intense contrasts among them in scale, texture, and form. In order to further distinguish this assemblage from the assemblage of the city, Le Corbusier introduced the raised podium, which provides a ground plane and organizing geometry separate from the street. From the perspective of the street, the parts of the building are collaged against both each other and the surrounding scene. From the perspective of the podium, the compressed sequence of the entry dominates; the architectural journey begins. Thus, in Cité de Refuge Le Corbusier created a building complete as a metaphor yet still a piece of the larger urban fabric.

Atelier Ozenfant 1922

53, avenue Reille
75014 Paris

Le Corbusier and Pierre
Jeanneret

VISITS: Private residence visible from street, in good but altered condition. The original saw-tooth skylights and the first-floor cornice have been partially removed; the garage door has been filled in; a new door has been added at the top of the stair; the second-story door is now a window; and the interior bears no resemblance to the original plan.

LOCALE: The neighborhood contains some of the nineteenth-century studio-workshops that influenced Le Corbusier's early houses, as well as buildings contemporaneous with the Atelier Ozenfant. Of special interest are the private houses of rue Villa Seurat, including nos. 4 and 89 by A. Lurçat (1926), no. 5 by Bertrand (1926), and Maison Orloff (1926) and Maison Muter (1928) by A. Perret. Maison Guggenbuhl by A. Lurçat (1926) is at 14, rue Nansouty, and Maison Braque by A. Perret (1927) is at 2, rue du Douanier.

A possible itinerary continues through Parc Montsouris to rue de la Cité Universitaire (no. 3 is by M. Roux-Spitz (1930)), then down to boulevard Jourdan and Cité Universitaire, to Le Corbusier's Swiss and Brazil Pavilions.

DIRECTIONS: Closest métro stops are Porte d'Orléans, line #4, and Cité Universitaire, line RER B.

THE CLIENT FOR THIS STUDIO-RESIDENCE was Amédée Ozenfant, Le Corbusier's collaborator in the development of Purism. Ozenfant was a painter and critic whose accomplishments include the design of a streamlined automobile body called the Hispano-Suiza (1912) and the establishment of the aesthetic journal *l'Elan* (1915). Soon after Auguste Perret introduced the two men, they began painting together in the evenings. Their communal efforts produced the manifesto *Après le cubisme* (1918) and the magazine *l'Esprit Nouveau* (1920-25). After a period of tension, the seven-year relationship between the two men came to an end, supposedly in a dispute over how to hang paintings, including their own, in the salon at Maison La Roche.

In his writings for *l'Esprit Nouveau*, Le Corbusier formulated a proposal for a universal dwelling called the Maison Citrohan, based on the potentials and demands of modern industry. Conceived as a standardized object of mass production, it had a reinforced concrete structure, metal sash windows, and other prefabricated parts. For the organization of this "architectural mechanism" Le Corbusier looked to various sources, including vernacular Mediterranean dwellings and a small bistro he frequented in Paris, which had a double-height salon and a small kitchen tucked below a mezzanine. As Reyner Banham has observed, however, it was in the nineteenth-century Parisian studio-workshop that Le Corbusier discovered a type combining the directness of vernacular architecture, the spatial formula of the café, and the forms of industry. Thus, as a studio-residence

Atelier Ozenfant was a particularly apt program with which to begin the exploration of his yet untested theoretical ideas of dwelling.

Like the Maison Citrohan, the Atelier Ozenfant has a reinforced concrete frame structure with smooth floor slabs and straight columns. This system frees interior and exterior walls of their load-bearing function and allows for large expanses of glass. At Ozenfant these freedoms are exploited in the arrangement of interior partitions that shift from floor to floor, in the continuous strip windows that bypass the interior walls, and in the glazed studio where large windows abut the slender, corner concrete post. Note that here Le Corbusier does not cantilever the slab in order to wrap the window completely around the building as he does in later works.

The industrial basis of building becomes a major part of the aesthetic as well. The stucco walls have a smooth, machine-like finish, and the windows have industrial sashes. Originally the house was crowned with factory saw-tooth skylights. In the studio, a metal ship's ladder led to a whimsical enclosed mezzanine that was half cockpit, half hut. Although on the second floor some curved walls were evocative of classical fragments, unlike the contemporary Villa Besnus there was no underlying classical model to temper the industrial flavor of the whole.

Spatially, as in the typical Parisian studio, the artist occupied a double-height loft space with a balcony at the top of the building. Circulation occurred along the edge. At Ozenfant, the lower floors were devoted to service space, maid's chambers, and a curious combination residence and art gallery. Le Corbusier resolved the awkward site configuration into a generic Citrohan-like box with a subsidiary, angled wing.

What differentiates Atelier Ozenfant from the Citrohan and the Parisian studio-workshop is its response to the corner and its corollary emphasis on the three-dimensional qualities of its box. While the Parisian studio tends to be symmetrical and the Maison Citrohan, despite the fact that it is freestanding, has basically blank sides and a symmetrical front, Atelier Ozenfant's studio is set like a transparent cube at the corner of the solid block of the house. Below, the abstracted cornice line wraps the corner above the odd double door and leads the eye to the stair. The facades are symmetrical, not internally but around the corner column—two strip windows, two squares, two doors—as if reflected across the edge of the box.

The other aspect of Ozenfant that distinguishes it from the traditional studio and modern versions by such noted architects as Perret and Lurçat is its tortuous architectural promenade. This procession travels from the exterior

Ground floor plan

spiral stair to the compressed foyer at the intersection of the two geometries of the site, up a second interior spiral stair and a ladder to the mezzanine, which had a trap door to a small roof garden. Herein lies the personality of the occupant of this house, the cerebral artist who is as much Le Corbusier as Ozenfant. He leaves his vertical trail on the outside of the house, in the long window and in the stair that barely touches the ground as he ascends to this first, light-filled cube of his creation.

Pavillon Suisse 1932

7, boulevard Jourdan
Cité Universitaire
75014 Paris

Le Corbusier and Pierre Jeanneret

VISITS: The building is a dormitory. Public rooms may be visited with permission of lobby attendant.

LOCALE: Le Corbusier's Swiss and Brazil Pavilions are both located in the Cité Internationale of the Cité Universitaire. The campus has other modern buildings of note, including the Netherlands College by W. M. Dudok (1930). From the curved side of the Swiss Pavilion, continue along the driveway for about 200m to reach the Brazil Pavilion. For an extended itinerary see Atelier Ozenfant.

DIRECTIONS: Métro stop is Cité Universitaire, line RER B. The Swiss Pavilion is at the eastern end of a row of international dormitories facing onto an athletic field. Le Corbusier intended visitors to arrive by car on the north side, in front of the curved stone wall.

UNDER THE GUIDANCE OF PROFESSOR R. Feuter of Zurich and the influence of Raoul La-Roche, Siegfried Giedion, and Karl Moser, a federation of Swiss universities awarded Le Corbusier and Jeanneret the commission for a dormitory for Swiss students. The award was intended as compensation for the disaster of the League of Nations Competition, where the architects were initially granted but finally denied the prize. Despite its small size and limited budget, the Swiss Pavilion emerged as a major work in terms of both Le Corbusier's own development and the influence it exerted on the Modern movement.

The influence of the Pavilion derives from its organization. Here and at the contemporaneous Cité de Refuge, Le Corbusier developed an architecture based not on the play of forms within a box-like perimeter, but on the expression of the elements of the program as independent volumes. No single building envelope subsumes the parts. The particular format of the parts—slab on pilotis with a free-formed public zone beneath—became the model for a multitude of postwar buildings.

Each part is a statement of several themes, including material, form, and social program. Together they fulfill the agenda of the linear apartment blocks of Le Corbusier's utopian Radiant City (Ville Radieuse) of 1931. In the early Radiant City dwellings, single-story apartments are organized along a corridor in relation to natural light and view. Within the block are collective facilities for housekeeping and recreation, as well as workshops and meeting rooms.

The whole is raised on pilotis so that the earth can flow beneath as a continuous garden. This proposal was easily adapted to the program and campus setting of the Swiss Pavilion. The dormitory has the form of a section of the Radiant apartment slab. The campus is the imagined continuous arcadia. The curved volumes house the communal facilities. The students occupy individual cells along the south side of single-loaded corridors. The glass skin *(pan de verre)* sheathing the rooms is conceived as a biotechnical machine for providing them with light, air, and view. Because the skin did not produce the optimal interior environment, shading devices were soon added, lessening the wall's slick, technical appearance. Reinforcing the logic of the southern glass wall, the northern wall along the corridor has small punched windows in a stone facing. The side walls are blank, suggesting that the slab is but a fragment of a possible utopian environment.

In contrast to the weightless glass wall of ambiguous scale, the pilotis have a muscular form, as if to express the raising of the slab in terms of human effort. Le Corbusier first proposed them in the form of slender steel posts, as a practical solution to the problem of constructing foundations on the site's weak soil, but when Swiss engineers questioned their ability to take wind loads, he would not abandon them; they were necessary to his utopian vision. In response to the need for strength, drainage, and forms consonant with the curves of the lobby, he decided to have them made of sensual, curved concrete.

Although the earthy curves found in the pilotis, the refectory, and the stair tower had appeared in Le Corbusier's sinuous viaduct city plans for Brazil and in his paintings of women, they had never so obviously appeared in his architecture. He cryptically described them as "acoustic," as if to suggest the

North facade

connection between perceptions of sound and space made by the surrealist and symbolist poets. He explained that, given the small site, "the slight curve in the wall gives a suggestion of tremendous extent and seems to pick up, by its concave surface, the whole surrounding landscape." The grounded stone shapes thus engage the site in a way the floating slab cannot.

On the interior of the pavilion, the column line and walls are also bent or, as Le Corbusier described them, "deliberately deformed," and so create a space that is at once continuous and layered in the cubist manner. Because the zones of vestibule, stair, lobby, and refectory are compressed and transparent, they are experienced almost simultaneously as one fluid space. Only the irregular line of columns reveals the divisions so apparent on the exterior. The cause of this irregularity seems to be the coming together of slab, stair tower, and bridge on the floors above. The bending suggests that the confluence of volumes has warped space itself and that this warping has created a shear line between the light and dark grey columns along the refectory.

On the opening of the pavilion, Le Corbusier was attacked for his materialism. The ascent from the complex stimulation of the lobby toward the purity and light of the monk-like cells suggests the spiritual value Le Corbusier attributed to his salubrious environment, but the mechanistic overtones of the glass wall, the exposed concrete, and the original lobby photomural of magnified, microscopic nature, convinced some critics that his was a soulless vision that could pervert young minds. At this point Le Corbusier still felt that machine-age civilization held the key to utopia. In the Swiss Pavilion he monumentalized ideas of building as machine. The presence of natural materials and of biomorphic forms suggests, however, the emergence of a less exclusive vision which could also embrace nature, primitive technology, and matters of the spirit.

Repainted by Le Corbusier in 1948 to complete the building's restoration after World War II, the mural in the refectory is an example of the roles of the natural and mythological in his late art. The dream-like sequence of symbol-laden images relates to his "Poem to the Right Angle," a kind of personal cosmology. On the right side of the mural, an open hand, symbol of reciprocal giving and receiving, holds a winged, female creature. The inscribed quotation from "Another Fan," by the symbolist poet Stéphane Mallarmé, translates as, "To keep my wing in your hand." To the left, some see crescent-shaped figures associated with the moon, the head of a bull or minotaur, and a medusa. The stone wall of this early building makes a fitting canvas for the late spiritual vision of the mural.

The complete stanza reads:

O rêveuse, pour que je plonge
Au pur delice sans chemin,
Sache par un subtil mensonge,
Garder mon aile dans ta main.

My dreamer, that I could plunge
Into sheer, errant delight,
Know how by a subtle lie
To keep my wing in your hand.

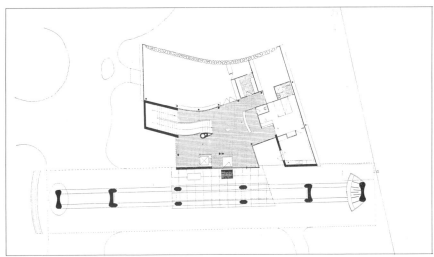

Pavillon Suisse, ground floor plan

Pavillon du Brésil 1959

*4, avenue de la Porte
Gentilly
Cité Universitaire
75014 Paris*

Le Corbusier and Lúcio Costa

VISITS: Public rooms of this dormitory are generally visitable with permission of lobby attendant.

LOCALE: See Pavillon Suisse and Atelier Ozenfant.

DIRECTIONS: Closest métro stop is Cité Universitaire, line RER B. The Pavilion faces onto avenue de la Porte Gentilly at the east end of campus. It is 200m from the Swiss Pavilion.

LUCIO COSTA DREW THE INITIAL PLAN FOR this building and then collaborated with Le Corbusier on design development. The final drawings were executed and supervised through construction by Le Corbusier's office.

In form and concept the Brazil Pavilion is the direct descendant of its neighbor, the Swiss Pavilion, designed by Le Corbusier nearly thirty years earlier. Like its neighbor, the Brazil Pavilion has a dormitory slab on pilotis that straddle the curved volumes of the communal rooms. The pilotis give the slab a monumental identity and create the potential for continuous passage through campus greenery. The dormitory cells are arranged along a corridor so that they have equal access to the "essential joys" of light and view. Thus, in the relations it suggests among individual, nature, and community, the Brazil Pavilion sustains many of the attitudes of the Swiss Pavilion and the legacy of the Radiant City.

The differences between the two buildings reflect Le Corbusier's gradual shift away from the machine-age aesthetic embodied in the Swiss Pavilion's glass wall and toward the primitive materials and plastic forms suggested by its stone refectory. Implied in this change is a certain loss of faith in modern, technological culture and a renewed interest in the individual's direct connection to a spiritually charged natural world. The rough concrete of the Swiss Pavilion's pilotis becomes the primary building material in the Brazil Pavilion. In contrast to the earlier sealed glass "machine for light," the Brazil Pavilion's concrete brise-soleil and operable windows are nonmechanical modulators of climate. The unit of the individual cell has increased importance within the dormitory slab because the brise-soleil are

View on approach

Entrance court

also balconies that outline each room and grant each student a framed connection to the landscape. Beneath the pilotis, a dark, walled court with a ritualistic looking stele replaces the liberated, flowing space symbolic of Le Corbusier's early faith in the Radiant City.

In terms of architectural character, exaggeration and extreme contrast override the balance and restraint found in the Swiss Pavilion. Shapes are activated until they seem almost out of control. Every volume tilts in section. Every curve induces a counter-curve. On the northwest side, the slab itself seems bent in two across the hinge of the central balconies. At both ends, the roof of the ground-level wing slants down, exaggerating the sense of distance and pulling the visitor along its edge.

Ground floor plan

Beginning with the rise in the portico floor, the ground plane defines a procession through the interior characterized by tense relations and strong movements in space and quality of light. From the dim, compressed vestibule, both floor and ceiling slope upward toward the light of the lobby windows. Following the fall and tilt in the floor, the path leads through a pinched space between two glazed curves, one interior, one exterior, before it arrives at a skylit alcove.

Some have criticized the Brazil Pavilion as an extreme and surreal version of the earlier, more controlled Swiss dormitory. Its intense pitch seems a product of Le Corbusier's increased primitivism combined with his and Costa's love for the culture and landscape of Brazil. Le Corbusier's trip to Rio in 1928 inspired his first use of sensual forms. In the 1930s he joined Costa and a group of native architects in a search for a modern Brazilian style, which produced, initially, an energetic interpretation of the established Corbusian vocabulary. Standing on the dark stone path outside the curved glass cage, which is bathed in a pool of light, we could be in an urban version of a South American rain forest.

Maisons La Roche-Jeanneret 1923

8-10, square du Docteur Blanche
75016 Paris
Tel. 42.88.41.53

Le Corbusier and Pierre Jeanneret

VISITS: Home of the Le Corbusier Foundation and the Le Corbusier Archives. Maison La Roche is open Mon.-Fri., 10-12.30 and 1.30-5. It sometimes holds special exhibitions. Maison Jeanneret contains the Foundation offices and is not open to the public. Its library is open to students and scholars from 2 to 6, only by appointment. Both buildings are closed for most of August.

LOCALE: This neighborhood in the sixteenth *arrondissement* was developed during the first third of the century as an affluent and stylish residential quarter, and so it has remained. It consequently contains many buildings of interest in relation to Le Corbusier. Works by Hector Guimard include: Hôtel Guimard (1910), at 122, avenue Mozart; Villa Flore at no. 120 (1924); no. 3 (1922), on Square Jasmin; and 18, rue Heinrich Heine. Down the street from the Foundation is rue Mallet-Stevens (1927), with houses designed by that architect at nos. 7, 10, 11, and 12. No. 65, rue La Fontaine is by Henri Sauvage (1927). More Guimard houses are located to the east on rue La Fontaine: nos. 14-16, nos. 17-21 (1912), and no. 60. Avenue de Versailles boasts no. 25 by J. Ginsberg and B. Lubetkin (1932), no. 29 by Boesse (1929), and no. 142 by Guimard (1905). To the north of La Roche is 25 bis, rue Franklin by Auguste Perret (1903). Le Corbusier worked for Perret there. A possible itinerary continues south to Le Corbusier's apartment house at 24, rue Nungesser-et-Coli.

DIRECTIONS:. The villa is a 5-min. walk from métro stop Jasmin, line #9.

THE YOUNG BANKER LA ROCHE WAS A patron of Le Corbusier's purist ideas. Following his introduction to Le Corbusier at a dinner party of Swiss emigrés, La Roche became a benefactor of his journal *l'Esprit Nouveau* and a collector of purist paintings. In partial compensation for La Roche's support, Amédée Ozenfant and Le Corbusier acted as bidders for La Roche at the Kahnweiler auctions of the early 1920s, acquiring a group of paintings by Braque, Picasso, Léger, and Gris that are now located at the Museum of Contemporary Art in Basel. The gallery of Maison La Roche was built to house this new collection.

The history of the villa's design and construction is typically long and difficult. Le Corbusier was involved in the acquisition of the property and in the search for additional clients. In the end he bought a compromised site facing north; it had height and depth limitations and two trees at the front that had to be preserved. The original U-shaped scheme for three clients became an L-shaped villa for La Roche and for Le Corbusier's brother and new wife, who were to have an apartment in part of the long slab.

Despite constraints of site and a complicated program with two very different clients, Le Corbusier produced a building with a level of spatial complexity and resolve new to his work. It became the basis of the first of his Four Compositions; he described it as "picturesque and full of movement but requiring classic hierarchy to discipline it." Le Corbusier used the word picturesque precisely, for he sited the house along the edge of a cul-de-sac according to picturesque principles of street design enunciated by Camillo Sitte, among others. The irregular massing of the house along an L-shaped plan derives from Gothic Revival architecture of the late nineteenth century. The multiple axes of the plan organize the picturesque but also achieve a modern or purist layering of space.

The multiple axes of the house arise from the overlapping of cubic volumes and a related sequence of centerlines and symmetries all placed very close together. For example, the house's stepping profile can be understood as a series of cubes shifting back in space, each with its own centerline and set of axes. The multiplicity of these relations is most evident in the entrance hall. Alternating bands of solid and void divide the room into parallel layers of space related to the axes of the house. As Siegfried Giedion has noted, "the cool concrete walls have been cut and levels arranged so that the hall is in touch with all adjoining spaces." For example, the space rushes through the open balcony into the darkly painted library. On the opposite wall, handrails dampen the flow of space from the hall to the narrow layer of the balcony, but the axes to the stair and dining room at either side pull the eye beyond this tense equilibrium. Kenneth Frampton has described these spatial effects as cubist *coulisse,* in reference to the moments of

great depth that occur through the gaps in the overlapping planes of cubist paintings. Standing on either stair landing and looking diagonally across the room through the windows to the building exterior, it seems that the house and its surrounding space impinge on this hall.

The entrance hall retains this primacy in relation to movement through the house. In this early instance of the Corbusian architectural promenade, the path from the beginning of the cul-de-sac through the house to the roof terrace returns constantly to the entry hall each time at a different position and aligned with a different axis. For example, on entering one crosses the hall, moving through a sequence of parallel layers of space defined by the balconies, doors, and stairways. One then ascends the stair to the left and thus faces the hall from the landing, passes behind a wall only to face the hall along the bridge, and then moves through the gallery, only to return to the hall at the highest level.

Most independent from the hall is the gallery wing, which has its own particular structure. Together, its pastel colored planes, curves, and lines seem a transposition of Le Corbusier's purist compositions into an architectural lan-

Maisons La Roche-Jeanneret, entrance hall   *Ground and first floor plans*

guage of fireplace, wall, and ramp. The ramp, which became a standard part of Le Corbusier's vocabulary, appears for the first time in the gallery. As an inclined floor plane, it was for the architect the ultimate unifier of time and space. Here, because of its curves, it moves in three directions simultaneously. On the exterior, the curved wall establishes a tense play between slight advance and recession while below, the space rushes back through the pilotis as in a cubist *coulisse*.

The forms of Maison La Roche have multiple sources, from the atrium of the Pompeian House of the Tragic Poet to the multilevel entrance halls advocated by Hermann Muthesius. The gallery facade even recalls Le Corbusier's own Villa Schwob. Along with modern principles of construction—concrete frame structure, flat roof, free facade with strip windows, pilotis—it adopts modern images from factory windows, streamlined trains, and ships. However, all these sources are important to the house not as quotations but as part of a search for an authentic architecture. Even today, Giedion's first response to what was a novel house for 1923 rings true: "a new statics which had been thought possible only through the use of overhanging slabs of concrete [is] here realized through spatial vision alone."

Apartment House with Le Corbusier's apartment at Porte Molitor 1933

*24, rue Nungesser-et-Coli
75016 Paris*

Le Corbusier and Pierre Jeanneret

VISITS: Private apartment house. Le Corbusier's associate in later life, André Wogensky, now occupies Le Corbusier's apartment.

LOCALE: Porte Molitor is within walking distance of many contemporary buildings of note. To the west is 18 bis, avenue Robert Schuman (1930), by Faurré-Dujarric. To the south in Boulogne are 52, avenue de la Tourelle (1927), by U. Cassan, and several houses on rue du Belvédère, including no. 9 by A. Lurçat (1927) and nos. 6, 8, 8 bis, 10, and 12 by P.Hillard (1930-33). The Parc des Princes was completed by P. Taillibert in 1970. A half-hour walk from Porte Molitor will take you to the interesting neighborhood of Maisons La Roche-Jeanneret. Maisons Lipchitz-Miestchaninoff, Ternisien, and Cook are even closer.

DIRECTIONS: Métro stop Exelmans, line #9.

ACCORDING TO LE CORBUSIER'S OWN statements, the Apartment House at Porte Molitor is as much a fragment of his Radiant City (Ville Radieuse) as a building within the fabric of Paris can be. It is an attempt to present the elements of the new urbanism, "sky, green, glass, cement, in that order of importance." Originally, the building lot had the gardens of Boulogne to its rear and an athletic park on the site of ancient fortifications in front. In this greenery Le Corbusier inserted a concrete structural frame sheathed in a composite curtain wall of glass and glass block to ensure the "penetration of light and air deep into the building." According to the architect, this environment, together with the building's provision for communal domestic services, inspired the first residents to proclaim that the apartment granted them a "new life." Even the domestics experienced the benefits of this new order. Liberated from the traditional Parisian attic, they occupied ground floor and basement chambers opening onto a two-tiered garden.

Despite the utopian premise, the apartment facade is probably the most traditionally contextual of Le Corbusier's mature work. Strict zoning codes specified parapet height, conformance to the established street wall, and even the placement of balconies and bay windows. As a result, the design uses the new material of glass bricks in a composition that seems rather neopalladian, especially in contrast to Le Corbusier's own first sketches and to the Maison de Verre by Pierre Chareau, which is most likely a source for the building. The balanced symmetry of the facade is not at odds with Le Corbusier's classical tendencies, but it represents only one voice of his typical architectural dialogue. The decidedly anti-classical column at the center of the window bay and the asymmetrical composition of the entry in relation to it set the stage for the dialogue within.

As the ground level of the facade hints, the architectural play involves the deformation of a center line of columns. The arrangement of structure down the middle of the building is a strategy Le Corbusier first used in Maison Cook. As in Cook, the division of the building, and especially of the apartment floors, to either side of a central axis can be understood as a reinterpretation of the usual eighteenth-century French *hôtel* plan. But whereas at Cook the circula-

Street detail with windows and column

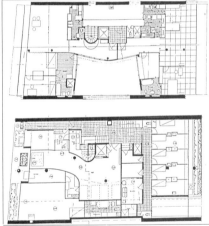

Ground floor (bottom) and typical floor (top)

tion adapts to the column location, at Porte Molitor the demands of the architectural promenade appear to warp the column line. Deep inside the building the columns are shifted to either side of center so that, after winding around, the promenade can occupy the middle of the lobby. On the typical floors, five columns define a central line that is warped at its middle in order to accommodate the entrance to the larger apartment. This shift in turn bows the exterior wall. The logic of these column patterns is clearest in the plan of the basement, where all columns are present. There we see how the center line of structure splits into pairs of columns at the wide middle bay, and how the second pair is pushed to one side by the elevator core. Note how, by reflecting a column, the lobby mirror recreates the illusion of the center pair and so, from the start, informs the visitor of the total order. The walls, as they move along the displaced columns toward the center of the lobby, convey a sensual force in opposition to the controlled rationality of the imaginary center line. Together with the tilting floor, columns and walls lead to a deep interior space illuminated from above by the diffuse glow of the skylight.

These dim, enclosed spaces, and sensual, primitive forms began to emerge in Le Corbusier's architecture and painting at the time of Porte Molitor; they assumed increasing importance in his later work. In the 1940s he developed a rather spiritual description of natural forces in his illustrated "Poem to the Right

Le Corbusier's studio

struts support Monol-type vaults derived from Mediterranean vernacular architecture. A curvaceous stair connects the levels. Here, on the roof terrace fragment of his Radiant City, Le Corbusier used the vaults and bricks of an earthy and earthbound architecture.

A former member of Le Corbusier's *atelier* has described the reaction of Le Corbusier's wife, Yvonne, to the life at Porte Molitor. A vibrant but nonintellectual woman, she preferred the society of the street, cafés, and bars to the monkish isolation of the roof dwelling. Laughingly she would complain of too much light and air. Her response to the bidet frankly placed at the bedside was to cover it with a tea cosy. The careful contrasts between the materials and values of the Radiant City and those of vernacular architecture expressed the principles Le Corbusier chose to live by and hoped others (including his wife) would accept.

Angle," which now covers the lobby wall. This vocabulary also has an important place in the design of Le Corbusier's own apartment and studio at the top of the building. There, in contrast to the technology of the glass and concrete, the brick party wall is left exposed and rough. Massive, V-shaped

Maisons Lipchitz-Miestchaninoff 1924

7, allée des Pins—3, rue des Arts
92100 Boulogne

Le Corbusier and Pierre Jeanneret

VISITS: Private houses visible from street in fair-to-good condition.

LOCALE: See Maison Cook.

DIRECTIONS: Métro stop Marcel Sembat or Porte-St-Cloud, line #9; bus #52, République.

LE CORBUSIER AND HIS SCULPTOR CLIENTS envisaged a small artisan colony of three connected dwellings around a communal garden, with M. Lipchitz's house at the center, M. Miestchaninoff's at the corner, and a third, undetermined resident's toward rue des Arts. Eventually, M. Canale obtained the third site and engaged Le Corbusier as architect, but he never had the project built.

As combination studio-residences, the completed buildings were variations on the house type that Le Corbusier had first developed for Ozenfant, based on nineteenth-century Parisian studio-workshop, industrial architecture, and his own Maison Citrohan. In response to the functional requirements of large sculpture, Le Corbusier inverted the section of Atelier Ozenfant by placing the studios at ground level and the dwellings above. The resulting relation of industrial sash window to simple shed and of shed to street heightened the buildings' resemblance to the first Citrohan project as well as to Parisian warehouses.

As in his other early studio designs, here Le Corbusier focused on the interrelation of prismatic volumes rather than on the issues of column and grid set forth in the Maison Dom-ino. The larger context of the colony of studios provided for an increased play among sculptural forms appropriate to the clients. The cubes of the two houses are modulated in reference to each other. The cornice and fenestration of the smaller cube imply the missing third story of the larger one. The corner stair tower of the larger reappears as a suspended spiral on the garden facade of the smaller. Thus, across the central axis of the service gate the two similar boxes stand as mutual reflections. This connection of masses through symmetry continues in the relation of windows to the tower. While this symmetry suggests that the

chaninoff and Canale but rather as a freestanding frame for the interior garden and as a nautical bridge from which the sculptor could survey his private domain. Thus, Le Corbusier created a

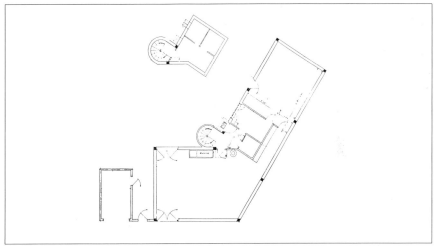

Ground floor plan

building surface is a thin, continuous plane wrapping the volumes within, the massing of the tower and the bridge assert that the building is composed of solid forms. Sketches show that Le Corbusier never intended the raised passage as a connection between Maisons Miest-

dialectical conversation between surface and mass, fragilely wrapped boxes and a bridge that bursts their confines. In Le Corbusier's development, these houses present a bolder imagistic and sculptural use of form in relation to the still central figure of the box.

Maison Ternisien 1926

*5, allé des Pins
92100 Boulogne*

Le Corbusier and Pierre Jeanneret

VISITS: Private residence visible from street. Virtually nothing remains of Le Corbusier's design. The house appears much as it did in 1936, after George-Henri Pingusson's addition.

LOCALE: See Maison Cook.

DIRECTIONS: Métro stop Marcel Sembat or Porte-St-Cloud, line #9; bus #52 République.

LE CORBUSIER DESCRIBED THE HOUSE AS A *jeu d'esprit,* referring to his witty adaptation of the studio-residence type developed for Atelier Ozenfant to a peculiar site and idiosyncratic program. The curved wall he gave Paul Ternisien's piano room was both a playful reference to purist instrument shapes and a graceful way to engage the corner. At the other end he placed Mme Ternisien's paintings in an updated version of the standard nineteenth-century Parisian studio, a double-height, prismatic volume with large, industrial-looking windows. A small, glazed dining room and entrance connected the two artists' spaces and framed the site's one small tree.

Le Corbusier conceived of the design also in terms of a larger site extending to the studio-residences he had recently built down the street for Lipchitz and Miestchaninoff. In the Ternisiens' painting studio, he continued the theme of thin-skinned cubic volumes begun at Lipchitz. Expanding on a nautical motif, he balanced the "smokestack" of Miestchaninoff's stair with Ternisien's pointed "bow."

Since from the first the Ternisiens planned to extend their house, Le Corbusier's initial design provided for the eventual addition of a story above the piano room. However, the clients' dissatisfaction with the architects' services and future plans led them to engage George-Henri Pingusson for the addition. The expansion of the house in 1936 virtually obliterated Le Corbusier's work, except for the ground-floor street wall at the distinctive corner.

Original ground floor plan

Maison Cook 1926

6, rue Denfert-Rochereau
92100 Boulogne-sur-Seine

Le Corbusier and Pierre
Jeanneret

VISITS: Private house visible from
street, in good condition. Ground
floor has been altered.

LOCALE: At the time Maison Cook
was built, there was extensive
development in this neighborhood
on the outskirts of Paris. Consequently, the adjoining houses are
no. 8 by R. Mallet-Stevens (1925)
and no. 4 by R. Fischer (1925); no.
7 is by P. Patout (1928). Placards
on the street in front of Cook suggest a brief architectural tour. Yours
might begin with Le Corbusier's
houses for Lipchitz-Miestchaninoff
and Ternisien on allée des Pins,
and finish in the neighborhood of
his own apartment building at Porte
Molitor.

DIRECTIONS: Bus stop Boulevard
d'Auteuil, line #52, République.
Metro stop Porte-St-Cloud or Marcel Sembat, line #9.

THE CLIENTS FOR THIS HOUSE, THE EX-
patriate American journalist William Cook and
Jeanne, his French wife, belonged to the artistic
circle that included many of Le Corbusier's clients,
the Steins among them. In fact, the Cooks commissioned their house within weeks of the Steins, but
moved into it long before their friends could inhabit
the palace at Garches. The speed with which the
house was designed reflects, in part, the extent to
which it expressed a set of thoroughly formulated
ideas concerning art and industry. As Le Corbusier
stated, "here are applied very clearly the certitudes
acquired to this point."

Maison Cook presented Le Corbusier's Five
Points in almost canonical form. The strip windows
were, for the first time continuous across the facade.
Round pilotis raised the main volume completely off
the ground. The roof garden was the natural culmination of the circulation through the free plan.

Le Corbusier called the Cook house "the true
cubic house" (*le vrai maison cubique*). Deriving its
plan and elevation from the same square, it was truly
cubic. This organization constituted a distinct plan
type within Le Corbusier's *œuvre*. Rather than adopt
the system of bays outlined by his prototypical
Maison Dom-ino, in which the proportions of the
golden section (3,5,8) were superimposed on a datum
of squares, at Cook he divided a square into quadrants hinged on the middle of a single line of
columns. This organization is based on an earlier
project for an artisan's house, in which a freestanding
cube focused on a sole center column is divided by a
diagonal balcony. Although there is no built diagonal
at Cook, there is a diagonal path of movement
throughout the house induced by the placement of

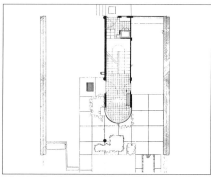

Maison Cook, ground floor plan

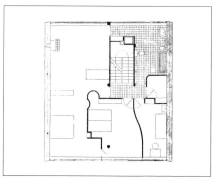

First floor plan

the stair opposite the center line from the doors and the major spaces. The wall along the column line on each floor thus becomes a second facade through which one moves from room to room. The "front" door to the house is in this wall perpendicular to the front of the house. Richard Etlin has elucidated how this central cross wall is on one

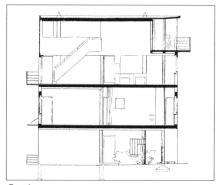

Section

hand a cubist construct, a portrait in both profile and full face. On the other hand, it divides the house into suites in the tradition of the French *hôtel*.

The compositional principles of the house are all visible on the street facade. It too is divided into four squares by the center lines that run vertically through the column and horizontally between the strip windows. The stairs, terraces, and rooms occupy particular

quadrants much as they do in plan. Consequently, the facade resembles a composite house plan "flipped up" ninety degrees to become a vertical plane. As in plan, much of the architectural play among quandrants again takes place along a visual diagonal. One diagonal connects the protruding balcony across the center line and back in depth to the stair; the other runs from the void of the terrace to that of the entrance.

Even the space in front of the facade is brought into this architectural conversation across the center lines of the house. The straight driveway leading to the enclosed garage designates the lower-right-hand quadrant for the automobile. The curved garden path passing under the house to the backyard makes the lower-left-hand quadrant the realm of the pedestrian. The visual diagonals then connect the upper quadrants to this set of relationships.

Peter Eisenman has observed that Le Corbusier established a radically modern relation between viewer and building in which all viewpoints are presented to the viewer simultaneously. At Cook the facade describes the space in front, the plan behind, and even the section with its rotated second facade. It separates the private realm from the public, the city of streets from the city of gardens, while containing them all.

Maisons Jaoul 1956

*81 bis, rue de Longchamp
92200 Neuilly-sur-Seine*

VISITS:Private residence only partially visible from street.

LOCALE: Neuilly is a fine residential district in greater Paris bordering the Bois de Boulogne. Not far from the house, at 34, avenue de Madrid, is the eighteenth-century Folie Sainte-James by F.J. Belanger. A possible itinerary continues on to the Bois, toward the Parc Bagatelle and the Musée des arts et traditions populaires.

DIRECTIONS: The métro stop Pont-de-Neuilly, line #1, is several blocks from Maisons Jaoul, along rue de Longchamp.

WITH THE CONSTRUCTION OF MAISONS Jaoul and the chapel at Ronchamp, the architectural world first took notice of Le Corbusier's expressive use of rough masonry, finding it at odds with the apparent machine aesthetic and rational principles proposed in his early architecture as the basis of Modernism. James Stirling questioned whether Maisons Jaoul were a retreat from "participation in the progress of twentieth-century emancipation" into the realm of "art for art's sake." Primitive and vernacular sources did take on increasing importance for Le Corbusier, but they had had a place in his architecture from the first. In particular, the antecedent for Maisons Jaoul, the vaulted prototype Maison Monol, appears as early as 1923, in his book *Vers une architecture.*

In both parts of the Jaoul residence, the front house of the elder Jaouls and the rear house of their son, Le Corbusier used a version of an authentic vernacular structure, the Catalan vault. The interior tile finish acts as a permanent shuttering for the bricks, which are set in cement without real form work. Steel tie-rods at 15-foot intervals take the diagonal thrust. The roof covering of soil and grass helps resist thermal expansion. A load-bearing spine wall of exposed brick runs along the groin of the vaults. The concrete boxes on the exterior are alternately bird-nesting boxes and rainwater heads. Stirling caught the building's aura in his statement, "built by Al-

Maisons Jaoul, interior with fireplace

gerian workmen equipped with ladders, hammers and nails," the house is "technologically no advance over medieval building." In fact, there is at least one significant revision of the Catalan structure in the design of the concrete edge beams. Their deep sections, capable of spanning long distances, allow for large openings in the bearing walls and thus for the pattern of exterior fenestration and the spatial flow between the interior vaults.

What distinguishes Maisons Jaoul from the Monol prototype and its built exemplars, Maison de Weekend (1935) and the contemporaneous Maison Sarabhai in India (1956), is its manipulation of the basic linear unit of the vault. Each Maison Jaoul combines two vaults of different widths into a multistory block with an identity as a cubic form rather than as a simple linear extrusion. The complex patterning of the walls and the perpendicular arrangement of the blocks also lessen the sense of continuous linear form. Stirling associated the pyramidal massing of the blocks with traditional Indian architecture. Because the profile of the arches appears only on the upper levels, as if the volume were a single, double-height vault, the arches have a monumental quality suggestive of Roman vaults as well. A sophisticated play thus occurs between ideas of undifferentiated vernacular form and particular, articulate objects.

The principles of the site plan, like those of the vault, derive from Le Corbusier's earliest theories. The small walled gardens are treated as "architectural enclosures" in keeping with Le Corbusier's adage of thirty years before—"every exterior is an interior"—made in reference to the Roman house. The front house has an imposing street facade made more monumental by the grading of the hillside, which protects and defines the enclave within. The upper level of the enclave is the product of regrading the slope and of constructing a plinth above the sunken garage. At terrace level the houses appear as smaller, two-story volumes scaled to the size of the adjoining gardens. Together, the built forms and walls define a group

Garden

of three connected exterior "rooms": a paved entrance terrace and two side yards. The passage among these enclosed garden areas—from the ramp at the edge of the site, to the center of the entrance court, and then to the long yard with its focal balcony—recalls the grading of axes and the shifts between center and edge that Le Corbusier associated with the architecture of Pompeii.

Along this promenade, the houses are viewed either episodically or on the oblique, so that their corners become prominent features. The elaborate articulation of the corners with wood panels acknowledges the importance of the oblique point of view. Le Corbusier discovered the possibilities of the three-quarters view in the architecture of the ancient Greeks, who angled their temples; however, he compressed the exterior spaces and manipulated the path of movement to create the desired perspective.

At Maisons Jaoul, Le Corbusier used Mediterranean vernacular sources in association with the architecture of antiquity, sensing their common basis in the vault and the wall. From the viewpoint of the street, Jaoul abuts the neighboring villa, which is made of similar brick, like a piece of "monumentalized vernacular," a conscious affront to suburban pretensions. From the garden it seems a less ironic proposal for a new type of "house-palace," replacing the earlier white temples of machine-age culture with an architecture focused inward on the play of shadows and light against textured masonry walls.

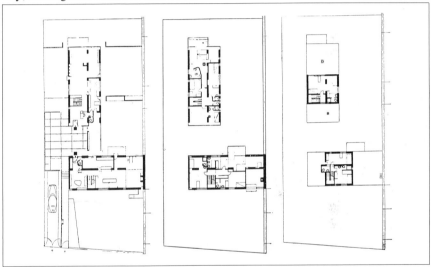

Ground and upper floor plans (above), section (below)

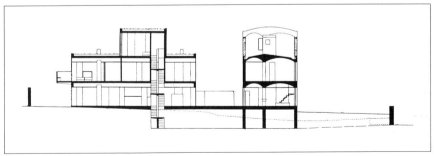

Villa Besnus (Ker-ka-ré) 1922

*85, boulevard de la République
94400 Vaucresson*

Le Corbusier and Pierre Jeanneret

Paris 19km, Versailles 5km

VISIT: In 1935, shops were built along the front of the house and a tile roof was added. Today the villa is clearly visible from the street but barely recognizable.

LOCALE: The suburbs of Paris where Le Corbusier's early villas are located are, in fact, older villages that still have town halls and some vintage buildings. They are close to such major sites as Versailles and could be included on a day trip to such monuments. They could also be included on an itinerary that begins with the recent building complex of La Défense.

DIRECTIONS: Villa Besnus is located in the center of the village of Vaucresson, on the main street just beyond the train station. Commuter trains that stop at Vaucresson leave Paris frequently from Gare St Lazare. You can also take the métro (line RER A) to La Défense and from there a bus that stops at the center of each suburban village, including Garches and La Celle-St-Cloud. In either case, the trip is under one hour.

M. AND MME GEORGE BESNUS COMMIS-sioned Le Corbusier to design their house after reading his articles in *l'Esprit Nouveau* and seeing his exhibit at the Salon d'Automne in Paris (1922). Although the clients requested that the house resemble the display model of Maison Citrohan, Le Corbusier did not translate his universal prototype directly into a built work. Instead, he chose to develop the idea of a purist architecture in which cubist design principles were reinterpreted in light of the French neoclassical tradition. The two facades of the house presented the different sides of Le Corbusier's aesthetic argument. The garden side of the house, at the top of the sloped site, was a two-story, symmetrical block with a clearly separate stair tower behind. In its tripartite division, its proportions, and its symmetry, the main block strongly resembled le Petit Trianon, designed by Gabriel for Louis XV at nearby Versailles. It had a cornice and a low ledge, equivalent to the palace's top and bottom balustrades. The wall brackets recalled the window entablatures of its model. Le Corbusier had analyzed the neoclassical monument in an essay in *l'Esprit Nouveau* on the subject of *tracés régulateurs* (lines related by their angles to the ratios of the golden section). To proportion the facade at Villa Besnus he used a similar system. However, he had to impose its rule with some effort, for behind the symmetrical facade lay an asymmetrical plan. In order to center the garden window, he had to blind part of the salon on one side and the entire kitchen on the other. While these compositional devices resembled the stripped-down classicism of the earlier Villa Schwob, their extreme abstraction and their setting within the white prismatic cube reflected a new set of principles that were more clearly enunciated in the street facade.

Le Corbusier ironically relegated the formality of le Petit Trianon to the backyard of Besnus. On the street facade, asymmetry, decentralization, and peripheral incidents held in tense equilibrium replaced a classical sense of balance. Le Corbusier set the stair tower in the same plane as the main body of the house, making the entire composition asymmetrical. Within this perimeter he then used overlapping sets of symmetries to create competing centers. For

First and second floor plans.

example, the center of the block remained strongly marked with a projecting box, but it ceased to be the center of the whole. As the visual junction between stair tower and the main block, the small vertical window became the true pivot of the composition. Tension existed among the elements in depth as well. The windows suggested a plane just behind the datum of the wall. The balcony and window box pushed out beyond it.

As soon as the house was built, structural problems became apparent. Since concrete slab construction was still a new technique in domestic building, Le Corbusier's contractor, Summer, had to assume a major role in the invention of the details. In any case, the house leaked and the clients complained. Within a decade of its completion it was transformed beyond recognition into a vernacular building with a pitched tile roof. The low architectural language of bungalow with sunporch easily obliterated Le Corbusier's abstract manipulation of the French neoclassical tradition.

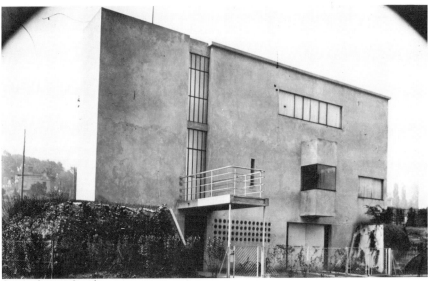

Original street facade

Villa Stein/de Monzie ("Les Terraces") 1927

17, rue du Prof. Victor Pauchet Garches

Le Corbusier and Pierre Jeanneret

Paris 19km, Vaucresson 2km

VISITS: The villa has been divided into condominiums and the original plan consigned to history texts, but the exterior is mostly intact. The rear stair has been filled in and the front service door altered to align with the window above.

LOCALE: Garches is a suburb of Paris that has maintained its identity as a town with pleasant, hilly neighborhoods and nineteenth-century houses. The villa is beyond town, opposite a golf course. Le Corbusier's Villa Besnus and Maison le Weekend are in villages nearby. The town of Malmaison begins 500 meters west of the villa.

DIRECTIONS: Commuter trains stopping at Garches leave frequently from Gare St Lazare, Paris, and take less than half an hour. To get to the villa, either take the bus or walk (25 min.) from the train station up the hill to rue du Prof. Victor Pauchet. Boulevard Foch is the most direct route.

IN HIS PURIST ARCHITECTURE OF THE 1920s, Le Corbusier attempted the simultaneous exploration of current technological culture and of the architectural systems of the past. He chose the house as the type through which to conduct his exploration. To focus on the dwelling as the object of architectural discourse was, he felt, to bestow dignity on modern life. The dwelling was the problem of modern architecture; every building was in essence a house. He expressed all these ideas in the rubric *une maison-un palais* (a house-a palace). While Le Corbusier intended to monumentalize all classes of dwelling, with the commission of a weekend house by Gabrielle de Monzie, the former wife of Minister of Construction Anatole de Monzie, he found patrons with the status, culture, and wealth to support the grandeur of a palace. The other joint clients in the venture were Michael Stein, the brother of Gertrude, who had earned his fortune from the San Francisco street-car system, and his wife, Sarah, a painter and early collector of Matisse. Having often vacationed together at various country estates, including the Steins' Italian Renaissance villa, the clients now requested that Le Corbusier create for them a personal and modern equivalent. In response, he developed the second and "most difficult" of his Four Compositions—an unremitting envelope of walls, which he called a "mask of simplicity," around the Dom-ino structural frame.

In the tradition of Choisy and Viollet-le-Duc, Le Corbusier searched the past not for stylistic features but for principles of spatial organization and rational structure. Scholars such as Richard Etlin have elucidated how the relation of column to wall in the Egyptian pylon temple informed the ordering of

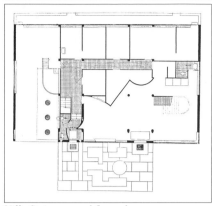

Villa Stein, ground floor plan

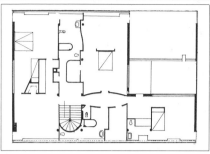

Villa Stein, plan, second floor

space at Villa Stein. But most central to this villa's architectural dialogue are the principles of symmetry, centrality, hierarchy, number, and proportion, as used by Palladio in his articulation of the Renaissance villa. Colin Rowe has demonstrated the specific correspondences between Villa Stein and Palladio's Villa Foscari, from the identical proportions of their volumes (8x5.5x5), and the rhythm of their structural bays from side to side (ABABA) to the placement of their stairways. Le Corbusier's humanistic mission to aggrandize the house has its Renaissance parallel in Palladio's domestic use of the temple front.

For Le Corbusier, the fundamental diagram of modernity was the Dom-ino reinforced concrete frame of columns and slabs and the continuous layers of space generated by it. Where in the Palladian villa the load-bearing walls fix the plan from floor to floor but allow space to be developed vertically in section, at Villa Stein the Dom-ino frame frees the walls inside and out and eliminates the figures of dome and pediment. At Villa Stein, the Dom-ino structure within appears on the facades in the horizontal banding of the windows. Although this non-bearing wall is free from the internal exigencies of struc-

ture, not needing to conform to the divisions of rooms, it does more abstractly express the layering of space from front to back. This continuous layering of space is consonant with the compositional devices of overlapping planes, shifting relations of figure and ground, and deconstruction employed in Synthetic Cubism's pictorial space. For example, the facades are organized as a series of overlapping planes, some real, others implied, that recede or emerge in relation to the reference plane of the white wall. On the front elevation, the windows appear both as background to the white wall and as bands coplanar with it. By wrapping the corner of the house, they suggest a layer of space parallel to the villa but separate from it. They draw emphasis to the extreme periphery of the facade much as in the centripetal compositions of cubist paintings. On the back wall, the proportions of the stripes are reversed, but their ambiguity and their power to dissolve the surface are similar. Where the space of the house seems collapsed onto a taut front facade with many implied planes, on the garden side it explodes into surfaces distant from one another. The horizontal bands of the stair landing, terrace, and roof garden describe a visual procession that moves up and back in relation to the reference plane of the wall to the right.

The brilliance of Villa Stein lies in the manner in which these systems of

Rear facade

historical and modern architecture are brought into relation to one another so that they create many readings and relationships simultaneously. For example, in the front elevation, the recognizable Palladian figure of the loggia, or balcony, that marks the center is placed unconventionally high, perhaps to suggest the upper pediment of Villa Foscari. The two flanking doorways, which establish a symmetrical triangle with the loggia at the apex, are not balanced in importance; the smaller door is a service entrance. (Originally, their symmetry was disturbed by a deliberate misalignment of the left-hand service door with the balcony above, which later owners "corrected.") The continuous striping of the facade undermines this almost classically balanced triangle by failing to clearly differentiate between center and edge, bottom and top. On the interior as well, the Palladian schema of Villa Foscari was reflected not intact but transformed according to modern precepts. The S-shaped plan suppressed the great central room; the portico was shifted to the edge. The particular curves and slants that once filled the interior, and which can still be seen on the roof, manifest the same sensibility as the curvaceous bottles of Le Corbusier's still lifes, but they do not represent those objects. Rather, they spring from an eclectic repertoire of architectural sources, machine-age and historical, stripped of their original ornamental features. The dining-room apse may have been an episode from a Turkish bath, the roof structures a Roman aedicule or steamship funnel, the toilets a figure from a Parisian *hôtel*. Behind the demeanor of Palladian restraint, Le Corbusier's imagination ran free.

Condition today (above); original condition (below)

Maison de Weekend 1935

49, avenue du Chesnay
78170 La Celle-Saint-Cloud

Paris 20km, Malmaison 7km, Versailles 4.5km

Le Corbusier and Pierre Jeanneret

VISITS: Private residence barely visible from street. There have been major alterations in wall finishes, exterior decoration, and garden, but the overall dimensions and placement of the building remain striking.

LOCALE: La Celle-Saint-Cloud is one of a chain of small towns to the west of Paris with verdant residential neighborhoods and a village center. From La Celle-Saint-Cloud to neighboring Vaucresson and Le Corbusier's Villa Besnus it is a 20-min. walk or a 5-min. local bus ride east along avenue de Verdun. From Vaucresson continue east to the adjacent town of Garches and Villa Stein/de Monzie.

DIRECTIONS: Trains stopping at La Celle-Saint-Cloud leave Paris (Gare St. Lazare) frequently and take a half hour. From the station walk uphill along avenue du Chesnay (5 min.) until it meets avenue de Verdun. The house is easy to miss because it is so low to the ground and stands behind a tall, overgrown fence.

FOR SEVERAL YEARS BEFORE HE DESIGNED Maison de Weekend, Le Corbusier had used primitive materials and construction techniques in his rural commissions, sometimes in a vernacular framework, as in Villa le Sextant, sometimes in combination with more current technology, as in Villa de Mandrot. At le Weekend he combined rough stone with Nevada glass block in appreciation of the beauty and utility of both primitive and sophisticated means. The vaults that compose this house derive from both Mediterranean folk architecture and vernacular industrial building. They had already appeared in his prototypical Maison Monol, which was in turn based on Auguste Perret's docks at Casablanca. Contemporaneous with the weekend house, he used the vaults as the typical roof in his Cooperative Village, an agrarian project.

Within the environs of Paris, Maison de Weekend seems an ideological critique of its immediate cultural context. Its associations with mass-produced workers' housing, warehouses, barns, and peasant huts suggest images alternative to bourgeois ideas of dwelling. The 2.6-meter-high vaults are covered with sod and placed against a high soil embankment so that they form a cave-like shelter appropriate to a modern-day, ornamental hermit. Early photos of the house show a finely finished interior filled with light

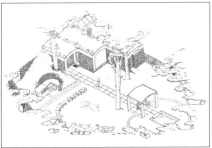

Maison de Weekend, aerial sketch

and open to the garden. From inside as well as out, the simple house had an intimate relation with its intensely private landscape that evoked "*ur*-shelter," or primal dwelling, in an Edenic setting.

This critique of dwelling has implications for the language of architecture as well. As Alan Colquhoun has noted, "it is not so much the case that vernacular elements are added to high architecture as that the tradition itself is modified to include them." When the basic vault unit is bare, as it is in the garden kiosk, it looks like a classical canopy or baldachino. However, as part of the house these units lose their classical identity and become part of a continuous, conceivably endless extrusion. From the outside, the house appears an assemblage of three such extrusions cut at various lengths. The axis from house to kiosk describes the imagined path of growth of the first vault. This architecture of continuous growth undermines the classical precepts both of a finite, composed whole and of a dominant frontal facade. Le Corbusier exaggerated this condition of lost front by placing the entrance of Maison de Weekend on the side of the vault and by setting the flat planes against the embankment.

Whereas in some late projects Le Corbusier took these ideas to their extremes, creating buildings like cellular fabrics, at le Weekend he composed the cells into a more traditional form. Accepting "the elements of construction as the only architectural means," he crea-

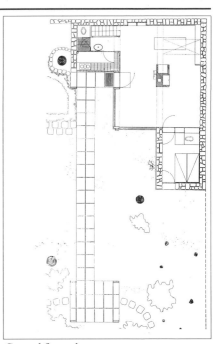

Ground floor plan

ted an architecture based on "precise relations." His placement of the kiosk twice as far from the kitchen as from the middle of the bedroom fixed the location of the vault ends. The ambiguous L-shape of the three vaults is resolved on the interior as a large, square room flanked by two small wings. The entrance aligns with the hearth and with the center of the dominant room.

In two important commissions of the 1950s, Maisons Jaoul and Sarabhai, Le Corbusier returned to the vault structure of le Weekend. As monumental residences they forced the question of high architecture's relation to low—and non-western—architectural language. Especially in the tropical, Indian Maison Sarabhai, the primitive forms had much the same value as in the modest weekend house of twenty-five years earlier. For Le Corbusier the vault in an enclosed garden would always approximate the sheltered position that once existed for man in nature.

Villa Savoye ("Les Heures Claires") 1931

Chemin de Villiers
78300 Poissy

Le Corbusier and Pierre Jeanneret

Paris 38 km

VISITS: The villa is now a historic monument. Visiting hours are 10-12 and 2-4, November through March; 10-12 and 2-5, April through October. It is closed Tuesdays. If the gate is locked, ring the intercom to call the concierge. Admission is free, but it is recommended that you tip the concierge in thanks for the informative tour.

LOCALE: Once a rural village, Poissy is now part of the greater Parisian megalopolis. Traces of the old town include a church and an old priory. The villa is located on a hill above the shopping district, next to a high school and athletic complex. On Saturdays there is a fine farmers' market in the parking lot across the street.

DIRECTIONS: Commuter trains run from Gare St Lazare in Paris to Poissy about twice an hour and take 20 min. From the station in Poissy, take the bus "Hôpitaux" up the hill (5 min.) and get off in front of the high stone wall on your right. This wall encloses the villa. If you pass the high school, you have gone too far.

VILLA SAVOYE IS PERHAPS THE BEST known of Le Corbusier's buildings and an architectural icon for many. The last of the purist villas, it freely and confidently expresses a decade of ideals.

The creation of such a house required a certain type of client. M. and Mme Savoye belonged tangentially to the crowd of artists and patrons that included Le Corbusier. Monsieur was an important administrator in an insurance company. The couple's requirements were for a weekend home well equipped with servants' quarters, where they could enjoy the rustic landscape in style. As for the architectural style of their house, the clients were, according to the architect, "totally without preconceptions either ancient or modern."

Villa Savoye reflects Le Corbusier's belief in the connection between the ancient and the modern. As Banham has observed, in Le Corbusier's *Vers une architecture* (1923), pictures of a Bugatti automobile and the basilica at Paestum stand side by side; "machine-design stands as a necessary intermediary stage between certain abstract fundamentals of design and the glories of the Parthenon." It is in this spirit that Villa Savoye was conceived as a natural consequence of classical architecture on the one hand and of the machine age on the other.

Modern technology appears at Savoye as a pure rendition of Le Corbusier's Five Points of a new architecture based on the potentials of the reinforced concrete frame. The entire major volume is raised on pilotis (1), sheathed by simple planes disengaged from the columns within (2). A single, elemental strip window dominates each of the four facades (3). The free plan (4) culminates in the roof terrace (5).

Le Corbusier viewed this pure villa as an *objet-type,* the ultimately refined, standardized dwelling for the elite. He proposed for a neighborhood of Buenos Aires, Le Vingtième, a grouping of twenty Villa Savoyes each with its own curved driveway. In the small lodge by the gate at Poissy, many of the villa's standardized themes—e.g., the strip window and the floating white box—appear in combination with a vernacular stone wall. This blending of prefabricated elements with products of the local mason's trade also characterized Le Corbusier's prototype for a regional mass-housing, the Maison Locheur.

Despite his vision of a suburban colony of prefab Villa Savoyes, Le Corbusier also understood the building as a mythic entity wedded to a particular setting and complete in its meanings only as a object in isolation. Originally, it stood in an open field surrounded by countryside. Le Corbusier described the setting in *Précisions* (1929): "The house is a box in the air…in the middle of a prairie overlooking an orchard….The inhabitants contemplate the countryside, maintained intact, from the height of their suspended garden. Their domestic life will be inserted into a Vergilian dream."

In the quotation, Le Corbusier suggests that the classic pastoral of Vergil's *Georgics* provides the proper mythic context for this villa. Colin Rowe has demonstrated how this classical allusion includes Palladio's interpretation of the Vergilian landscape and how Villa Savoye corresponds to Palladio's Villa Rotunda. Both villas are cubes with a single motif repeated on all four facades; both are thus disengaged from their pastoral settings. As expressed at Villa Savoye, the Five Points are a reformulation of Palladio's classical language. Pilotis correspond to the rusticated base, the white box to the *piano nobile.* The strip replaces the aedicular window, just as the roof terrace replaces pediment and dome. As Palladio used the temple front as a domestic porch, in order to monumentalize his house, so Le Corbusier took the temple's fundamental elements of post and lintel as the basis for his villa design. The pilotis stand like a porch spanned by the simple horizontal entablature of the white wall. The glass enclosure seems the shadow of a *cella* now housed within the figure of the lintel.

For Le Corbusier, as for Auguste Choisy before him, only by moving through architecture could it truly be appreciated. He described the experience of the villa as *l'espace arabe,* in reference to the common architecture of North Africa, with its unfolding spaces and shifting viewpoints. The column placement, bay dimension, even window mullions consciously orchestrate the promenade. Originally, the promenade began when the Savoyes' chauffeur pulled out of their garage in Paris, preferably in the late-model Voisin auto of which Le Corbusier was so fond, for the hour drive to Poissy. Following the lead of the pilotis, the green planes, and the vertical mullions receding beneath the white box, the chauffeur would drive around the glass enclosure, designed specifically to accommodate his car's turning radius, and drop the passengers at the front door. Although a perimeter piloti blocks the path from this front door to the landscape, inside the house it is replaced by a more classically disposed pair of columns framing a reception area. A sink, visible down the hall, suggests the values of cleanliness and health provided by this new architecture and, perhaps, that ablutions are appropriate before continuing on to the ceremonial ascent.

Throughout the house runs the sculptural counterpoint of the two contrasting means of ascent: the spiral stair

Villa Savoye

Master bath detail

for the servants and the ramp for the Savoyes. For Le Corbusier, the ramp was the preferred route because, as a kind of tilted floor plane, it connects the separate stories in a continuous path through space-time as incremental stairs cannot. Siegfried Giedion found this sense of space-time continuum radically modern, an artistic equivalent of relativity theories in physics.

At the second level, a much more fragmented composition of colored planes in space replaces the initial impression of the house as a pristine cube hovering above the landscape. While the ramp unifies the space vertically, it also slashes apart the box. It shifts from inside to outside, from the center of the house to the edge of the terrace, in a continual state of tension. The glass walls, the strip windows that wrap both interior and terrace, and the roof that extends beyond the boudoir, all further dis-integrate distinctions between outdoors and in. In the master bathroom, the skylight and a tiled chaise evocative of the undulating landscape bring the values of the outdoors deep inside the house.

The ramp reaches its resolution in the roof terrace's framed view of the countryside. Originally, Madame Savoye's bedroom was to have occupied this level, but the window in the screen wall seems culmination enough. Gazing through the frame, from behind one picture plane into another, it is tempting to question which side is more illusory, the Vergilian landscape or the ambiguous realm of the villa.

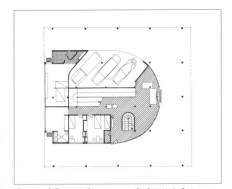

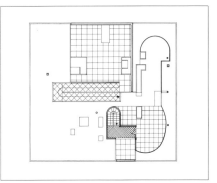

Ground floor (above); roof plan (right)

France

Unité d'habitation, Briey-en-Forêt 1961

*Route D.137,
Meurthe-et-Moselle*

Luxembourg 50km, Metz 40km

VISITS: Apartment house, in fair condition. Public spaces visitable.

LOCALE: Briey-en-Forêt is a separate township about 2km outside of Briey, a small, picturesque place of Roman ancestry. The economy of this region along the Orne River is dependent on iron smelting; most of the surrounding towns are industrial. A possible itinerary moves south from Briey to the cathedral and main square of Metz, then into Alsace, toward towns with buildings by Le Corbusier: St-Dié, Mulhouse, and Ronchamp.

DIRECTIONS: Briey is very difficult to get to by public transportation; several transfers are required. Trains to Metz, on the other hand, are frequent and take 2.5 hours from Paris Est. The building is located off the Longuyon-Briey road 40km northwest of Metz.

LE CORBUSIER INTENDED THE UNITÉ d'habitation as one cell of a community composed of similar units. The original project for Briey-en-Forêt came closest to placing the Unité in its proper context (for a description of the Unité type, see the original Unité d'habitation at Marseille). In 1949, the mayor of Briey, Pierre Giry, conceived of a new township in the midst of greenery to provide the laborers of the region with an antidote to their working environment. The town was to have not only a Unité of 339 apartments, but also 49 terrace dwellings, 200 smaller housing units, and separate community facilities. Le Corbusier was to design the Unité and the cultural and commercial center. During Le Corbusier's lifetime only the Unité was completed.

Built to house poor laborers, many of them migrant, the Unité at Briey-en-Forêt relates more directly to the Unité at Nantes-Rezé, also built for the working class, than to the original block at Marseille. As with Nantes, Le Corbusier considered the apartments inadequately small. The original furnishings were simple: rubber flooring, plywood interior partitions, one freestanding storage unit serving as a room divider, electric wall outlets but no lighting fixtures, and a swivel tap to fill the kitchen sink on one side and an awkwardly small tub on the other. The only planned communal facility was a nursery on the roof and a tobacco stand in the lobby. Recreation facilities were to be housed in a separate building where they could serve the community at large.

At Nantes a cooperative of workers commissioned Le Corbusier out of respect for the idea of the Unité.

The building at Briey has rental units for a population that had little say in the design process. One senses the residents' disapproval in the dilapidated condition of the building. However, the pilotis, the sheer mass of the building, the modulor proportions, the colors, and the isolation in a forest, whatever their social value, give the building its architectural presence.

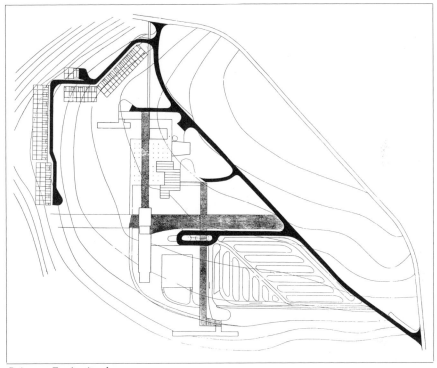

Briey-en-Forêt, site plan

Manufacture Duval 1951

Avenue de Robache
88100 St-Dié
Vosges

Paris 388km, Belfort 128km, Colmar 56km, Mulhouse 100km, Strasbourg 90km

VISITS: Private factory visible from street. M. Jean-Jacques Duval, a personal friend of Le Corbusier, is dedicated to the ideals represented in the architecture of his factory. He enjoys showing his building to students of Le Corbusier's work. Those with a half day to spend in St-Dié should arrange a meeting with M. Duval by writing him in advance at the factory.

LOCALE: St-Dié is located in the picturesque mountains of Alsace. Although much of it was destroyed during World War II, portions of the impressive cathedral and a chapel survive. M. Duval was also involved in commissioning Le Corbusier's famous but unrealized proposal for the reconstruction of the town. A possible itinerary moves south from St-Dié to Le Corbusier's canal station outside Mulhouse, perhaps stopping at Colmar (see l'Écluse de Kembs-Niffer and Ronchamp).

DIRECTIONS: St-Dié is not on a major rail line. Trains depart from Nancy, Epinal, and Strasbourg about twice daily; most buses from Strasbourg, Mulhouse, Basel, and Belfort require a transfer at Sélestat. From the St-Dié train station walk (30 min.) along the main street to the cathedral. The factory is on the left, just past the cemetery.

THE FACTORY, WHICH SERVED AS A MODEL for so much of Le Corbusier's thinking, became at St-Dié the subject of the architecture itself. In his early treatise, *Vers une architecture*, Le Corbusier praised facories for their plastic forms shaped by methods of construction, but distinguished from them architecure as products of the Law of Economy rather than objects that move the spirit. He gave the utilitarian Manufacture Duval an "integrated architectural message," but one still grounded in issues of factory production and technology.

This architectural message involved the self-conscious definition of the factory in terms of both its own past and the current state of its industry. The Duvals commissioned Le Corbusier to rebuild their factory after a fire had left the back buildings intact but the major, front site empty. The Duvals also intended to modernize their textile manufacture. Le Corbusier framed the new building within the memory of the old by constructing the end walls of stone taken from ruined local buildings and inserting a concrete structure in between.

Inside, the building is a diagram of the modernized manufacturing process. Originally, the raw materials of fabric and thread arrived and were stored on the ground floor. The fabric was transported to the third floor for cutting; it descended by toboggan or lift to the studio, where it was sewn on the main gallery and ironed on the balcony, then to the ground floor to be packed, and down a final chute to storage and the loading dock. The central portion of this loop, the studio, has the typical Corbusian house section of double-height space, with balcony facing a glazed wall, but at an enormous scale. Everyone is in touch with this window and placed according to their roles—ironers on a small balcony, seamstresses on the main floor, finishers underneath the balcony, and supervisors in a glass-encased lookout post at the upper level. The enlightened industrialists who created this salubrious setting filled with light and air have offices on the roof. Thus, while fulfilling the requirements of the industrial process, the factory also provides a forceful image of the structure of the factory community.

tems of "life-supporting" substances, they suggest bodily functions as well.

First seen in his buildings of the early 1930s, this biomechanical metaphor here takes on a new character as organic materials and primitive methods of construction infiltrate the earlier vocabulary of glass and steel.

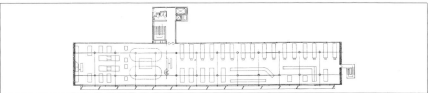

Manufacture Duval, typical floor plan

quirements of the industrial process, the factory also provides a forceful image of the structure of the factory community.

In his architecture, Le Corbusier used form metaphorically, taking objects and systems from outside the realm of building as part of the image or metaphor. Here, in the context of a factory, some of his most symbolically charged elements take on more directly utilitarian roles: the ramp as a chute for goods, pilotis as a porch for bicycles and storage. But many continue to function metaphorically. The pipe rails, deck levels, "funnel"-shaped conference room, and "smokestack" stair all refer to a ship, Le Corbusier's model container for a utopian-socialist community. Unlike the Unité d'habitation at Marseille, an ocean liner designed for dwelling and recreation, the factory is a freighter designed for work, with a communal interior but no cabins, and a deck that belongs to the captain.

Le Corbusier joined the idea of factory as large machine to concepts of organic functioning. The exposed, color-coded mechanical systems—green for air conditioning, yellow for electricity, and blue for water—connect the building more graphically than the abstract procession of goods. As circulation sys-

The end walls of used stone and the rough concrete replace the machined finish of the earlier buildings. The northwest glass wall recalls the hermetically sealed curtain of his "factory of good," the Cité de Refuge (1933), but in place of the metal frames are oak windows proportioned according to the anthropometric Modulor system. The southeast facade has concrete brise-soleil as an architectonic rather than a mechanical control of climate.

Prefabrication and standardization are still seen as viable means of production, but are employed in the creation of a more organic product. Standard-sized, prefabricated wood frames with pre-drilled screw holes were installed in a continuous trough in the concrete sill, but these frames were paired and reversed to create a varied fenestration. In imitation of nature, where objects are infinitely varied but relate to a larger geometric pattern, the independent rhythms of column, brise-soleil, and fenestration overlap so that no bay repeats but all relate to the Modulor. This, Le Corbusier's first postwar building, proposes an integrated architecture in touch with timeless ideas of construction and with the spirit of nature, but still idealistic in its attitude toward the workings of modern industry.

Chapelle Notre-Dame-du-Haut 1954

70250 Ronchamp
Haute-Sâone

Belfort 21km, Besançon 91km, Lure 12km, Vesoul 43km

VISITS: Open to public Mon.-Sat., 9-12 and 2-5, and for religious services on Sunday. It remains an important pilgrimage site. It is better to tour the site when mass is not in progress.

LOCALE: Ronchamp is a tiny village with exactly one inn, which is closed in the winter and does not have a restaurant. If you intend to spend the night close to the chapel, you might stay in Belfort. It has a noted medieval citadel and some excellent restaurants. From Ronchamp, possible itineraries include trips to Besançon, the region of Alsace (see l'Écluse de Kembs-Niffer), or Geneva.

DIRECTIONS: Ronchamp is difficult to reach by public transportation. A train to Ronchamp leaves Belfort every morning at 6:30 am and returns from Ronchamp at 6:45 pm. There is also one morning train from Lure, with a return in the evening. A cab ride from Lure station to the chapel takes less than twenty minutes and costs 70 francs. The ride from Belfort is twice as long and costs twice as much. You can call for a cab from the pay phone at the café below the chapel. From Lure and Belfort, train service to major towns is fairly frequent.

The road from Belfort to Lure is the main road of Ronchamp. To get to the chapel turn north off the main road at the stone arch and proceed uphill for about 2km to the café and chapel. For a true sense of pilgrimage, climb the hill on foot. It is possible to walk to the chapel from the Ronchamp train station; take the road toward Belfort.

LE CORBUSIER AT FIRST REBUFFED THE INvitation to design the chapel at Ronchamp, which came soon after Church authorities had rejected his project for the shrine of Saint Mary Magdalene. But believing that modern art could rejuvenate the Church, Canon Lucien Ledeur of Besançon and Père Alain Couturier promised Le Corbusier design freedom and eventually prevailed on him to accept the job. Couturier went on to be instrumental in offering him the commission for La Tourette as well.

Dissent within the Church was to be expected, but the completed chapel shocked the architectural world as well. Those who revered Le Corbusier as champion of the machine age, reason, and type solutions to universal problems, saw the chapel as an irrational, expressionist aberration. Others saw its organic form as a humanistic enrichment of modern architecture and its modulor proportions as evidence of its underlying rationality. In retrospect, the chapel still seems a singular work in Le Corbusier's *œuvre*.

Throughout his life, Le Corbusier displayed two opposing tendencies, one toward the generation of universal types applicable to any setting and the other toward site-specific responses to landscape. At Ronchamp the site was inspiration for the design. Le Corbusier wrote, "One begins with the acoustics of the landscape, taking as a starting point the four horizons.... They are what gave the orders.... To them the chapel addresses itself." As in the earlier Swiss Pavilion, Le Corbusier employed the term visual acoustics to describe how "the curved walls simultaneously gather and open to the landscape." They "give a suggestion of the great extent of the landscape...far beyond the building's boundary." Le Corbusier's initial sketch of the four lines of the horizon became the basis for the final plan and did not vary in the five years between conception and completion of the chapel.

The site's history as a sacred place also inspired Le Corbusier in his design. Worship on the hilltop dates back to a megalithic cult of the sun, continuing uninterrupted through Roman times until, in the twelfth century, it became associated with an effigy of the Virgin with magic powers. The chapel stands on the foundations of a Gothic church destroyed in World War II and has much of the rubble from the ruin incorporated in its walls.

Ronchamp, aerial view

Beyond the force of its own *genius loci,* the site had power for Le Corbusier by virtue of its resemblance to two other landscapes: the Jura Mountains of his youth and the Acropolis. The Juras are actually visible on the northwestern horizon of the site. As a boy immersed in studying nature and John Ruskin with his teacher L'Eplattenier, Le Corbusier spent a lot of time roaming through the Juras; with his classmates he even designed a forest shrine. On his trip to Greece in 1911, he learned how to compose with nature. He witnessed how "the Acropolis extends its effect to the horizon" and how the Parthenon and Erectheum are placed "outside this forceful axis" and at an angle to it.

Based on the qualities of the site and his own sense of the sacred, Le Corbusier fashioned a personal acropolis of forms at Ronchamp. His Parthenaic procession begins at the bottom of the hill and passes by an artificial hillock with a door before reaching the propylaeum formed by a youth hostel and parish house. The temple rises up like a Greek temple in three-quarters view, drawing the pilgrim around it past the available entrances in a procession most critics describe as magnetic. As on the Acropolis, the procession is orchestrated by a sequence of axial perspectives defined but not enclosed by the built forms of ziggurat, chapel, and youth hostel. For example, the view from the top of the hillock and from the ziggurat has the distant mountains at its center and the corner of the chapel at its periphery.

Each of the built outcroppings encountered on the procession suggests a symbol open to interpretation. The artificial hillock with a door recalls the ancient burial mounds, or dolmens, of Brittany. The ziggurat is officially a memorial to the War dead, but it also has significance as an ancient altar place, a sacred mountain, and a necropolis. In Le Corbusier's own work, it appeared in the Mundaneum project (1929) as a museum of man's complete knowledge. The fountain, since there is no subterranean well on the hilltop, has a utilitarian role as a basin for rainwater, but its sculptural forms also suggest a microcosm complete with heavens, sea, and mountain. The bells opposite the fountain seem a literal realization of acoustic landscape. Le Corbusier intended that they be electronically programmed to play modern music by Edgar Varèse, so that Ronchamp would have a "limitless voice coming from the most distant ages and reaching the most modern hours of today."

As at the Acropolis, the procession comes to rest outside the *cella* door. At Ronchamp this resting place is the open-air altar, the primary place of worship for groups of pilgrims. Le Corbusier explained, "Inside, a little talk with oneself. Outside, 10,000 pilgrims before the altar."

Ironically, after years exploring a kind of modern classical language based on the piloti, Le Corbusier chose not to make his small "temple of plastic

Site plan

events" a "matter of columns." Enclosive, battered, and thick, the walls evoke images of Romanesque churches and of Mediterranean vernacular buildings, including the North African mosques of M'zàb, which Le Corbusier had visited. On the inside of the chapel, the small, cave-like altars lit from above have their source in the stone chambers of the Serapeum at Hadrian's Villa.

At odds with this sense of thick bearing wall are the reality of the structure, consisting of concrete columns imbedded in the rubble, as well as the illusion of the wall as a weightless plane. Much of the drama of the building comes from the explosion into separate planes of what first seems a solid mass of a building. Both the slot of space left between roof and wall and the exposed post supporting the roof, make the non-bearing nature of the wall quite clear. From the perspective of the open-air pulpit, the western wall seems a

stretched membrane that, together with the roof, drapes the altar like a tent. As a structure of posts and light membranes, the tent is antithetical to the idea of a cave depicted in the interior altars. As Frampton has suggested, it derives from Le Corbusier's image of the Hebrew temple in the wilderness, illustrated in *l'Esprit Nouveau* thirty years before and given a modern technological interpretation in the catenary tent of the Pavillon de Temps Nouveau (1937) and, following Ronchamp, in the hyperbolic curves of the Phillips Pavilion (1958). The roof of two 6cm-thick concrete shells, held 2m apart, makes the chapel part of this search for a new structure for the primal tent. Also related to the chapel's roof are the architect's sketches of airplane wings and dams with curved double profiles.

In keeping with his basic belief in the structural parallels between man-made technologies and nature, Le Corbusier also likened the roof of the chapel to a seashell found on a Long Island beach. The choice of a shell is also significant in the realm of nature it suggests, namely, the sea. Le Corbusier saw mountain and sea as opposite but complementary poles of the natural world. At the Acropolis, the great axis runs from the mountain to the sea at Piraeus. At Ronchamp, the absent sea is recalled in the exterior water basin, the shell of the roof, and an inscription on one of the stained glass windows. In the dim chapel, the roof swells up, the floor dips down, and the western wall ripples like a wave, all as if the space were somehow related to water.

The sea is not the only image or reading suggested by the inside of the chapel. The altar wall, known as the constellation wall because of its pattern of tiny scattered openings, immediately evokes an association between the darkened interior and the heavens. After the activity of the exterior surfaces and surrounding forms, however, what is most striking about the interior of the chapel is its subdued and empty quality. The ancillary chapels, with their dramatic lighting effects, are hidden. Tafuri has commented, "the sloping floor contributes to the programmatic loss of center. [We see] his art in search of its own origins." The supposed point of arrival, the interior, is like another point of origin and another site awaiting the pilgrim.

Ronchamp, interior view

Écluse de Kembs-Niffer 1962

Canal du Rhône au Rhin Embranchement de Huningue-Rhin

Basel 25km, Colmar 60km, Mulhouse 18km

VISITS: Toll station open on request of manager during working hours, approximately 9-12:30 and 2-5:30.

LOCALE: The lock is located in Alsace-Lorraine, just south of a group of towns renowned for their nineteenth-century textile industry as well as for pork dishes, onion tarts, and white wine. The closest accommodations are in Mulhouse, an interesting town with museums dedicated to fabric and an old town complete with an elaborate Rhenish Renaissance town hall. L'Hôtel de l'Europe, 11, avenue Foch (tel. 45.19.18), is pleasant. Nearby Colmar has noteworthy Renaissance dwellings and a hotel with a good restaurant by the train station, l'Hôtel Terminus Bristol. Either Mulhouse or Colmar make good bases for a two- or three-day tour of the region (see Manufacture Duval and the chapel at Ronchamp).

DIRECTIONS: Buses leave the Mulhouse train station for Niffer and Kembs about eight times daily (tel. 89.44.41.90). The lock is located just beyond Niffer, about 35 minutes by local bus from Mulhouse. Get off at the town hall in Niffer and continue walking in the direction of the bus route for five minutes. The lock will be on your right.

Customs house

IN HIS DESIGN FOR THIS CUSTOMS HOUSE station and watchtower on a branch of the Rhône-Rhine Canal, Le Corbusier restated in architectural terms the elements of the sluiceway and its extended landscape. The vertical section of each building reflects the canal's drop in level, while the flights of stairs are mimetic of the water's fall. The customs house is half carved from the ground, half built above it so that its main floor coincides with the upper level of the lock. The architectural promenade first descends a flight of steps built into the hillside, to the machine room, and then ascends a concrete stair to the main floor. A columnar chimney emerges from the sod-covered roof of the machine room as a vertical axis through the several ground planes. The watchtower is part of a much larger vertical axis connecting the levels of the sluiceway. Stairs extend from the higher canal up the tower to the lookout station and down along the natural cliff at the tower's base to the lowest plane of water.

The architecture also dramatizes the parting of the canal water in relation to its source and destination. As the stairway ascends the axis of the watchtower it establishes two distinct views to either side of the central concrete panel, one toward the Rhine, the other toward the main canal, each with its own horizon. The views are joined in a continuous panorama only from the lookout station, which is twisted off the orthogonal of the tower. The twist of the customs house roof and the lateral pull of its end columns seem to have split the building in two parts and thus created the central path between them. The "columns" are, in fact, huge drainpipes fed by the angles of the oversized roof-umbrella. The building

Watchtower

is thus a water-machine with a symbolic function in its depiction of the division of continuous rainwater into two streams. From a distance the roof describes a V-shape engaging the broad sky and drawing it deep into the crux of the building, much as depicted in Le Corbusier's early drawing of the Er-razuris house with its butterfly roof. Here, on the flat Alsatian plane, the diagonals also appear as lines in

perspective leading to the opposite horizons at either end of the canal and intersecting above the building passageway. Their juncture can be interpreted as either vanishing point or the origin from which the two levels of water spring.

Many of Le Corbusier's buildings elevate the flow of water to a level of significance. The idea of roof as umbrella dates from his Villa Baizeau (1929) and appears in the posthumously completed Centre Le Corbusier in Zurich. The sluiceway of the Rhône-Rhine Canal created a unique, hybrid landscape in which man's intervention in nature made water into part of a machine for lowering ships, while maintaining the semblance of the river from which this water flowed. In response, Le Corbusier created an architecture that operates in several ways: as a self-referential system of planes, analogous but not identical to the levels of the lock, and as a building wedded to its site. Ultimately, he described the sluiceway as a realm in which nature and architecture, ordered according to similar geometries, abide in harmony.

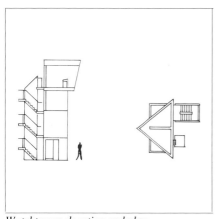

Watchtower elevation and plan

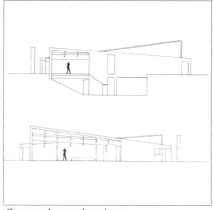

Customs house elevations

Couvent de La Tourette 1960

69210 Eveux-sur-l'Arbresle
Rhône
Tel. 74.01.01.03

VISITS: Hours are usually 9:30-12 and 2-5:30. Off-season, call at least two days in advance and mention your professional interest in the building. With enough notice it is possible to spend the night at the monastery or in the farmhouse next door.

LOCALE: The monastery is located on a hill above the small, old, and rather quaint town of l'Arbresle. A visit to la Tourette can be made as a day trip from Lyon, with a picnic lunch on the hillside.

DIRECTIONS: The 40 minute train ride from Lyon-Perrache to Eveux departs at 7:00 and 12:00, returning at 12:30, 1:30, and 5:30. From the track side of the train station take the road up the hillside; signs point to the monastery. It is a 25-min. walk.

COMMON TO THE PHILOSOPHY OF THE NINE-teenth-century dialecticians are assertions of the "reciprocal or ideal adequacy of content and form in art." For Le Corbusier, this ideal existed in the acropolitan temple, which he felt compelled to reinvent throughout his lifetime. The program perhaps best suited to his mode of invention was that for the monastery of La Tourette. Le Corbusier personally embraced certain monastic values, including material simplicity, self-discipline, and denial. Moreover, as Rowe has elucidated, "it was after all a Dominican monastery. An architectural dialectician, the greatest, was to service the requirements of the archsophisticates of dialectics." One is meant to experience the monastery as a series of intense contrasts in form which build upon one another and thus gradually assert the dualistic structure of the whole. This dualistic tension is not a rift. Rather, in the manner of Heidegger, it reveals "the intimacy with which opponents belong to each other" and the source of their common ground.

The elements of the argument were long established tenets of Le Corbusier's architecture, formulated from the first dualistically: the social pairing of the individual-collective, the spatial pairing of wall-column, and the opposition of architecture- nature. The "indissoluble binomial" of the "individual-collectivity" was Le Corbusier's recipe for the ideal community. It was inspired by monastic life and form as he first observed them in his visit to the Tuscan Charterhouse of Ema in 1907. (At the suggestion of his patron, Father Couturier, he also adopted as a model the Cistercian convent of Le Thoronet, outside Toulon.) Thus at La Tourette he addressed the design of a type that was already an essential part of his architecture, having influenced the form of his Maison

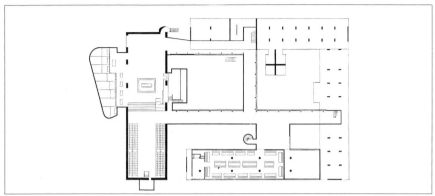

La Tourette, ground floor plan

Citrohan, the villa-apartments, and the apartments with individual balconies of the Unité d'habitation. In a kind of reverse transformation, these apartments became the basis for the design of the cells at La Tourette. Le Corbusier had previously accommodated communal life in the central garden of his *immeuble-villa* as well as in the corridor and the roof terrace of his Unité. At La Tourette, the cloister, its passages, and the roof garden recall these previous forms. The sanctuary has a more ambiguous lineage identifiable in part as the Maison Citrohan box expanded to house the monastic family, with individual altars for solitary prayer.

In Le Corbusier's architecture there is also a long-standing duality between spaces defined by the columnar system and those enclosed by walls. Where the columnar system generates continuous horizontal spaces exemplified by the Dom-ino concrete frame, the wall architecture creates vertical, "tunnel" space as in the Monol and Citrohan types. At La Tourette, the U-shaped dormitory on pilotis, with its horizontal bands of balconies, presents the Domino diagram placed in clear opposition to the walled block of the sanctuary.

Le Corbusier placed this monastery in the landscape according to a third duality of nature and architecture. Here, without being disrupted, a savage nature passes through an equally rough architecture. Monastery and hillside are almost independent of one another. Claiming that the project budget left him no choice, Le Corbusier struck his own horizontal level at the highest point and continued it out over the slope, letting the pilotis below hit the ground as they may. The monks' cells define the top level, with refectory and meeting rooms suspended underneath. The placement of the monastery in its "austere and brutal setting" atop a mountain and the architectural promenade around it recall Le Corbusier's descriptions of the Parthenaic procession as well.

Within each individual element of the monastery are further dualities. For example, not only is the first view of the monastery blank—there is neither door nor window—but it is the side of the chapel, not its front. The idea of front is suggested only to be denied. As Rowe has described, while this wall first appears a regular, static solid, the barely perceptible oblique of the parapet in conjunction with the slant of the belfry imply both a depth and a rotation at odds with our initial understanding. The manipulations, only subliminally recognized, inject a sense of unresolved tension into this apparently singular element.

La Tourette, altar

Despite the seemingly lucid positioning of the building in relation to the shifting ground, the levels within the building confuse our initial perception. In crossing the building we are thrown from the secure horizontal level the building so adamantly establishes in opposition to the landscape, and are instead forced to descend with the hillside. Le Corbusier observed that in the sanctuary, the raised pulpit is placed downhill so that "the lowest place becomes the highest, the highest the lowest." The murky atmosphere and the light from above evoke both ocean depths and celestial heights. As Rowe has suggested, in the sanctuary's darkness, "negation becomes positive."

The elements of the collectivity—cloister, corridor, and garden—are fraught with internal oppositions as well. From outside the building our first impression is of a massive rectangular block, which is later revealed to be a hollow court with a tenuously connected perimeter. The cloister is simultaneously defined by this perimeter and denied by the fall of the land and the crossing of the cloister passages. These passages occupy the center of the court, but their centrality is undermined by one blank and one glazed wall. The other corridors of the monastery have continuous glazing with mullions spaced according to the harmonic rhythms of the Modulor, but they end in

Corridor

windows that are blocked by concrete panels to deny the view. Le Corbusier intended that the roof be used not as a communal garden but as a solitary walk for monks selected by the fathers. Even without this enforced regulation, the roof provides its own frustration: its parapet is built so high as to eclipse the very panorama it might have offered.

Though an obstruction to a promised delight, the parapet presents in its place something of equal power, an artificial horizon across an open sky punctuated only by the vertical forms of the chimney and bell tower. In this fabricated line is the spirit of the Acropolis as Le Corbusier understood it. He wrote, "The Greeks on the Acropolis set up temples which are animated by a single thought, drawing around them the desolate landscape and gathering it into the composition. Thus, on every point of the horizon the thought is single." The horizon enthralled Le Corbusier in part because of its dualistic nature. In conjunction with its opposite, the vertical force of gravity, it defines "the full power of a synthesis," a right angle that is the "sum of forces which keep the world in equilibrium." By itself, the horizon is the "line of the transcendental plane of immobility," an abstract place where mathematical order and the perceived order of nature coincide. But while this line brings together reason and nature, it does so at an unfathomable distance. It is always present, never reachable, perceptible but never palpable, single but infinite. It thus represents the boundary of the human condition as Le Corbusier found it. Perhaps this explains why he chose dualistic tension as the architectural basis of La Tourette.

Cloister

Section

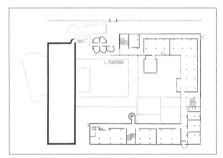

First floor plan

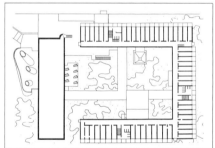

Third floor plan showing monks' cells

Firminy-Vert

La Maison des
Jeunes et de la
Culture 1965

Unité d'habitation
1968

Athletic complex
Stadium 1969

*42700 Firminy-Vert
Loire*

Lyon 67km, Montbrison
39km, St Etienne 12km

VISITS: La Maison des Jeunes (tel.
77.56.07.07), a youth center, is
open Tues., Thurs., and Fri. 4-6,
Wed. and Sat. 2-6, and Sun. for
special exhibitions only. The public
areas of the Unité are visitable.
The stadium is always visible.

LOCALE: Firminy and the adjacent
development of Firminy-Vert are at
the center of the coal and iron mining district that encircles St
Etienne. Besides Le Corbusier's
athletic complex, Firminy-Vert contains mostly low-cost, high-rise
housing set on a green hillside; it
has very little commercial activity.
Neither the old nor the new town offers much in the way of tourist at-
tractions or accommodations. A
possible itinerary spends a few
nights in Lyon with day trips to Firminy and La Tourette.

DIRECTIONS: The trip from Lyon
to Firminy is about 1 hour by car
and 1-3/4 hours by train. From
Lyon's Part-Dieu station take a
train to St Etienne and then switch
to a local line that stops at Firminy.
Trains run the complete circuit
about five times daily. From downtown Firminy, either walk (15 min.)
southwest on rue Jean-Jaurès and
then turn east (left) up the hill, or
take a bus from Place du Breuil.

AFTER BOMBINGS IN WORLD WAR II DE-
stroyed much of Firminy, the French government
decided to construct Firminy-Vert as a new town for
the working class on the site of an old iron mine. Le
Corbusier was not involved with the original planning or design of the apartment towers. He did,
however, discretely advise the mayor of Firminy-
Vert from 1953-72, Eugène Claudius-Petit, his
longtime supporter who as Minister of Reconstruction had helped in the realization of the first Unité.
With the approval of the town architects, Roux and
Sive, Le Corbusier received the commission for the
design of the athletic center, the Unité d'habitation,
and the church. Although the site plan for these buildings was designed by Le Corbusier, only the youth
center was completed during the architect's lifetime.
He did not choose the color scheme for the Unité.
André Wogenscky, his former partner, designed the
pool complex. The church remains incomplete.

As Petit explained, through its architecture and
planning Firminy-Vert was "to lay the foundations
for a renaissance of the human being, the family, and
society, to effect an authentic revolution in the gestures of everyday life which would directly affect
mothers and which would largely determine the be-
havior of children," as well as "to create the site, the
everyday urban landscape, spaces and volumes,
shapes and colors; to make the history of the
town...."

These proposals for a humanist future coincided
with Le Corbusier's constant desire "to introduce the
sacred into the home, to make the home the temple of
the family." The call to fill the tabula rasa of the
mine with volume, shape, and color reiterates Le
Corbusier's own definition of architecture as the play

of prismatic solids in light, as done in antiquity. For Le Corbusier, man's search for his history meant a return to classical sources rather than local precedents. Thus, to fulfill the vision of Firminy-Vert, he placed his Unité like a Greek temple on top of the hill and his athletic complex like an agora below.

Firminy-Vert, Unité

Le Corbusier's association of house with temple took its most monumental form in the Unité, where the pilotis form a great portico of columns and the apartments define a block of individually walled *"cella."* The roof terraces of these buildings are designed as vaguely ancient landscapes, with amphitheaters and hippodrome/running tracks. At Firminy, the roof playground has curious, low, curved walls evocative of ancient foundations.

As low-cost housing, the Unité at Firminy resembles more the Unité built at Nantes-Rezé than the original block at Marseille, which has luxurious finishes and dramatic sculptural effects. Like the building at Nantes, Firminy has apartments Le Corbusier considered inadequately small, and it lacks the commercial facilities he thought essential to the communal life of the inhabitants. In general profile and planning, however, this Unité adheres to the principles of its model, as described in the entry for Marseille.

The athletic complex mimics the Greek agora in its organization but transposes freely the functions of the original parts. For example, the playing field replaces the central marketplace of the agora; the youth center assumes the formal role of a stoa at the agora's edge. Had this public precinct been completed as planned, an open-air theater and stage for electronic spectacles, and an enclosed theater called a *boite à miracles* (box of miracles) would have approximated the Greek amphitheater and *odeion*. The unfinished church in the forecourt, which, according to Anthony Eardly, resembles the ruins of the Telesterion at Eleusis, would have constituted a mystical transmutation of cube into pyramid into cone.

The distinctive shape of the youth center originally had a utilitarian purpose: shading a grandstand built into its base. When the Ministry insisted that the youth center be opposite the stands, Le Corbusier followed their directive

Maison des jeunes

but raised the building above the field onto a remaining ridge of the mine and kept its profile, thus increasing its visual and symbolic importance. More akin in spirit to a work of Roman than Greek engineering, the building has a catenary structure of cables attached to the top of reinforced concrete columns. The curve of the roof is the parabola of the cables draped from post to post. The posts and exterior walls cant slightly outward as an expression of the tension force on the cables in between. The frieze of small rectangular openings marks the positioning of the cables. Each opening provides access to a tie-rod that secures a pair of cables and thus allows the tension to be regulated from the outside by adjusting the rods. The roofing plates are Celium auto-matted, cellular concrete, 10cm thick, resting directly on the cables.

The bas-relief on the gable end of the building includes many representations of the forces of nature favored by Le Corbusier. At the center is a bull's head with a feminine face floating horizontally within it. On the lower left are a human ear and a conch shell. By each of the four linear "branches" are small leaves and curved shapes like faces.

Today the youth center and the Unité bear signs of neglect; they are marked with graffiti. Their condition not only reflects the general state of economic depression in this mining region but also raises doubts as to the effectiveness of the town's architecture in accomplishing its humanist ideals. While some critics claim that the Firminy-Vert townscape of "towers in a park" does not accurately represent Le Corbusier's Radiant City of Unités and terrace apartments, others state that it descends from his proposal and that its failures can be blamed on him. Across the entire site of this townscape, Le Corbusier's sports complex and Unité establish a dialogue focused intently on both the landscape and each other, less concerned with their relation to the other solitary towers than to a timeless, ideal city.

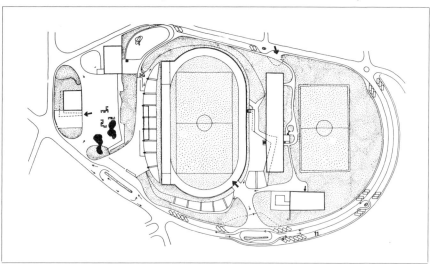

Athletic complex and Maison des Jeunes, site plan

Unité d'habitation, Marseille 1952

2800, boulevard Michelet 13000 Marseille, Bouches-du-Rhône

VISITS: Apartment house. Public areas visitable. Within the building is a small hotel, comfortable but not extravagant, intended as lodging for the guests of the residents but open to the public.

LOCALE: The Unité is located beyond the center of town, on a wide residential boulevard lined with apartment complexes. The picturesque port is several kilometers away but easy to reach via the subway and bus system.

DIRECTIONS: Take the subway to Rond Point, which is the end of the line, and then bus #21 or #22 to stop Le Corbusier. From the train station, the trip takes about 35 minutes with good connections.

THE MARSEILLE BLOCK IS THE FIRST BUILT example of Le Corbusier's Unité d'habitation *à grandeur conforme*. It was derived from the Unité d'habitation dwelling of his ideal Radiant City. First conceived as continuous linear blocks with setbacks, the Unité type appeared as a rectangular slab in schemes for Nemours, Algeria (1934) and Zlin, Czechoslovakia (1935). It emerged as the basic unit of housing in his plans for the postwar reconstruction of St-Dié and La Pellice/La Rochelle, and was developed as a block of the proper size for Marseille and, later, for Nantes, Briey, Berlin, and Firminy. The initial plans for Marseille and for most of the Unités included either three or four residential slabs with community facilities and garden apartments. However, no such context was ever realized, and the built Unités stand in isolation.

At Marseille the construction of even one building met with opposition. Only with the unwavering support of the Ministers of Reconstruction Raoul Dautry and Eugène Claudius-Petit, as well as seven successive city governments, was it completed amid complaints from architects that it violated building codes and from doctors that it would mentally damage its inhabitants. Since its completion, many have deemed its social program a failure, pointing out its underutilized communal facilities, its dim, lengthy corridors, and its anti-urban siting on enormous pilotis; however, its present occupants value its architecture. Le Corbusier argued that without its imagined urban context the Unité as a community would be doomed to failure through no fault of its own. While clearly cognizant of its limited representation of his ideas, he so much valued the Unité as an aesthetic accomplishment that he toured it with Picasso, whom he greatly admired as another artist of the Mediterranean. The building's character reflects this complex intersection of general type based on a lifetime of social thinking and its conceptual location on the "edge" of the Mediterranean, which had always been Le Corbusier's great source of inspiration.

The Unité concept of a single dwelling in a collective framework dates to Le Corbusier's 1907 visit to the Charterhouse of Ema, where the monks' cells are grouped about a communal cloister but open onto private gardens with a view of the Tuscan hills. He referred to the Charterhouse as the "indissoluble binomial, the individual-collectivity." Since the monastic life has limitations as a universal model for dwelling, Le Corbusier absorbed other, more widely applicable schools of thought relevant to his binomial proposition, which Reyner Banham refers to as the "cottage-cooperative" and "monumental-revolutionary" traditions.

The cottage-cooperative includes the Garden City tradition and variants of it, such as the worker towns of Tony Garnier's Cité Industrielle, where the unit of the family and dwelling remain distinct within a community that encourages mutual dependence and, in some cases, shared ownership of the means of production. Le Corbusier's "cottage" is his model Maison Citrohan, a free-standing house characterized by its rectangular perimeter, its double-height living room opening onto a large window, and its blank side walls.

In his writing on the Unité, Le Corbusier critiqued suburbia as a demonstration of the value and failure of the cottage model. He praised the "sacred idea of the nuclear family, the symbolic fire or hearth at the center of family existence, and the close contact with nature provided by the little house," but decried its repression of the

wife chained to the demands of housekeeping, the poor use of the 24-hour day devoted to work, commuting, and home maintenance, the financial problems involved in home construction, and the weak sense of collectivity.

Le Corbusier saw a possible antidote to these suburban problems in the monumental-revolutionary models for housing, from ocean liners and Charles Fourier's Phalanstery to early-twentieth-century Soviet social condensers. In these models, the individual home is subsumed and dignified within a monumental whole. The communal services of the "house-palace" liberate the individual from bourgeois domesticity. A variety of accommodations provides for the individuality and mobility of the inhabitants, who are freed from the biological family and from any fixed social role.

In the Unité d'habitation Le Corbusier tried to preserve the values of the cottage family while integrating it into a monumental form with some of the freedoms of Fourier's collective. For a community of 1,600, approximately Fourier's ideal as well, Le Corbusier provided twenty-three types of units, from bachelor studios and single hotel rooms for transients to apartments for families of ten. Le Corbusier called the apartments *logements prolongés* (extended dwellings) because they are extended through the provision of twenty-six services available to all the Unité inhabitants.

Halfway up the block is an interior commercial street with professional offices, shops, and services to liberate the housewife. The street is visible on the outside as a band of vertical lamellas. On the roof are communal facilities, including a nursery, a gymnasium, an outdoor theater, and a running track. The two-story apartments with overlapping sections generate a circulation system of internal corridors every third floor, called interior streets.

Once off the community thoroughfare of the corridor, the apartments present the essence of the individual cottage dwelling as Le Corbusier understood it. The isolation of the individual units extends to the very concept of the building's structural frame as a concrete bottle rack into which the apartments are inserted like bottles. He envisaged that someday the apartments would be prefabricated off site and then hoisted into the frame. The perimeter of the individual cell is carried through the skeleton onto the facade in the outline of the brise-soleil. The apartments within are in the mode of the Maison Citrohan: long, walled boxes with double-height living rooms opening onto large windows. The kitchen is the symbolic hearth, and the balcony is a high-rise equivalent of the cottage garden, with views to mountains or sea by means of which the resident can "commune alone with nature." Most apartments have two balconies, one facing east, the other west, positioned according to the solar cycle. According to Le Corbusier, the balcony links the apartment to "the most ancient traditions" and basic forms of dwelling because it is also a portico, "such as Socrates advocated, [which] allows the inhabitants of the house to savor the good things that a Bountiful God dispenses to men. It gives coolness in the summer and warmth in the winter."

In the wake of World War II, with metals in short supply, Le Corbusier brought to maturity at Marseille a style based on the plastic use of exposed concrete. Sometimes called brutalist, this aesthetic is characterized by its rough surface qualities, its forceful and organic forms, its strong colors, and its radical reconsideration of the wall. At Marseille, the glass wall of his earlier architecture is placed behind the thick but permeable wall of brise-soleil. Whereas in the purist style a single surface gives the illusion of having layers or depth, here, to the mobile observer, the wall both reveals and dissembles its thickness, appearing alternately as an open grid, a series of colored planes, and a

Apartment interior, ca. 1953

dense mass. As a system of brise-soleil, the thick wall represents the rejection of an architecture dependent on mechanical systems of air conditioning in favor of one with a symbiotic relation to climate, where breeze and shade are naturally manipulated. As loggia or balcony, it is a habitable extension of the house into nature. Once a transparent yet emphatic glass membrane, the wall is now occupiable.

Inherent in this sylistic shift is the idea of a new kind of humanistic architecture. The balconies are proposed as a new unit of wall that brings human scale to a large building. Endowing his building with anthropomorphic qualities, Le Corbusier likened the surface of concrete to human skin, which shows its age and character through its flaws. It was at Marseille that he first employed the anthropometric system of the Modulor to determine every dimension, from balcony to slab thickness. The figure with an outstretched arm impressed on the lobby walls is the Modulor man on which the system is based. Le Corbusier reported that the bright colored panels at Marseille were to disguise errors in the window proportions and thus to reassert the Modulor. Whether the Modulor's aesthetic effect is perceptible is often questioned. Jencks believes "the building is composed from five basic dimensions related by the Modulor which gives it a semantic strength greater than its particular dimensions, a fullness, a dignity."

As the classically rooted Modulor and the references to Socrates indicate, Le Corbusier's late style continued his early romance with antique Mediterranean culture, but with a different emphasis. Instead of limiting his references to the high culture of the Greek golden age, he evoked more archaic attitudes of Greek sources, its "raw materials" and "brutal order." The thickened masonry of the brise-soleil suggests analogies with ancient Roman and vernacular Mediterranean walls. The roof terrace, with its outdoor theater and totemic smokestacks, has the aura of a ritualistic

Roof detail

site or acropolis. The high parapet masks the immediate context and directs views to the mountains and Mediterranean, so that the roof becomes like the deck of a Homeric ship. In the Marseille block, Le Corbusier invested his utopian vision of dwelling with values connected to both the primal hearth and the ancients' landscape.

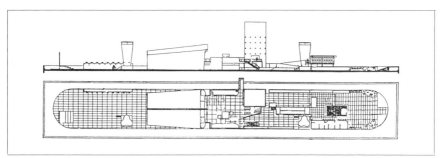

Roof terrace, plan and elevation

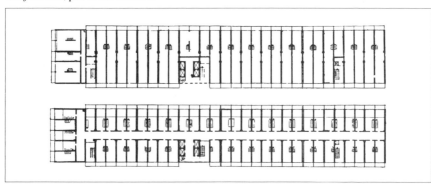

Typical floor plans

Villa de Mandrot 1931

Chemin de l'Artaude
83220 Le Pradet

Le Thoronet 70km, Toulon 4km

VISITS: Private residence in fair but unaltered condition visible from the street. Le Pradet has plans to establish hours for visiting the interior of the house, beginning in summer 1987. Check at the tourist office in the center of town, avenue de la Première D.F.L.

LOCALE: Le Pradet is a small town less than half an hour outside Toulon by public transportation. The terrain beyond the village is a high, gently rolling plain that provides many of the houses with dramatic views of the surrounding mountains. A possible itinerary travels north to the twelfth-century Cistercian Abbey, Le Thoronet, a model for Le Corbusier's monastery of La Tourette. The abbey is open daily except holidays (tel. 94.73.87.13).

DIRECTIONS: To get to the villa, take buses #39, #49, or #9 from avenue General LeClerc in Toulon to the center of Le Pradet. The walk to the villa takes about 15 minutes. Continue moving away from Toulon along rue St-David, which will eventually become chemin de l'Artaude. Opposite a new housing development called le Verger de Beauvoir there is a private road with a sign to that effect. The villa is the second house on the left. It is not visible from the main street. If you pass the camping grounds l'Artaudois on the chemin, you have gone too far.

LE CORBUSIER CITED THE REMOTE LOCAtion of the villa and the limitations of local craftsmen as the justification for this, his earliest foray away from the pristine surfaces of Purism. The first scheme for the house was a refined version of his Maison Locheur, his prototypical dwelling for rural areas in which prefabricated metal walls imported from Paris are combined with the rustic masonry walls that local contractors preferred to erect. The final design also adapts the purist concerns of his Parisian villas to the situation at hand. In between the stone end walls, at the center of the house, is a concrete frame of columns and beams set in from a free facade. The thin infill panels of glass and stucco together with the masonry create an ambiguous composition of transparent and overlapping planes. Even the terrace steps and dining table are articulated as abstract horizontal slabs. A dynamic geometry of asymmetrical and overlapping parts figures in the composition of the site plan as well. For example, the main block of the house continues beyond the forecourt along a narrow slot of space defined by the end of the garden wall. From the perspective of the lower courtyard, the garden wall is a vertical plane that continues below the terrace along the edge of the podium and into the ground.

In contrast to these purist qualities are the expressive use of rough stone and the manipulation of the landscape, both of which hark back to the naturalism of Le Corbusier's earliest Swiss architecture. As in the early chalets, masonry walls distinguished from stucco infill panels and earthen terraces are major elements of the architecture. Like the Swiss houses, but unlike the purist villas, Villa de Mandrot is wed to the hillside and sited according to the mountain view. Both the organization of the villa's forecourt and the curve and counter-curve of its podium recall in particular the terrace of Villa Jeanneret.

The confrontation of purist and naturalistic qualities in Villa de Mandrot affects the understanding of

Villa de Mandrot, wall detail

both. It creates a hybrid environment in which initial impressions are contradicted, expectations reversed, and experience consequently intensified much as in surrealist art. For example, because the natural stone is articulated as a flat plane, it "looks almost more painted than real." Because of the peculiar garden wall with a window, the natural terrace becomes a mysterious salon, complete with a dining table. The displaced room as an ambiguous realm of space and consciousness is a common theme in surrealist painting as well. The culmination of the architectural promenade through Villa de Mandrot is a view of the mountains, but a shocking one, because the final door opens in mid-air instead of on a level with the podium. Le Corbusier described the effect: "The site offers the striking spectacle of a vast, unfolding landscape, and the unexpected nature of this has been kept by walling in the principal rooms to the view and by having only a door that opens onto a verandah, from which the sudden vista is like an explosion."

In each case of theatrical effect, Le Corbusier revealed the artifice through which it was created. From the lower terrace he exposed the garden wall as a stage flat with struts fastened to the edge of the stage, or podium. He exposed the metal frames around the fieldstone panels to suggest how and why they look like paintings. He thrust the visitor into space on a level with the horizon only to admit it is a staged effect, complete with a ladder to descend to earth. This self-conscious shifting between artifice and nature, the sophisticated world of Purism and the primitive, gives the villa its surreal aura and suggests that the architect's initial peace with nature has been disturbed.

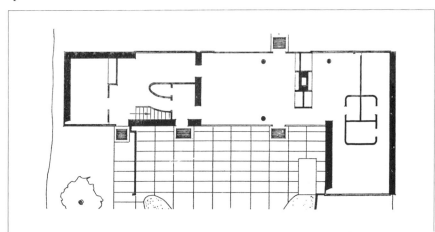

Terrace level plan

Le Petit Cabanon 1952

Path parallel to Sentier du Bord de Mer, Plage du Buse 06 Roquebrune-Cap-Martin

Menton 5km, Nice 26km

VISITS: A visit to the interior of Le Petit Cabanon requires permission from the town hall, which is granted with a letter of introduction from La Fondation Corbusier or a comparable institution. M. Rebutato, a relative of Le Corbusier's wife, has his own studio next to the cabin and keeps the keys.

LOCALE: Roquebrune is a beautiful hilltown with a network of paths leading up to an old château and down to the sea. One itinerary continues up the hillside from Le Petit Cabanon past a house designed by Eileen Grey (1926), to Le Corbusier's gravesite in the town cemetery, and then to the château. Menton is larger and livelier, with a notable Cocteau Museum.

DIRECTIONS: Trains run regularly from Nice to Menton. In summer, buses run from the center of Menton to Roquebrune several times an hour. Off season take a 10-minute cab ride from the Menton Casino to the center of the old village of Roquebrune.

The best route to Le Petit Cabanon is a scenic twenty-minute walk from the tourist office in the old village of Roquebrune. The office can supply maps. Take avenue Virginie Herriot to the sign for the hotel Europe Village. Walk down its private drive and around the outside of its garden wall along a narrow path leading to the sea. Beyond a concrete platform and drainage station the path divides. Take the right fork which emerges on a cliff at the water's edge. Cross the bridge suspended from the railroad wall. To the left is a gate to the property of M. Rebutato. Le Corbusier's cabin and studio are the two buildings just before the gate.

FOR HIS VACATION RETREAT, THE ONLY house he ever built for himself, Le Corbusier abandoned for a moment his search for new housing prototypes and chose for his dwelling an archetype. The two neighboring sheds, a log cabin for dwelling and a flat plank studio for working, are less a radical project of invention than *objets-types*, those banal, found vessels he put in his paintings. The cabin shell was actually a kit, prefabricated in Ajaccio, Corsica, which was then customized according to Le Corbusier's modulor dimensions. He described the studio as a worker's shed from a construction site. Both structures also resemble the outbuildings of the neighboring villas. The cabin differs slightly in that it is made of logs rather than planks or masonry. In its intentional rusticity it suggests the image of a primitive hut. The primitive hut, man's first constructed dwelling, has been the subject of endless speculation for architects and has often been depicted as a cabin of tree trunks crowned with branches or thatch. At Roquebrune, Le Corbusier placed his windows and finished his interiors with care, but in deference to the most basic of existing types he suppressed his will to invent.

The architecture of Le Petit Cabanon lies in the precise relations among the two buildings and the landscape. (The siting of the sheds brings to mind a conversation reportedly held between the young Le

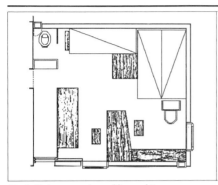

Petit Cabanon, plan of log cabin

Corbusier and his teacher L'Eplattenier. The teacher, who was entrusted with the design of a monument, asked Le Corbusier whether he thought an obelisk would do, to which Le Corbusier replied, "One obelisk—that's nothing. Two obelisks—that's architecture.") The cabin sits against the hillside almost like a cliff dwelling. Its roof aligns with the ground level above; its width coincides with the width of the terrace. A path leads from the cabin door, along the cabin front, to the side door of the studio. Thus, in connecting door to door, the path switches its geometric relation from the edge of one building to the center of the other and so implies a rotation of ninety degrees. Note that while the door is shifted from the rectangular face of the cabin to the slanted side of the studio, the volumes of the sheds have identical relations to the cliff, with their roofs slanting up and toward the sea. Because the terrace of the hill is not much wider than the buildings, a visitor cannot see both the front of the cabin and the sea at the same time. The view belongs to the occupant of the cabin, the man at the center looking out.

Le Corbusier rejected the theory, popular during the Enlightenment, that the Greeks translated the tree into the column and the primitive log hut into the stone temple. He contended that the geometry of the architecture was a "pure creation of the mind" linked to a cosmic order, not earthly nature. At Le Petit Cabanon, Le Corbusier stated his attraction for both "the hut of the savage and the Parthenon, distant as they are in their degree of order and understanding." He began with a shelter of logs related more to nature than to the history of architectural form, and built inside of it a modulor shell dimensioned according to his own version of the Greek system of measure. Standing between hut and horizon, one cannot help but muse on the character of the man who placed himself inside this double philosophical embrace.

Grave of Le Corbusier and his wife, Yvonne 1957

*Roquebrune Cemetery
Chemin de Pancrace,
Roquebrune-Cap-Martin*

VISITS: Public cemetery open daily.

LOCALE: See Le Petit Cabanon for general directions and description of region.

DIRECTIONS: The cemetery is a half-hour walk uphill from the tourist office. The most picturesque route is up the chemin du Pontet, past the chapels of St-Roch and la Pausa to the town château. Just before the entrance to the château take a right on to chemin de Pancrace. The entrance to the cemetery is on your left. Le Corbusier's grave is located beyond the second arched gateway on your right as you climb the central terrace.

LE CORBUSIER DESIGNED THE GRAVE IN 1957, the year of his wife's death. The tombstone summarizes the architect's lifelong belief in the connection among nature, geometry, and beauty. Within the four-square plot stands a hollow cylinder as a feminine vessel for Yvonne and an ambiguous angular solid for Le Corbusier. His headstone suggests many interpretations: a primitive shelter, a cube that has been rotated around an axis aligned with the plane of the ground, and a cube in exaggerated perspective. Its top plane slants down toward a horizon line that appears again in the bright, horizontal stripes on the enamel nameplate. Embedded in the plinth are Yvonne's cross and the impression of a seashell, one of the forms of nature Le Corbusier appreciated for both its organic curves and its inherent regular patterning. Thus Le Corbusier presents us with the most personally compelling aspects of his cosmos: prismatic solids, natural objects, and that ever elusive horizon line. But looking up from the grave to the Mediterranean he loved, it is clear he intended this landscape, unframed by any window, to be his final statement.

Quartier Moderne Frugès 1926

Rue Le Corbusier, rue H. Frugès, rue des Arcades 33600 Pessac

Le Corbusier and Pierre Jeanneret

Arcachon 57km, Bordeaux 7km, Lège 50km

VISITS: Neighborhood of private residences visible from the street. Many of the houses have been altered or are in disrepair, but there is at least one example of each house type in original, if not restored condition. The original site plan is also recognizable though overgrown and slightly obscured by added garden sheds.

LOCALE: When visiting Pessac, be sure to include enough time for a tour of Bordeaux. Much of the housing stock as well as monuments, plazas, and the spectacular Grand Théâtre date from the eighteenth century. Then there are the surrounding vineyards and the three-fork restaurants. In nearby Lège, Le Corbusier and his patron Frugès built a group of ten houses as a dry run for Pessac, but there the houses have been so completely altered by the inhabitants that the original architecture is virtually unrecognizable.

DIRECTIONS: Local buses on line P, destination Toctoucau, Magonty, or Clairière-aux-Pins, run from Quai Richelieu in downtown Bordeaux along avenue Jean-Jaurès, past Château Haut-Brion, directly to Quartier Frugès (20 min.). Get off at the stop just beyond avenue des Aciéries. To reach Lège continue from Pessac east on the Bordeaux-Arcachon road.

EVEN BEFORE HE TESTED HIS PURIST NOtions in the design of Parisian villas, Le Corbusier proposed a scheme for a Contemporary City of Three Million Inhabitants (see Pavillon de l'Esprit Nouveau). In this scheme a wide greenbelt separated a central city of business from the industrial district and from garden communities for the working class beyond. Though Le Corbusier conceived these workers' settlements more as suburbs economically dependent on the city of business than as independent towns, they are still in the tradition of the nineteenth-century British Garden City. The site plan of garden lots along orthogonally ordered streets, and the Mediterranean style of the houses, also owe a great deal to the residential district of Tony Garnier's Industrial City.

Early in his career, Le Corbusier had the opportunity to test a fragment of his working-class community outside an urban center, thanks to the patronage of Henri Frugès, an enlightened industrialist, artist, and man of letters who was impressed by the young architect's writing and work at the Salon d'Automne in 1922. Frugès sought to stabilize his sugar-cube factories' workforce by building housing first in a small development of ten houses, at Lège, and then in a community of over a hundred units, at Pessac.

The houses of Pessac evolved from Le Corbusier's vision of a new type of dwelling based on the potentials of modern industry. Like his prototypical Maison Citrohan, the houses have reinforced concrete frames with non-load-bearing walls, continuous ribbon windows in these "free" walls, roof gardens on top of the flat concrete roof slabs, and simple geometric volumes. Their designs use a handful of modular variations on a group of standardized elements. All the houses are built from combinations of two basic volumes, a square cell and a

Towers and terraces

rectangular half-cell. The standard window is a strip of alternating square and half-square bays. It has two independent subunits: a single square window and a Palladian grouping of a square flanked by two half-squares. Through this modular design Le Corbusier hoped not only to taylorize the building process by involving prefabrication but also to develop the house as a "tool for living in" (*machine-à-habiter*), fulfilling modern needs with standardized forms.

Adhering to his favorite adage of the eighteenth-century theorist Abbé Laugier—"wild variety in layout, uniformity in detail"—Le Corbusier tried to generate a great variety of types from his modular elements. The housing types include "towers" of two, three-story dwellings placed back to back; "arcades" of dwellings connected to one another with arch-covered terraces;

Z-shaped terrace

rows of attached "terrace houses" with alternating facades, one entered from the street, the other from the garden; Z-shaped "terrace houses" of two L-shaped dwellings facing opposite directions; and single residences with work-

shops on the ground floor. Although Le Corbusier articulated his types with stairs and arches, the spare, geometric uniformity of the complex was initially so severe that, under pressure from Frugès, he painted the different sides of the houses pale green, blue, yellow, and maroon. The colors broke the cubes into planes, expanded the sense of space, related the houses to their gardens, and added variety.

In siting the houses Le Corbusier grouped them according to type and massing along modest axes. The original project included a more formal sector with a broad avenue leading to a square plaza. The sector that was built has a central garden axis running be-

Terrace houses

tween the terrace units, interrupted by the cross-axis of single residences. A row of "towers" defines the edge of the complex and frames the central garden. The arcade is a special incident along an angled cul-de-sac.

Pessac also has sources outside Le Corbusier's modern agenda, in both the vernacular of worker housing and the history of the region. On the basis of his employees' tastes, Frugès insisted on detached and semidetached units rather than the larger towers Le Corbusier first proposed. Le Corbusier studied texts on vernacular housing and derived from them a five-meter module for all his elements. The southwest region of France provided models in the thirteenth-century *villes neuves* (new towns), planned communities on grids with arcaded

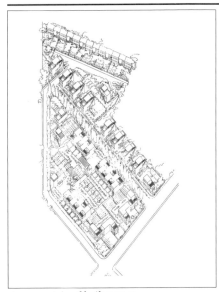

Axonometric of built sector

plazas bordered by commercial properties with dwellings above. The original plan of Pessac owed its square, avenue, and ground-floor workshops in part to the ancient towns.

Pessac was neither completed according to its original plan nor inhabited as intended. Bureaucratic and technical problems abounded during construction. The inadequacy of the site's drainage and sewage facilities delayed occupancy of the project for years. In his zeal to taylorize building practice, Le Corbusier insisted on using a tool, a cement spray gun for coating the wall panels, that the workers could not operate. Eventually, after bringing his Parisian contractor to Pessac at great expense, he changed the wall infill to traditional masonry, also at great expense. By the time he prevailed upon Minister de Monzie to let him complete fifty of the houses under a new housing provision, not only did the dwellings cost too much for workers to inhabit them, but

Frugès had suffered a nervous breakdown and moved to Africa. At first, a few daring bourgeois moved to the settlement. The Loucheur Law (1929) eventually made it possible for workers to afford to live there as tenants.

For one brief moment the empty project planted with fruit trees and painted pastel colors attracted international acclaim and visits from people like Mies van der Rohe and E. S. Rasmussen. But Rasmussen wrote in 1926 that despite the evocative nature of the objects, "the value of Le Corbusier's architecture for the future will be entirely dependent on his conception of the task of this architecture. If the program is wrongly conceived, then no matter how ingenious the solution, [the houses] cannot express our times." Events revealed that Rasmussen's doubts had been well founded. The occupants began to add to the cubic houses the pitched roofs and windows of the vernacular sheds of Bordeaux. If the task was to accommodate the needs of the users, then Le Corbusier had misjudged the conservative nature of these provincial citizens. If the task was to transform their nature, then he had failed. Although to this day residents appreciate the privacy achieved within the dense settlement, and although many have come to like the floor plans despite features that first shocked them, such as the small bedrooms and the entrance through the kitchen, they cannot tolerate the blankness of the facades. In response to the changes at Pessac, Le Corbusier commented, "You know, it's life that's always right and the architect who's wrong." It seems both a truthful and ironic statement, one that recognizes the paradox of an architecture so severe that the inhabitants want to transform it, so flexible and blank that they can.

Villa le Sextant (Maison aux Mathes, Maison l'Océan) 1935

Avenue de l'Océan
La Palmyre
17570 District Les Mathes,
Charentes-Maritimes

La Rochelle 85km,
Marennes 21km, Paris
520km, Royan 17km

VISITS: Private residence, visible from street.

LOCALE: La Palmyre is a summer beach resort that caters to families of campers. During the winter even the more substantial residences along the main avenue are empty. The surrounding countryside is quiet and agricultural. Most of the small villages have one short commercial street and a Romanesque church worth visiting. The closest city is Royan, a beach resort. The beautiful resort town of La Rochelle, 85km away, has good hotels and restaurants open all year, including the Hôtel Terminus and Hôtel Urbis, which is located in an old church.

DIRECTIONS: Getting to La Palmyre without a car is almost impossible. During the winter a bus goes from Royan to La Palmyre on Wednesdays, leaving at 12:30 and returning at 2:30. During the summer it runs daily. The winding, scenic route takes about 40 minutes. You can also take the more frequent bus to La Tremblade, walk 3km to Les Mathes, and then take a cab the 4km to La Palmyre. The road from Les Mathes, rue du Clapet, changes its name several times, but eventually reaches La Palmyre as avenue des Mathes. There it meets a major traffic circle and emerges on the other side as avenue de l'Océan. The house is less than 500m from the Atlantic.

LE CORBUSIER EXPLAINED HIS USE OF vernacular materials and forms at Villa le Sextant as the natural adaptation of his interest in prefabricated dwellings to rural circumstance. He employed fieldstone walls, timber framing, and prefabricated panels of glass, plywood, and asbestos cement in such a way that the three systems could be erected independently and without supervision. He explained the unusual butterfly-roof, with pipes that run along the center ridge, as a technical solution for heavy rainfall using concealed drainage. Although Le Corbusier saw the site only in photographs, the villa's strong resemblance to local barns suggests that he was quite familiar with the countryside. In fact, a barn of this type, a two-story stone box with an adjoining wooden shed beneath a continuous roof, stands on the road from Les Mathes.

On this updated regional model Le Corbusier imposed purist constructs such as the abstract relations of solid and void and the ambiguous nature of walls. The masonry box of the barn is pulled apart into two L-shaped planes joined by timber infill. The infill panels of wood and glass give the illusion of a transparent plane that continues behind the face of stone. Consequently, the masonry appears as both a weighty, load-bearing material and a surface that does not even touch the roof. This reading of a shattered box is reinforced by the opposition of solid and void. On the front of the villa, the void of the dining porch balances the solid block of the house. On the back, this relation is reversed. The solid rear wall of the porch balances the void of the linear balcony. This diagram of similar forms reflected diagonally across a center line often appeared in Le Corbusier's purist houses and in his paintings as well. Here he

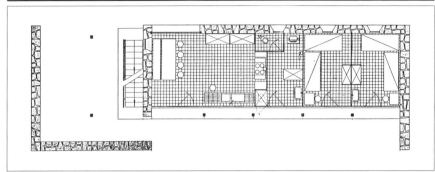

Villa le Sextant, ground floor plan

Balcony on rear facade

the possibility of an alternative architecture characterized by a more primitive technology, vernacular sources, direct expression of the means of construction, and the sensual primacy of the masonry. Whereas in the purist villas the illusion of transparent planes had required that a smooth stucco hide the cinderblocks beneath, here architectural illusion depended on the simultaneous expression and contradiction of the physical properties of the wall.

This alternative architecture was not an isolated incident in Le Corbusier's *œuvre*. It dates to his rustic Swiss chalets and his early admiration for the bricks and cement of ancient Roman walls. With Villa de Mandrot and Maison de Weekend, it developed in the 1930s as a critique of his own theory of a machine-age architecture. Frampton has observed that Le Corbusier designed le Sextant on the eve of World War II. It was perhaps "the vision of a forbidding future" that led Le Corbusier to confront his purist ideas with a humble, more earthbound dwelling.

marked the center with the sign of the sextant and a curious projecting shelf.

In applying purist principles of composition to the stone barn of le Sextant, Le Corbusier modified his original purist polemic. Initially, Purism was an architecture for the machine age, with slick white walls, floating cubes, and industrial images. Le Sextant presented

Unité d'habitation Nantes-Rezé, La Maison familiale 1953

19, rue Crebillon
44400 Rezé-les-Nantes

Angers 88km, La Rochelle 146km, Nantes 6km, Pornic 45km

VISITS: Public areas of the apartment house are visitable.

LOCALE: Rezé-les-Nantes is just across the Loire from Nantes, the principal city of Brittany. About 20km from the Unité is a hotel housed in the eighteenth-century Abbaye de Villeneuve (tel. 40.04.40.25), route des Sables d'Olonne, off route D178. A possible itinerary continues on from Nantes to the coast and Le Corbusier's Maison le Sextant.

DIRECTIONS: Local train and bus lines from Nantes stop near "Cité Radieuse Le Corbusier."

LA MAISON FAMILIALE WAS THE SECOND Unité built and the first to serve the organized working class that Le Corbusier envisioned as its proper tenants. Impressed by the recently finished Marseille Unité, a private cooperative composed primarily of laborers and foremen from the port of Nantes commissioned the building.

The Unité at Nantes differs from the model block at Marseille due to the combined factors of budget restrictions (which eliminated the sculptural treatment of the pilotis, portico, and roof garden), improvements in construction, and client demands. Improvements include detailing of the glass and wood exterior wall, and the surface finish of pebble aggregate in place of exposed concrete. In furtherance of the principle of standardized construction, a box frame of precast concrete slabs replaced the "bottle rack" system of Marseille. In this "château of cards," as Le Corbusier called it, there is no proper skeleton. The concrete "shoebox" of each apartment is the building frame as well. For acoustic purposes, bands of lead separate the boxes vertically, and fiberglass mattresses fill the space between. The four plate-like pilotis are the cross-walls of the apartments brought down to the ground to act as bracing as well as columnar supports. The stair towers also act as stiffeners.

For the large kindergarten on the roof terrace, Le Corbusier devised a thick wall reminiscent of Ronchamp, with a dense pattern of punched windows filled with colored and textured glass. This "optical glitter" breaks down the massive volume of the

Unité at Nantes, aerial view

school and provides a visual foil to the restrained surface of brise-soleil below.

Le Corbusier considered several of the modifications at Nantes-Rezé disruptive to the social vision of the Unité. He claimed the apartments were too small to be either comfortable or architecturally distinguished. The double-height living rooms of the Marseille block were totally eliminated; instead, the upper-level bedrooms were extended over the living room to the window. At the clients' request, there is neither an interior commercial street nor communal services other than the nursery on the roof, a laundry room on the fourth floor, and a tobacco stand and post office in the lobby. Despite the sluggish life of the interior street of Marseille, Le Corbusier considered commercial facilities vital to the social life of the Unité. In returning them to the traditional public realm of ground level, he acknowledged the benefits of an expanded clientele and relation to the community at large.

La Maison familiale's most distinctive feature is its siting. Several of its feet dip into an ornamental lake that fills an old red-granite quarry. The siting accentuates the building's resemblance to a great ship. It also suggests another source of fascination for Le Corbusier: the prehistoric lake dwellings on stilts found in central Europe. Like an expanded version of these dwellings, this "family house" is both raised above and immersed in nature. Le Corbusier intended the bridge across the lake as symbolic proof that the Unité was a viable and economical alternative to the modern suburb. He described how its 1,400 inhabitants passed over the single 1.83m-wide bridge daily without discomfort. He wrote, "Authorities require three kilometers of roads, communications, water, and gas in [suburban] family houses. Here there is a bridge over water. Impossible to cheat. 50 meters long. That's all."

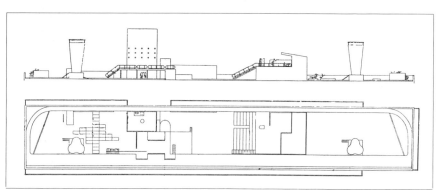

Plan and elevation of roof garden

La Chaux-de-Fonds and Switzerland

LA CHAUX-DE-FONDS, THE BIRTHPLACE OF Le Corbusier, contains many products of his life's work, including six early buildings. The town library, the Bibliothèque de la Ville at 33, rue du Progrès, has a marvelous collection of his sketches, correspondence, and memorabilia, which is accessible to scholars who request permission in advance. Le Corbusier's teacher, L'Eplattenier, was involved in the design of several murals and buildings in town, including the Crematorium, the Museum of Fine Arts, and the paintings in the post office.

The town retains many of the features that exerted an influence on Le Corbusier in the late nineteenth century. Like his own first city plans, La Chaux-de-Fonds is rationally ordered according to a preconceived plan. Following a fire in 1794, the town was rebuilt on a grid with a major avenue and pleasant town squares, many of which remain today. Two of Le Corbusier's buildings, the Cinéma Scala and the Villa Schwob, are located downtown on the grid. The other four houses he designed are located on a hillside path above the commercial center, on chemin de Pouillerel. At the time they were built, the neighborhood was a more rural colony of houses belonging to the intelligentsia. Today, nature is still close at hand in the forest paths that begin just behind Villa Jeanneret.

Villa Fallet	1907
Villa Stotzer	1908
Villa Jacquemet	1908
Villa Jeanneret	1912
Villa Favre-Jacot	1912
Cinéma Scala	1916
Villa Schwob	1916
La Petite Maison	1924
Immeuble Clarté	1931
Centre Le Corbusier	1967

Villa Fallet
1907

1, chemin de Pouillerel
2300 La Chaux-de-Fonds

Le Corbusier with René Chapallaz; decoration by students from the local School of Art.

VISITS. Private villa visible from street.

LOCALE: See La Chaux-de-Fonds.

DIRECTIONS: Take bus #10 to the chemin de Pouillerel or take bus #6 to rue du Nord and climb the hillside steps.

LE CORBUSIER WAS SEVENTEEN YEARS old when L'Eplattenier obtained this commission for him and arranged for the established architect René Chapallaz to supervise the project. The client, Louis Fallet, was a small manufacturer of watches, a member of the board of the School of Art, and a supporter of L'Eplattenier's educational ideas. While the house is imbued with Le Corbusier's spatial sense, it is, above all, a testament to L'Eplattenier's search for an architecture appropriate to the region of the Jura Mountains.

Sympathetic to the principles of the Arts and Crafts movement, L'Eplattenier advocated respect for local culture, materials, building methods, and landscape. In this spirit, Le Corbusier's first house incorporates most of the basic features of the region's vernacular architecture: overhanging eaves, complicated gables, and the clear disposition of materials according to their structural role. There is a typical rusticated stone base of yellow Neuchâtel stone and an expressed, heavy timber frame with infill stuccoed panels. The building is placed like most of the houses of the region—major axis and gable toward the view—but with a heightened sensitivity to its site. The land drops away beneath the house so that the entrance level is high on the hill and intimately scaled, while the south facade is vertical and imposing. The living room opens onto a balcony dramatically suspended over the slope. In contrast, the hollowed-out corner of the rusticated base hugs the ground. The plan follows the outlines of the Arts and Crafts and Hermann Muthesius in its separation of public and private areas and in its organization of the rooms around the surprisingly lofty space of the stairwell in the north gable.

Villa Fallet, facade detail

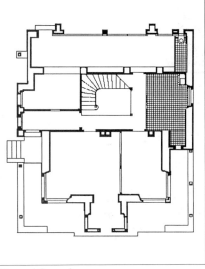

Ground floor plan

L'Eplattenier's curriculum is most clearly expressed in the ornament, based as it is on the nature of the Juras. The villa is covered with forest imagery. The naturalistic orientation of the trees, with mullions placed like branches reaching up and eaves carved as pine cones hanging down, reflects L'Eplattenier's own Ruskinian emphasis on direct observation of nature. All the ornamentation is depicted at some level of abstraction, however, according to a belief in the connection among natural forms, spiritual essence, and mathematics. Following the precepts of the grammar books of Owen Jones and Charles Blanc, and the more mystical texts of Henri Provensal, L'Eplattenier had his students extract the essential forces of natural forms by drawing their geometric structure. For example, on the villa, pine boughs are depicted as compositions of cubes. The abstracted ornament of the building as a whole is more decorative than severely Pythagorean. Its patterning relates to Art Nouveau and Jugendstil in its fluidity and in the equal weight given to figure and ground, branches and the spaces in between.

L'Eplattenier exposed his students to a spectrum of formal and philosophical ideas that contributed to his brand of national Romanticism as embodied in his search for a local style. Villa Fallet is the most complete evidence of Le Corbusier's youthful attraction to these ideas.

Villa Stotzer 1908

6, chemin de Pouillerel
2300 La Chaux-de-Fonds

Villa Jacquemet 1908

8, chemin de Pouillerel
2300 La Chaux-de-Fonds

Le Corbusier with René Chapallaz

VISITS: Private residences visible from street.

LOCALE: See La Chaux-de-Fonds.

DIRECTIONS: See Villa Fallet.

Villa Stotzer (above); Villa Jacquemet (below)

BOTH IN TERMS OF THEIR STYLE AND ORganization, Villas Jacquemet and Stotzer can be grouped as a single entry in Le Corbusier's work. Their difference in demeanor relates to the slight variations in their adjacent sites. While in Vienna on his grand tour, Le Corbusier designed the villas in tandem, mailing his drawings and models to La Chaux-de-Fonds. As in the case of Villa Fallet, René Chapallaz advised the younger architect, completed the drawings, and supervised construction.

The architectural similarity of the villas is a consequence of their nearly identical patrons and programs. Relatives of Le Corbusier's first patron, Louis Fallet, both clients shared his progressive bourgeois views. Each requested that his house contain two apartments designed to appear as a substantial single residence. In plan, Le Corbusier's solution for all the apartments called for a living-dining room on the south side, bedrooms on the north, east-west service wings with hooded bay windows, and a distinct entrance/stair hall half

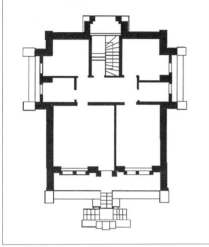

Villa Stotzer, ground floor plan

submerged in the main block of the house. Rather than use repetitive conditions to explore varied solutions, Le Corbusier formulated a modest typology. This attitude was to typify his design approach throughout his career.

Stylistically, Le Corbusier remained true to L'Eplattenier's philosophy based "on nature...and probity in the use of materials," while incorporating certain lessons from his travels. Like Villa Fallet, the houses have stone bases and piers, stuccoed walls, and heavy timber roof frames, but between the load-bearing masonry walls they have floor slabs of reinforced concrete built according to the Hennebique patent and the specifications of Samuel de Mollins, an engineer from Lausanne. The motif of the pine

cone and tree still appear in the eaves and windows, but massing and the bold treatment of structural elements displace surface pattern as the means of expression. The voluminous dormers are like foliage, the wooden supports like branches; Stotzer's masonry arch is an artificial grotto. The stone corbeling of Jacquemet's doorway suggests the interlocked forms of jagged pine boughs above the void of a stepped mountain. Le Corbusier's discovery of the stonework of medieval Florence contributed to this rejection of the Art Nouveau aspect of L'Eplattenier's regionalism.

The composition of the villas in relation to their site gives them recognizably distinct characters. Jacquemet, on the gentler slope, has the more placid appearance. The curved profiles of its stone piers ease its transition to the ground. The horizontal lines on the south side and the folded peak of the roof counteract the thrust along the major axis down the hill. Like a covered bridge, its vestibule spans the one abrupt drop in terrain. At Stotzer, on the other hand, the composition exaggerates the verticality of the slope, from the tilted roof to the cut in the high stone podium that leads to the elaborate stair. Subtly but insistently, Le Corbusier differentiated his boxes by placing a horizontal vestibule bridge on Jacquemet's front and a verticle exterior stair on Stotzer's rear, reversed but complementary devices for engaging the hill. In the quiet polemic of these two villas, Le Corbusier joined two ideas that are often dialectically opposed in his later work, the invention of a dwelling type and the response to a site-specific *genius loci*.

Villa Jeanneret 1912

12, chemin de Pouillerel
2300 La Chaux-de-Fonds

VISITS: Private residence visible from street.

LOCALE: See La Chaux-de-Fonds.

DIRECTIONS: See Villa Fallet.

IN THIS DESIGN FOR HIS PARENTS' HOUSE, Le Corbusier abandoned the modified chalet style of his early commissions for a restrained classicism. This change was inspired by his 1911 voyage to the Near East and by the book *Les Entretiens de la Villa du Rouet* by Alexandre Cingria-Vaneyre, which instigated his travel. Cingria argued that the French-speaking Swiss, or Suisse-Romande, descended from Mediterranean peoples and thus should have an architecture reflecting classical rather than Germanic values. His argument for buildings of pure, geometric shapes agreed with Le Corbusier's early lessons concerning the spiritual essence of Pythagorean solids; however, his description of calmly disposed, pale buildings distinct from the tones of the forest ran counter to the architect's use of natural motifs. Accepting Cingria's basic thesis, Le Corbusier intended the villa as a reconsideration rather than a rejection of the regional style.

For the particular forms of Villa Jeanneret, Le Corbusier turned to contemporary German neoclassicism rather than directly to antiquity. Behrens' Villa Shröder, Hoffman's villas at Kaasgraben and, through them, Frank Lloyd Wright's Winslow House were sources for his attic-story windows, floating hip roof, and axial planning. Still, the design indicates a consistent awareness of the classical precedents for these sources. The central salon, defined by four columns, has sources from Pompeii to Palladio. While evocative of a Mediterranean villa, the siting of the house, with its pergola and sequence of terraces, is Le Corbusier's first domestic representation

Upper terrace

Villa Jeanneret, side elevation

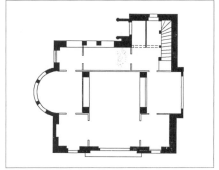

Ground floor plan

of the procession around the Parthenon, from natural slope to built podium, around the building to the rear entrance.

The regional aspect of the architecture lies primarily in the manner in which the building is wedded to the Jura hillside. Three terraces spiral about the villa, so that it engages the ground on several different levels. The upper terrace is an earthen extension of the villa wall. The rotated apse carved from the terrace, the winding stair, the protruding bay window, and the final patio, with its wave-like profile, together create a sequence of curve and counter-curve around the static, symmetrical box. Half built, half carved from the earth, part geometric, part organic, these curves mediate between the villa and nature. In his later work, abstract descendants of these curves appear inside buildings as representations of nature, but at Jeanneret the curves merge with the landscape. As in two earlier villas, Stotzer and Jacquemet, Le Corbusier took cues from the landscape and so created a new classical style for the Suisse-Romande.

Villa Favre-Jacot 1912

6, côte des Billodes
2400 Le Locle

Le Corbusier with
decoration by Léon Perrin

La Chaux-de-Fonds 8km

VISITS: Private residence visible
from access road.

LOCALE: Le Locle is a manufacturing town neither large nor
prosperous as La Chaux-de-Fonds
but similar in its landscape and feeling. Le Corbusier's client, M. Favre-
Jacot, owned the town's largest
operation, the Zenith watch factory,
and a lot of town real estate as
well. There is a watch museum and
a museum of fine arts in the town.

DIRECTIONS: A local train runs frequently from La Chaux-de-Fonds
and takes ten minutes. The best
view of the villa is not from côte
des Billodes. Instead, walk west
along the road in front of the station, following signs to the musuem
and hospital. After crossing the
train tracks, where the hospital
road turns back up the hill, continue
west to an unmarked drive lined
with trees. This is the entrance to
the villa. The côte des Billodes is
off the rue des Billodes just beyond
the small railroad bridge. There are
some good views of the villa from
rue des Billodes.

AT LE LOCLE, LE CORBUSIER CONTINUED
the search begun at Villa Jeanneret for a regional
style appropriate to the classical Mediterranean
heritage of the French Swiss. Again, for his forms he
turned to contemporary neoclassical models as well
as to the past. For example, the front of the house not
only recalls Behrens' Villa Cuno but has sources as
remote as the forecourt of the seventeenth-century
French Hôtel de Beauvais and Palladio's Villa Tris-
sino. Le Corbusier suppressed his original Jura
regionalism, understood as the need for architecture
to include images of nature, in favor of a classical
tradition. The shapes of pine trees that permeated the
early villas appear only as an abstract design on the
pilaster capitals. In his design of Villas Favre-Jacot
and Jeanneret, Le Corbusier reinterpreted
regionalism to mean the composition of classically
conceived, geometric solids that accord with the
spirit of the site.

Le Corbusier negotiated the steep hill at Le Locle
as he had at Villa Jeanneret, with a shifting sequence
of ground planes. The forecourt is the pivot point for
the various levels. Because the court is half carved
from the hillside, half built from the edge of the villa,
it connects house to garden at both balcony and
entrance level. As the court aligns with the access
road rather than the major axis of the house, it seems
to rotate and, through its rotation, to generate the
path down the slope. The asymmetry of the court
wall and the tilt of the ground plane increase the
sense of spin.

In elevation, the placement of the windows further
articulates the villa's ambiguous relation to the
ground. The window above the front door seems the
loggia of the *piano nobile,* but a similar window ap-

Villa Favre-Jacot, cliffside facade

pears on the cliffside at a lower level, as if the *piano nobile* were descending with the path. In fact, the forecourt does occur at mid-building: the cliffside win-dow marks the true *piano nobile,* while the front loggia is really on the third, bedroom floor. The game continues throughout the house.

In contrast to the descending path around the building, the interior prom-enade moves on the same level from the forecourt through the house, toward the view of the back garden and eventually to the terrace. Within this orthogonal framework are elements that repeat the themes of the exterior promenade, such as the cylindrical vestibule with a stair spiraling around it.

At Favre-Jacot, Le Corbusier placed every point of arrival or rest within a continuous sequence of spaces that, in the end, returns the participant to the landscape. By disrupting the static sym-metry of the design according to his desire for movement, he infused his classicized box with some of the charac-ter of the narrow terraces and winding paths of the Jura hillside.

Cinéma Scala 1916

52, rue de la Serre
La Chaux-de-Fonds

Le Corbusier and René Chapallaz

VISITS: Public cinema accessible during evening showings only. For the price of admission you can see a movie as well as what remains of Le Corbusier's design. Structural flaws required the front wall to be completely rebuilt. All interior finishes have been changed. The basic plan remains intact, however, and some of the original back elevation is still visible beneath the addition of a cantilevered projection booth.

LOCALE: See La Chaux-de-Fonds. The cinema is in the center of town.

DIRECTIONS: To get to Cinéma Scala from the train station take bus #10 to the corner of rue de l'Ouest, or walk.

IN THE COURSE OF TRANSFORMING A legitimate theater into a cinema, Le Corbusier used reinforced concrete to create a forty-foot clear span and a balcony cantilevered over four slender columns. Remarkable for the time, this structure still remains. On the other hand, the detailing of the pitched roof was disasterous. Water drained to the eave plates but then back down inside the walls, eventually leading to the structural failure of the cinema front. Le Corbusier claimed that this experience spurred his research into flat roof slabs with internal drainage, first used at Villa Schwob.

In elevation Le Corbusier created an architectural dialogue between rear and front facade. In both elevations he focused on the motif of an arch within a pediment, reminiscent of Claude-Nicolas Ledoux and Behrens, but he varied elements of size, placement, and stylistic nuance. The expansive arch on the front was part of a romantic-classic composition, with flanking colossal pilasters and two miniature temple fronts. It rose above the cornice line and thus accentuated the continuous planar quality of the wall. In contrast, the rear arch was the front layer of a composition with a great deal of actual depth. It was small and low, as if Le Corbusier conceived of it at a great distance from the cinema front, diminished in size according to the laws of perspective. This telescoping effect was carried further in the relation of the small pediment and lunette window to the arch below. Rather than the arch, the wide pediment and taut cornice dominated the rear composition and divided it into two distinct zones. Below the thin horizontal line, groupings of simple geometric pilasters created an ambiguous pattern across the facade. Although much of the central figure of the back elevation is now lost, the pilasters, the strong punctuation of the oval windows, the clear symmetries, and the overlapping pediments still com-

Rear elevation (original)

Front elevation (original)

municate the forceful severity of this rear composition.

Whereas in historical perspective the Cinéma's relation to the movements of romantic and rational classicism is clear, to the population of La Chaux-de-Fonds in 1916 it appeared radically abstract; the local paper even called it "cubist." In light of Le Corbusier's next work, Villa Schwob, where the cubist potentials of this simplified geometric style emerged in the conception of interior space as well, the public's response to the Cinéma appears justified.

Villa Schwob (Villa Turque) 1916

167, rue du Doubs
2300 La Chaux-de-Fonds

Le Corbusier, with bas-reliefs by Léon Perrin.

VISITS: Private residence visible from street.

LOCALE: See La Chaux-de-Fonds.

DIRECTIONS: The house is in a residential neighborhood on the eastern edge of the town grid. Either walk (20 min.) or take bus #6 from the train station to rue de la Fusion, then walk downhill to the villa.

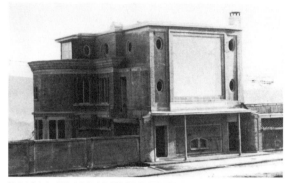

IN 1914, IN AN ARTICLE ENTITLED "RENEWal in Architecture," Le Corbusier publicly abandoned his search for a Swiss regional architecture and ornamentation. His interests had turned toward the international scene and the progressive, rationalist arguments of Perret. Villa Schwob was the first building designed at this juncture in his thinking and the first that he chose to publish (in *Vers une architecture*), implying that it fulfilled his new ideas. Although an eclectic array of sources both antique and contemporary is still apparent in the forms of Villa Schwob, the personal interpretation of these sources and the systematic application of rationalist ideas throughout distinguish it from his prior work.

While he had employed concrete in his architecture beginning with Villa Jacquemet, at Schwob Le Corbusier used it systematically in accordance with the abstract construct of his Maison Dom-ino. The salon has slender columns supporting smooth slabs at the center of a freely flowing space. The large window flooding the room with light is a direct consequence of the non-load-bearing wall. The flat roof slab holds a small roof garden and inclines slightly toward the center to provide a system of internal drainage. The central heating circulates warmed air through the cavity between the two nonstructural layers of brick. Despite a cost far in excess of traditional masonry, Le Corbusier maintained great faith in the future of the system, proudly announcing that Schwob was one of the first concrete villas in Europe.

For the particular forms of Villa Schwob, Le Corbusier turned to his prior sources of inspiration, striving for an increasingly personal and rigorous interpretation. Besides the usual references to Behrens and Hoffman, he looked to Perret's Théâtre Champs Elysées for the front facade and to the Byzantine architecture he saw on his travels for the house's massing. As in Villa Jeanneret, a four-columned court appears in the main salon, this time adjacent to a compressed stair hall reminiscent of F. L. Wright's Willits House. The biaxial symmetry of the plan and the tripartite division of the facade are both Palladian, perhaps influenced by that architect's Casa Cogollo.

Le Corbusier's new architectural logic begins with his abstraction of these sources in the spirit of Perret's rational classicism. In order to emphasize their pure geometric qualities, the forms of Villa Schwob are stripped of ornament. For example, the pilasters on the apses are semicircular cylinders, like the apses themselves. The cornice is three bare, overlapping planes. Most abstract is the front facade, which reads both as a massive extension of the garden wall and as a weightless plane stretched between the oval windows.

In the framework of this stripped-down classicism, Le Corbusier manipulated the size and shape of the elements to create a composition of intense contrasts. In elevation, plan, and massing these contrasts are powerful enough to threaten the harmony of the whole and require a strong opposing force to restore the balance. In elevation, the extreme delicacy of the porch columns plays off the severe quality of the wall behind them. The overblown cornice seems even more oddly scaled in relation to the small oval windows above. In order to control these contrasts and to draw the disparate elements into a unified whole, Le Corbusier proportioned the facades in the tradition of Choisy, with a system of angles related to the golden section, which he called regulating lines.

Front and back facades stand in contrast to one another. While the garden facade of Schwob is all glass, light, and

openness, the street side is blank, walled, and mysterious, with two identical doors only one of which leads to the main vestibule. The name Villa Turque resulted from this secretive, "seraglio" quality as well as from the Byzantine massing.

In terms of massing, the geometric clarity of front plane, apses, central cube, and corners break the building down into separate parts. Perhaps in homage to the "machined perfection" of the entablature of the Parthenon he so admired, Le Corbusier then used the huge chiseled cornice to wrap the separated volumes together.

On the inside of the house, the conflict occurs between the primacy of the central cube and the lateral pull of the many cross-axes. From the perspective

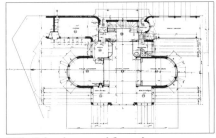

Villa Schwob, ground floor plan

of the entrance hall, the salon appears to be a unified and luminous volume with a strong axis leading to the garden window. Once in the room, however, the angled balconies and the layers of the apse and the library slice the room apart. A sense of spatial flow and instability dominates over the perception of the static position of the double-height cube. In his incipient search for a new architecture, eventually developed as Purism in the Parisian villas of the 1920s, Le Corbusier stretched to its limits the vocabulary and principles of his rational classicism.

La Petite Maison 1924

Route de Lavaux
Vevey

Le Corbusier and Pierre Jeanneret

Geneva 78km, Lausanne 19km, Montreux 7km

VISITS: Open Wednesday afternoons from 2 to 6 except Dec.-Feb. Call 52.78.61 to arrange for visits during the winter months.

LOCALE: Vevey is a resort town on the shores of Lake Geneva (Lac Léman). When Le Corbusier built his little house, only an old Roman road connected it to the sleepy village. Today the major thoroughfare to Lausanne runs right through the town and in front of the house. Still, the terraced vineyards that spill down the Alps to the lake are spectacular; they can be viewed from the funicular that runs from the town center.

DIRECTIONS: By train Vevey is a half hour from Lausanne and an hour from Geneva. Service runs hourly. From the train station walk west in the direction of Lausanne on avenue Général Guisan, which becomes route de Lavaux. The house is on the lakeside of the road about 20 minutes from the station and just beyond the Nestlé Headquarters.

THE "LITTLE HOUSE" WAS A VACATION home Le Corbusier designed for his parents just before his father's death. His mother spent time there throughout her life as did his brother, a composer who used it as a studio. Many photographs survive of family gatherings in the garden. The house still contains personal artifacts, such as Mediterranean pottery and an elaborate wood desk designed by the architect early in his career.

Vevey provides an interesting case study of Le Corbusier's ideas of general type and mass production confronted with a very personal program. Here and throughout his work he was constantly resolving the tension between his search for a modern, standardized, international architecture and his love for the timeless vernacular of the Mediterranean. These contrasting impulses had been combined previously in his prototypical dwelling the Maison Citrohan.

Le Corbusier described Vevey as a "dwelling-machine." Like Maison Citrohan it is a simple rectangular box with continuous horizontal windows that provide the interior with enormous amounts of sunlight and the exterior with a new, industrial aesthetic. At Vevey, one wall is slashed by such a strip window which bears no strict relationship to the particular division of rooms. To protect the north face of the masonry building several seasons after its completion, Le Corbusier himself covered the original stucco with corrugated metal and took pleasure in his then avant-garde use of a prefabricated material intended for airplane cockpits. He claimed that the dimensions of the box derived from the areas exactly required by the specific functions within. In order to satisfy those functions, he inserted a central "gear" of built form that generates the spaces along the garden wall. Some of the parts operate like tools. Have the attendant slide the bedroom wall to show you the storage cabinets below the floor.

La Petite Maison, wall detail with window

Interior view

Despite all these general and mechanistic attributes, the lakeside house has a Mediterranean vernacular aura. It is a low-slung, wall-bearing box wedded to the ground and opening quietly onto a garden. A whitewashed wall separates the house from the street and wraps the yard, transforming it into an outdoor room. The architectural promenade through the house culminates in this garden-room, at the cogent still life of a dining table before a stone wall with a window to the lake. Inside the house Le Corbusier used color and contrasting sources of light in order to enrich and modulate the simple sequence of spaces in relation to the landscape. For example, the end rooms, lit only from above and darkly painted, are a caesura from the view and light before the visitor passes to the outdoors.

Le Corbusier wrote that he and Pierre Jeanneret went in search of the "perfect site" for this house with the completed plan in their pockets. Contained within that plan was a romantic idea of dwelling that could fully express itself only in relation to its envisioned landscape. The strip window of the house needed the aedicule in the rough stone wall, the machine its garden.

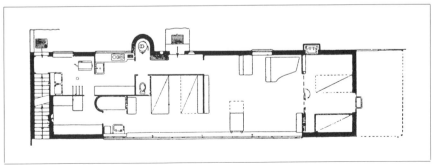

Ground floor plan

Immeuble Clarté 1931

2, rue St Laurent
Geneva

Le Corbusier and Pierre Jeanneret

VISITS: Apartment building with some professional offices. Public areas visitable.

LOCALE: The building is located on the southeast side of town, in a pleasant neighborhood not far from the Museum of Natural History.

DIRECTIONS: Rue St Laurent is a five-minute walk from the Rond-Point de Rive. Trolley or bus lines #12, #2, #11, and #15 all pass close by.

BY 1930 LE CORBUSIER HAD BEGUN TO revise his first scheme for a Contemporary City (Ville Contemporaine) to be the more egalitarian and expandable Radiant City (Ville Radieuse). A reformulation of his plans for the standard units of housing in his imagined city accompanied this shift. The apartments of the Radiant City stressed economy, standardization, and number of dwellings, where those of the Contemporary City focused on providing the elite classes living at the city center with a luxurious lifestyle. In the Radiant City, everyone was to live in long, horizontal blocks of single-story apartments called *blocs à redents* (blocks with setbacks). Gone were the *immeuble-villas* (villa-apartments) of the earlier city, with their alternating cells of two-story villa and hanging garden. Influenced both by CIAM's proposals for minimal dwellings and by current Soviet architecture, the plans of the Radiant blocks stressed the flexible use of space and rooms of small dimensions with built-in equipment instead of furniture. Thin sliding partitions as in a *wagon-lit* replaced traditional walls so that spaces could be combined according to family need. Basic to the character of these apartment blocks were pilotis, roof terraces, and the sheathing of glass wall *(pan de verre)* to provide interiors with the "essential joys of sun, space, and green."

The Immeuble Clarté was Le Corbusier's first commission for a multiple dwelling and, consequently, an experimental attempt to realize some of the housing principles from both his initial and emerging city schemes within the context of a preexisting urban fabric. In the alignment of the Clarté's major axis along the minor cul-de-sac and in the severe design of the avenue facade, Le Corbusier registered his dissatisfaction with the existing city street. The organization of the apartments along a horizontal slab conforms to the precepts and aesthetic of a Radiant City. The procession through the building moves from the shadowed lobby, with its classically placed columns, toward the "essential joy of light" to be found at the top of the skylit stairwell and in the apartments. Access to the apartments from a central interior corridor allows the units on both sides of the building to face uninterruptedly onto the balconies. The ideal of the glass wall is approximated by the large composite panels of glass and wood.

Most of the apartments derive from the housing of the Contemporary City, two-story units with balconies overlooking double-height living rooms. Even the single-floor flats have a generous breadth of dimension associated with the early, more luxurious dwellings. However, in the particulars of planning, such as the sliding partitions and built-ins, they reflect the later attitudes of economy.

The client for the Immeuble Clarté, the metals manufacturer Edmond Wanner, encouraged Le Corbusier to think in terms of standardization and prefabrication. One of those elite captains of industry in whom Le Corbusier placed hopes for the future of society, Wanner commissioned several large, idealistic projects from the architect, but only Clarté was built. As a consequence of Wanner's interests and capabilities as a contractor, Clarté is the first building in which Le Corbusier used a structural steel frame. From columns to windows, it is designed according to an unvarying module. Wherever possible, from wall panels to awnings, elements were fabricated in quantity off-site and then assembled "dry" in the building. Unfortunately, the techniques used in this relatively new construction process did not all have the clarity represented by the lobby's elegantly detailed metal stair. Within the steel structure, a subframe of wood supported traditional wood flooring and plaster ceilings. As a result, the building recently required massive restoration. Whatever the technological limits of this experiment in housing, the architectural repetition of the two monumental portals and lobbies confirms the intended message of standardization: that Immeuble Clarté is a slice of a *bloc à redents* that would continue well beyond its actual end in a future Radiant City.

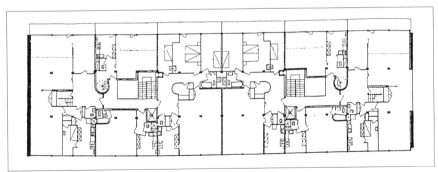

Immeuble Clarté, typical floor plan

Centre Le Corbusier, La Maison de l'Homme 1967

*Höschgasse 8
Zurichhorn Park, Zurich
110, A Postfach, CH-8034
(mailing address)*

VISITS: Open July 5-Oct. 5, Sat. and Sun., 2-6. Because of the extensive glazing and surrounding open space, it is possible to get a good sense of the interior even when the building is closed.

LOCALE: The Center is located in a small park complex that contains several other museums. Of special interest are the changing contemporary exhibits at the Gallery of Applied Art, across the street.

DIRECTIONS: The tram up Seefeldstrasse passes Höschgasse, but the 40-min. walk from the center of town, along the Seefeld Quai, is lovely.

THE IDEA OF TENT APPEARS CONTINUALLY in Le Corbusier's work, from the drawing of the nomadic shelter-temple in *Vers une architecture* to the exposition tent of the Pavillon de Temps Nouveau (1937), the huge pyramidal umbrella of the Porte Maillot project (1950), and its final realization in Zurich. Le Corbusier and Heidi Weber intended the pavilion as a proper architectural setting for the artwork of Le Corbusier, among others, and as an "example of dwelling." Although outfitted with a kitchen, bathroom, and possible bedroom, it was intended neither as a house for Weber nor as a demonstration house. Its title, House of Man, indicates that it was constructed "on the scale of man, for the disposition of man." This curious combination of ideas of domestic shelter with public exhibition is reflected in the relation of the cubes of the building proper to its monumental umbrella.

The construction of the building from modular cubes reflects Le Corbusier's late concepts of cellular growth. In unbuilt projects such as the dwellings of Roq et Rob and the Venice Hospital, he rejected traditional values of complete and predetermined form, proposing instead an expandable architecture composed through the repetition of identical units. The modular cubes suggest a limitless fabric that continues uninterrupted throughout the building, even by the ramp, which slides comfortably into a module. The half-bays at either end of the building emphasize the idea of infinite extension. The metal technology of the Center, interesting in itself as a departure from the brutalist concrete of the previous decade, has special relevance to this cellular idea of a standardized system. With the advice of Jean Prouvé, Le Corbusier developed a structural system similar to the one proposed for Roq et Rob, based on a single length of steel angle. That length, 226 cm, is the length of a six-foot man with an outstretched arm, the basic unit of Le Corbusier's Modulor system of measure. Here the prefabricated angles are bolted together to form cubes and filled with panels of glass or enameled metal. It is known as Le Brevet, or "226x226x226," in reference to the modulor dimensions of the basic building block. The consistent detailing of the cubes with reveals, so that the panels seem to float within the frames and above the ground, emphasizes the complete and independent nature of the system.

Onto this organization of dwelling cubes Le Corbusier imposed the larger order of the custom steel umbrella and the concrete ramp, two elements from his more monumental and ceremonial architecture. The umbrella defines a perimeter in three dimensions, beyond which the cubic grid cannot grow. Its supports at the center of the modules interrupt the rhythm of the expanding grid. The dialogue that typically occurs within the column grid of Le Corbusier's buildings here takes place between the umbrella and the cubes. For example, the umbrella support opposite the center of the entrance, like the perimeter piloti at Villa Savoye, blocks the axis to the door and thus a conflict with the interior grid. The posts of the grid, like the foyer columns of Villa Savoye, flank rather than occupy the center of this entrance. However, while this dialogue between center and edge occurs within a single structure at Savoye, at Zurich it takes place between the umbrella and the cubes.

The ramp further transforms the character of the pavilion by bringing ceremonial form to the architectural promenade through the building. It weaves an invented landscape, which extends from the subterranean exhibit room to the roof terrace, culminating in a framed view of the sky beyond. Even though the ramp impinges on the cubes only at the landing, this intersection is sufficient to connect the modulor House of Man to the more monumental expression of a shelter in nature.

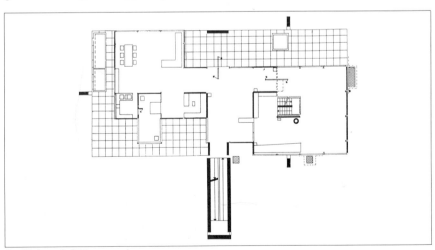

La Maison de l'Homme, plan

Belgium

Maison Guiette   1926

Germany

Weissenhof houses   1925
Unité at Berlin   1958

Italy

Pavillon de l'Esprit
  Nouveau   1925

Maison Guiette 1926

32, Popanerenlaan (in French, avenue des Peupliers) Antwerp, Belgium

Brussels 52km

Le Corbusier and Pierre Jeanneret

VISIT: Private residence currently under restoration. Both front and back visible from street.

LOCALE: Antwerp contains many examples of Flemish Baroque architecture. The home of Rubens, it holds many of his masterpieces as well as his house. Maison Guiette stands beyond the circumferential, beside a pleasant residential neighborhood. Visitors may either spend time touring the rest of Antwerp or visit Maison Guiette on a half-day trip from Brussels.

DIRECTIONS: From Brussels airport, buses run hourly to central Antwerp (50 min.). From Brussels Midi, the train to Antwerp runs every half-hour (40 min.). From the Antwerp train station take local bus #26 or #17 (15 min.). Get off several blocks after the bus crosses the Kleine Ringweg on Eglantierlaan, just before its intersection with Vare della Faillelaan. The house is on a rather forlorn street overlooking the freeway.

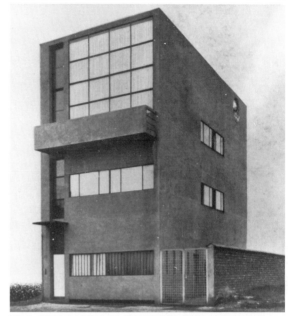

FOR THE PAINTER GUIETTE AND HIS FAMIly Le Corbusier adapted his mass-production Maison Citrohan (1922) to a standard Antwerp lot, six meters wide and very deep. Like Maison Citrohan, Maison Guiette is a freestanding rectangular volume with major facades facing front and back and rather blank side walls. As in the Citrohan, the posts of the concrete frame structure fall between the narrow bay for the linear stair and the wide bay with the living quarters. The double-height studio with balcony that Le Corbusier used as the living room in the Citrohan is returned to its authentic role on the top floors, as a painting workshop for M. Guiette. The living room of Guiette is on the ground floor facing the garden. Because of the site's depth, the typical Citrohan plan, with each room looking out either a front or back window, gives way to a linear sequence of three rooms, with the middle one looking onto a side garden. This plan recalls townhouse traditions both European and American. Le Corbusier wittily acknowledged the resemblance when he described the Guiette stair as the "Jacob's Ladder" of the tenement in Charlie Chaplin's movie *The Kid* (1919).

Like the Maison Citrohan, Maison Guiette was a demonstration of the new aesthetic and functional freedoms provided by the concrete frame structure. Nonbearing walls are free to curve and to have large openings. On the interior they become curving,

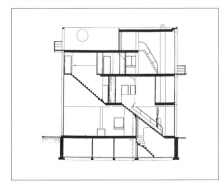

Section

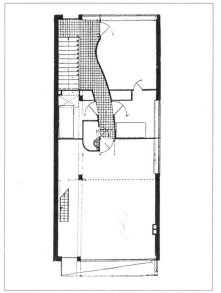

Maison Guiette, second floor plan

streamlined containers for efficient bathrooms, like ship or plane cabins. On the exterior their continuous horizontal openings bring light and air deep into the house. The concrete frame also generates a flat roof slab that supports a garden. Far from the grime of the street, this terrace replaces the ground lost to the building's foundations. Le Corbusier wrote in reference to the Maison Citrohan, "There is no shame in living in a house without a pointed roof, with walls as smooth as sheet iron, with windows like those of factories. And one can be proud of having a house as serviceable as a typewriter."

The new house Le Corbusier described is functionally precise yet aesthetically conceived. At Maison Guiette the balanced asymmetry of the windows and balconies owes something to De Stijl compositions of the period, but the insistent cubic volume of the house is particular to Le Corbusier. Whereas De Stijl architecture explodes volumes into abstract, independent planes, Le Corbusier's suggests interpenetrating volumes and planes beyond the literal relations of floors and rooms but within the confines of the cube. Most of the geometric play concerns the relation of front to back rather than the house as an object in the round. For example, the vertical strip window defines a layer of space

running continuously from front to back. The strip window below the balcony suggests a similar, horizontal slot of space. The front studio window describes both a void cube above the balcony and a plane of glass that passes continuously from the top to the bottom of the building.

At Maison Guiette, the building restrictions of the Antwerp lot complemented the parameters Le Corbusier set himself in his prototypical dwelling. The result is a lively and complex articulation of the Citrohan box.

Roof garden, Le Corbusier's sketch

Single-Family House and Two-Family House of the Weissenhof 1925

Am Weissenhof 30
7000 Stuttgart 1
Tel. 257 1434 (Architecture Gallery)

Basel 150km, Karlsruhe 80km, Ulm 92km, Zurich 230km

Le Corbusier and Pierre Jeanneret

VISITS: Private residences viewable from outside only. Complex open throughout the day. The Weissenhof Architectur-Galerie, which sells guides to the complex and holds exhibits of modern architecture, is open 2:00-6:00 Tues.-Sat. and 11:00-4:00 Sun.

LOCALE: From the top of the Siedlung one has a fine view of Stuttgart, with its picturesque vineyards within the city fabric. Stuttgart has many other buildings notable in relation to the Modern movement, including the Zeppelinbau by Bonatz and Celle Schoal by Haesler. More recently, it has become the home to the Kunstmuseum by James Stirling, which has a good restaurant and is near the train station.

DIRECTIONS: From opposite the Stuttgart train station, at bus stop "Kunstacademie," take the #43 bus in the direction "Killesberg." It is a ten-minute ride to the top of the Weisenhof hill (Weissenhofsiedlung). The complex will be on your right.

Two-family house

IN 1925, THE DEUTSCHE WERKBUND, A GERman national academy and workshop dedicated to the revitalization of art through industry, held its second international exhibition in Stuttgart. The exposition included temporary pavilions and an enclave of experimental dwellings intended to be permanent. The Weissenhof is that enclave recently renovated. Mies van der Rohe, vice president of the Werkbund and director of the exhibition, chose the participating architects and designed the site plan. His international roster included the Germans P. Behrens, W. Gropius, B. Taut, H. Poelzig, and H. Scharoun; the Dutchmen J. P. Oud and M. Stam; the Belgian V. Bourgeois; and the self-designated Frenchman Le Corbusier.

Given the suburban site and the exigencies of an exhibit situation, Mies realized the Weissenhof could not pretend to present a model ideal community. Rather, he intended that each architect present his concept of the basic unit of dwelling from which an ideal community could be built. Still, he incorporated innovative principles into the site plan. Instead of a series of lots along linear streets, he created a series of garden terraces for the individual buildings, each with its own yard, view, and pedestrian paths.

The Weissenhof exhibit was the first public forum for the post-World War I work of an international group of architects all concerned with the dwelling and the city in their relation to new means of production. More than their individual differences, the similarities among the exhibit buildings made a strong impression on the public and inspired the critic Alfred Barr to coin the name "International Style."

In his writings for the exhibit, Le Corbusier explained his houses as the product of a new system of structure based on the potentials of the reinforced concrete frame, a system he enumerated as the Five Points. Together the Points revolutionized every aspect

Single-family house

of the house. They provided "a roof garden for the top of the house, pilotis beneath it, a free plan inside of it, a free facade on the outside, and maximum illumination through strip windows." From columns to metal windows and prefabricated stairs, all its elements were industrialized, standardized, and taylorized in their means of production. The style of this architecture was thus to be derived directly from technical innovations serving human needs; it was not a matter of choice.

Implicit in the standardization of this structural system is the idea of a mass-produced, typical house. Le Corbusier emphatically argued that the system did not entail the production of a single type of dwelling. The standardized elements were calculated to satisfy the uniform physical needs of the human being, but the flexibility of the system produced an "absolutely revolutionary freedom" to invent a wide variety of dwellings for the spectrum of "moral types." In this spirit, Le Corbusier used his structural system and Five Points to create for Stuttgart two of the possible categories of dwelling.

He described the single-family unit

as a "dwelling that derives from the primitive hut a certain force and certain simplification in its manner of living." As in his prototypical Maison Citrohan, a double-height living room dominates the plan, organizes the facade, and determines the major axis from back to front. At the rear of the box is a sleeping balcony with kitchen tucked below. On the roof are the children's bedrooms and garden. The maid's quarters and service area stand beneath the pilotis. Circulation is along the building edge in a slot of space that extends through the facade onto the small balcony. This architecture provides for a kind of nuclear family life focused on a large communal space around a hearth, with a clear hierarchy of bedrooms for private activities. Formally, its curves and angles enrich the experience of the "simplified order." For example, the mechanical shaft becomes a vertical axis of sculptural form as it rises through the house, interlocking with the hearth, deflecting the balcony, and finally emerging on the terrace.

As a box raised on pilotis with a framed roof garden and a true strip win-

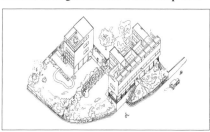

Aerial sketch

dow, the two-family house clearly employs the same system of structure as the single-family house and with a similar aesthetic effect. In plan, however, it differs from its neighbor according to the character of its imagined inhabitants. In contrast to the Citrohan type, here all the family dwelling rooms are on a single level along an axis that

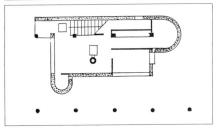

Single-family house, ground floor plan

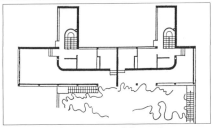

Two-family house, ground floor plan

runs parallel to the continuous window. Moreover, they are separated by sliding partitions rather than fixed walls. The maid has her canonical ground-floor chamber. Le Corbusier described this plan as "a sort of sleeping-dining car combined, with equipment for day and for night." During the day, with the partitions open, the space flows continuously through the slab. At night, the closed partitions create a series of cells along a very narrow corridor. As in a train, many of the desks, tables, and storage units are built in as equipment rather than furniture. Flexibility dominates over the sense of stable centrality that characterizes the single-family house. Banham has suggested that the variety of possible conditions for privacy, openness, and sleep hints at a radical social unit outside the nuclear family. Although a party wall divides the plan in half, the single rectangular volume and the continuous window divided only by a curious metal flag stress the merged identity of the two family units.

A walk through the Weissenhof places Le Corbusier's architecture in the stimulating context of contemporary avant-garde proposals. Mies's simple slab dedicated to hygiene achieves its elegance through proportion and detail alone. In the house Behrens designed, traces of romanticism linger in the modulated relation of the spaces. Gropius produced an inventive essay in mass production and modular construction. Oud's terrace units introduced an element of picturesque siting into a se-

vere vocabulary of form. The house designed by Scharoun interpreted the new, machine-age language in a decorative, almost mannerist fashion. In this context, Le Corbusier's architecture is distinguished by the inventiveness of its pieces and parts, the clarity with which he disposed them, and their precise relation to the landscape.

All of the exhibition houses, including Le Corbusier's, distinguish themselves from the hill as abstract, machine-age objects, but through position and color Le Corbusier's houses also establish a strong bond with the landscape. The pilotis of the single-family house let the surrounding garden flow continuously beneath it. The metal posts of the two-family house seem to rise out of the cliff itself. The houses are painted not the harsh white of Oud but pastel shades, labeled "space," "sky," and "sand," closer to those of the landscape. Having made a trip to Stuttgart to select his sites, Le Corbusier chose the edge of the complex and the hill, where his buildings could perch above the crest on pilotis, gazing out over the city and toward the slopes beyond. He placed them perpendicular to one another so both could face the mountains yet back onto contiguous gardens. Thus they are solitary in their unimpeded views but social in their adjoining turf. Le Corbusier's proposal for an ideal community hinged on the ability of the new architecture to redefine man's relation to nature as well as to his fellow man.

Unité d'habitation Berlin Charlottenburg (Le Corbusier-Hochhaus) 1958

Reichssportsfeld
Heilsbergen Dreieck 143
Berlin

VISITS: Public areas of this apartment house are visitable.

LOCALE: For a model reconstruction project of 1957, architects from fourteen countries, including Aalto, Gropius, and Taut, built residential projects in the Hansa Quarter (Hansa-Viertel). Le Corbusier's Unité is surprisingly far from this development, west of the center city, in an open field opposite the Olympic Stadium built for the 1936 Games.

DIRECTIONS: The Unité is located on the hill above Heerstrasse, not far beyond the Theodor-Heuss-Platz. It is in the Reichssportsfeld, between Scottsweg and Dickensweg. Bus lines from Bahnhof Zoo-Strassen to Olympia-Stadion stop at the Unité.

THE CITIZENS ADMINISTRATION OF BERLIN commissioned Le Corbusier to design the Berlin Unité on the occasion of the 1957 Interbau, an international exposition. Thus, thirty years after the Weissenhof Exhibition at Stuttgart, he again had a chance to present the world with a new model for mass housing (see Unité at Marseille for a description of the type). The Berlin building conforms to the basic form of the Unité but lacks the communal facilities Le Corbusier felt were crucial to its successful social functioning. It is a large example of the type, with four hundred apartments accommodating nearly two thousand people. In placing the Unité on the crest of the Olympic Hill, Le Corbusier emphasized its monumental quality and, perhaps, the acropolitan quality of the site, at the expense of its integration in the city.

As a result of an uneasy relations with his German collaborators and because German building standards conflicted with his personal system of measurement, Le Corbusier abandoned the proportioning system of the Modulor, increasing the floor-to-floor height by approximately one meter. This reproportioning adversely affected the brise-soleil. Consequently, Berlin lacks the sense of balance that characterizes the best of the Unités. In the end, extremely dissatisfied, Le Corbusier renounced it.

Pavillon de l'Esprit Nouveau 1925, 1977

*Piazza Constituzione, 11
Bologna*

Le Corbusier and Pierre Jeanneret; reconstructed under the direction of José Oubrerie and Giuliano Gresleri.

DIRECTIONS: Local buses run frequently from downtown Bologna to the Piazza.

THE PAVILION IS A RECONSTRUCTION OF LE Corbusier and Jeanneret's exhibit in the International Exposition of Decorative Arts held in Paris in 1925. Along with the Russian exhibit by Melnikov and the De Stijl "City in Space" by the Austrian Friedrich Keisler, it had a machine-age aesthetic at odds with the Art Deco style prevalent throughout the exposition. The Pavilion has two parts, one a full-scale mock-up of the *maisonette* dwelling unit from a proposed apartment building, the other a rotunda with dioramas of the urban scheme in which this apartment building belonged. The dioramas illustrate the Contemporary City for Three Million Inhabitants first exhibited in 1922 and a related proposal for the center of Paris entitled Voisin Plan after its sponsor, Voisin automobiles. The Pavilion's vision of machine-age culture in all its aspects, from furniture to town planning, was Le Corbusier's response to what he considered the untenable conditions of Parisian life: overcrowding and lack of sun and air. It argued against Art Deco as a superficial and stylistic answer to the serious problem of dwelling.

Contemporary City

Scientifically detailed by technicians, implemented and administered from above, the Contemporary City was to have combined nature and modern industrial culture in a single urban form. The geometric patterning of the plan based on the figure of the double square is an expresion of its ideal of unity. Within this complete environment, functions and classes are separated according to zones. At its center stand twenty-four cruciform, glass office towers for the heads of industry, finance, science, and the humanities, each 60 stories high and 800 feet apart in

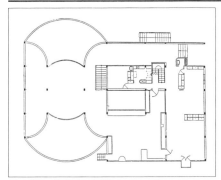
Pavillon de l'Esprit Nouveau, plan

Living room, ca. 1925

a continuous park. At night the zone is devoted to entertainment, with a night club on top of each tower. On the outskirts of this center are the municipal and administrative buildings and the museum and university. Throughout is a tiered circulation system of vehicular roads, park promenades, and elevated pedestrian malls with cafés and stores (see Fig. 6, p. 22). In the very center is a multilevel transportation nexus crowned by a landing plaza for airplanes, reminiscent of the drawings of the Italian Futurist St 'Elia. From this focus run the grand arterial thoroughfares. Le Corbusier wrote, "a city built for speed is built for success."

Beyond the business center are the residential neighborhoods for those who work in the towers. In order to accommodate more dwellings than Paris (to increase density) while simultaneously moving them further apart, the architects proposed two types of housing: the twelve-story perimeter block of *immeuble-villas* (villa-apartments) and the linear *bloc à redents* (linear blocks with setbacks). Both housing types have communal services, including house cleaning, a gourmet kitchen, and recreational facilities to free the individual from daily drudgery. Both have precedents in established utopian forms of dwelling. The influence of Charles Fourier's Phalanstery and Victor Considerant's re-

lated People's Palace can be seen in the linear blocks; Le Corbusier's personal impressions of the Carthusian Monastery of Ema inspired the alternating cells of dwelling and garden in the villa-apartments.

A wide greenbelt separates the white-collar city from the industrial zone downwind, which includes both manufacturing districts and the residences of the citizens who work in them. In these outlying communities, the former urban slum dweller lives in low-rise apartments with gardens reminiscent of the English Garden City and Tony Garnier's Cité Industrielle but more like garden suburbs than independent towns.

Exactly what the politics of this city are is unclear. As in Henri Saint-Simon's utopia based on the organization of industry, "the administration of goods replaces the government of men." The individual within this hierarchical collective is a "modern nomad" without property, who receives the "essential joys" of nature and the products of technology regardless of class, and further benefits according to his position of responsibility.

Voisin Plan

Le Corbusier responded not just to the problems but also to the glories of Paris. His admiration for the boulevards of Haussmann, the squares of Louis XIV,

Voisin plan, airport and surrounding towers

Detail of the immeuble-villa

and the power of Colbert, are evident in his own grand gridwork. It was in the spirit of past acts of bold destruction and monumentalization of Paris that he proposed in his Voisin Plan to raze over three square kilometers of existing urban fabric on the right bank of the Seine. He felt that it would create financial as well as urbanistic renewal by increasing land value and attracting international concerns to its centralized facilities. Similar in organization to the Contemporary City, it has eighteen glass towers located in a park, surrounded by luxury dwellings and connected by a tiered system of circulation. In the park, selected monuments of Paris past, including the Louvre and humbler private houses, stand as museum pieces or picturesque garden follies.

Immeuble-villa

The adjoining L-shaped pavilion wrapped about a terrace is one dwelling unit from the proposed villa-apartment block. Like Le Corbusier's freestanding type, the Maison Citrohan, the apartment is organized around a double-height salon with balcony facing a large factory sash window. From its open structural frame to its furnishings, the apartment demonstrates the potentials of machine-based culture to create new tools that fulfill human needs. Walls are

either factory produced concrete panels or large, metal-sash windows. Vases are laboratory flasks. Chairs are either the bentwood Thonet common to many French cafés or the English club model. The aesthetic of this "equipment for living" is the direct result of its production. As Le Corbusier wrote, his intention was "to illustrate how, by virtue of the selective principle (standardization applied to mass production), industry creates pure forms." Le Corbusier called these objects, purified over time by their evolution according to human needs, *objets-types*. Although they are expendable, in contrast to art, which is of lasting value, they are the subject of purist art and of the paintings that originally hung on the wall, by Le Corbusier, Léger, and Ozenfant. Like Adolf Loos, he recognized that manufactured *objets-types* were modern folk culture related in spirit to the apartment's anonymously crafted Berber rug, an appropriate possession for a "modern nomad." Scattered through the original display were stones and shells, reminders of the greater universal order to which both man-made and natural facts belong. This is the house of *"l'homme poli vivant dans ce temps-ci"* (a polite gentleman living in these times), supposedly anonymous but clearly the invention of Le Corbusier.

USA

UN Headquarters	1947
Carpenter Center	1963

Argentina

Maison Currutchet	1949

Brazil

Ministry of Education	1938

United Nations Headquarters 1947

*First Avenue, 42 nd-48 th St.
New York City
Tel. (212) 754-7713*

International Committee of Architects:
Australia, Soilleux; Belgium, Brunfaut; Brazil, Niemeyer; Canada, Cormier; China, Ssuch'eng Liang; France, Le Corbusier; Sweden, Markelius; U.S.S.R., Bassov; United Kingdom, Robertson; Uruguay, Vilamajo. Chairman: Wallace K. Harrison

VISITS: Tours daily between 9:15 and 4:45 in a variety of languages.

LOCALE: Le Corbusier visited New York City for the first time in 1935. He admired the ten-mile-long avenues that put the automobile at the city center, but he decried the congestion caused by skyscrapers that were "too small" to allow for surrounding parks. He loved the plethora of New York hotel silverware but objected to America's consumerism. For those who wish to visit the metropolis through Le Corbusier's eyes, his impressions are found in his book *When the Cathedrals Were White.*

The United Nations Headquarters is located in midtown Manhattan on the East Side, within walking distance of many of the towers that made an impression on Le Corbusier. From the United Nations west on E. 42nd St. are the Daily News Building (1930, 1958) at no. 220, by Howells and Hood; the Chanin Building (1929) at no. 200, by Sloan and Robertson; the Chrysler Building (1930) at Lexington Ave., by William and Allen; Bowery Savings Bank (1923) at no. 110, by York and Sawyer; and, across the street, Grand Central Station (1913) by Warren and Wetmore. At Fifth Ave. and 47th St. is Rockefeller Center, where in 1947 Le Corbusier and the U.N. design team had their offices.

DIRECTIONS: Walk from Grand Central Station or take the 42nd St. bus east. The E train (subway) stops at 53rd St. and 1st Avenue.

FOR LE CORBUSIER, THE UNITED NATIONS represented one more frustrated attempt "to create a point on the globe where the image and meaning of the world may be perceived and understood." Both the ideological framework for such a project and his desire to build it date from just after World War I, with his entry in the League of Nations competition and his design for a Mundaneum soon after. The Mundaneum combined the League concept of an international political forum with the idea of a cultural center to include a modern communications library and a cross-disciplinary museum.

As an official member of the international team of architects, Le Corbusier flew to New York in 1946 to join the search for an appropriate site and program for the United Nations. Plan 1 envisioned a world capitol in the spirit of the Mundaneum, with political organs, a cultural center, and a city for the functionaries of the entire complex. For this "city of international bureaucracy" Le Corbusier, among others, suggested a site twice the size of Manhattan on virgin soil far removed from any existing metropolis. When, however, John D. Rockefeller responded to pressures of time and planning by purchasing the 42nd-48th Street site, Le Corbusier changed his mind and accepted the edge of Manhattan as a suitable location, because it would bring to New York his own Radiant City of towers in the park as a shining example for future development.

Le Corbusier's scheme #23a, developed by March 1947, was accepted by the international team as the working model for the United Nations buildings. In this scheme, the Secretariat, a tower on pilotis with brise-soleil, stands above a curved General Assembly, and a low conference wing connects the two. The

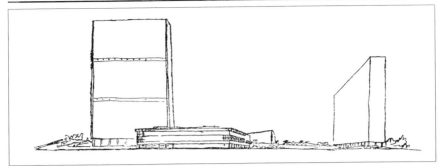

Le Corbusier's design sketch (23A)

other agencies are housed in another slab at the end of the site. Le Corbusier's definition of the separate organs of the institution as distinct volumes joined to the site and each other by strong axial relations derives from the Swiss Pavilion and, ultimately, from the elementarist composition of his League of Nations. The scheme suggests an elaborate sequence of spaces moving from the General Assembly's entrance on the avenue, through the building toward the water, ending in a great ramp to a dock. As in his other institutional buildings, the fluid circulation space and forms at ground level are balanced against the static slab of offices. In this case, as Lewis Mumford has observed, because the slab stands at the center of the project, the technocracy of the Secretariat, rather than the political forum of the General Assembly, seems the U.N.'s symbolic voice, ironically or otherwise.

At this point in the development of the United Nations, much to Le Corbusier's dismay, Wallace Harrison was entrusted with the execution of the project. While Harrison adopted the outline of scheme #23a, the built version includes many misinterpretations of the intended relations. The theater of the General Assembly is subsumed within the low block without a clear sense of its relation to the curves. The large end of the wedge, intended to hold the audience for the Assembly, became a vast lounge and lobby. Consequently, the entrance sequence is shifted perpendicular to the street, losing some of its clarity in relation to the building complex. Stylistically, a technical elegance replaced Le Corbusier's sense of weight, both physical and symbolic.

Carpenter Center for the Visual Arts, Harvard University 1963

24 Quincy Street
Cambridge, Mass. 02138

Le Corbusier with associated firm José-Luis Sert and Assoc.

Boston 8km

VISITS: University classrooms open weekdays 9am-10:30pm, Sat. 9-6, Sun. 12-10:30. Sert Gallery open 1-6 Tues.-Sun.

LOCALE: Carpenter Center is located on the main campus of Harvard University, just across from Harvard Yard, the original campus. The University boasts buildings by Charles Bulfinch, Henry Ware, H. H. Richardson, Richard Morris Hunt, Walter Gropius, José-Luis Sert, James Stirling, and others. Stop by the university information office, corner of Holyoke St. and Massachusetts Ave., for a map and tour of the University. The center of Cambridge is a student dream filled with fashionable stores and cafés. Cambridge accommodations range from the tidy Holiday Inn on Mass. Ave., up by the Radcliffe campus, to the chic Charles Hotel in Harvard Square, but nearby Boston offers more choice.

DIRECTIONS: Subway stop Harvard Square, Red Line. Walk through Harvard Yard to the Fogg Art Museum. Carpenter Center is on the right.

LE CORBUSIER ACKNOWLEDGED HIS DE-
sire to make Carpenter Center, his only work in North America, a didactic statement of principle. The building reads as a revisionist history of many of his basic ideas. Therefore, the vague building program emphasizing the Center as a vessel for communication among the arts encouraged him in this intent. Throughout his life Le Corbusier constantly reinterpreted and transformed his own architectural language. Already, in his Shodhan House and Millowners Building in India, he had reinvested his late style, characterized by rough concrete and primitivism, with some of the forms and spirit of his early, purist architecture. At Carpenter Center he continued that exploration, combining familiar elements with unexpected spatial effect.

Le Corbusier's late interest in natural forms and forces is evident here. The windows derive from a three-part system of glazing, brise-soleil, and ventilating panels he developed for India in order to architecturally control climate (see entry for Secretariat). Some critics interpret the building as an organic metaphor, seeing the two curved studios as lungs or ventricles on either side of the central circulation system of ramp and stair.

In order that Carpenter Center be consonant with the advanced technological culture of America, Le Corbusier adopted purist elements to correct what he considered any "artificial primitivism." He abandoned the rough, flawed skin of *béton brut* for the machined, polished look associated with his early architecture. At great expense, he insisted that the concrete's finish be absolutely smooth, without even the raised impression of lines from the sonotube formwork. Together, the cantilevered slabs and pilotis define, once more, his first image of the Domino structural skeleton.

In the combination of vocabularies there arise certain conflicts, which Le Corbusier acknowledged in the architecture. The confrontation of the earthbound sense of his late work with seemingly weightless forms of Purism appears, for example, in the siting of the pilotis. Even as the pilotis lift the studios up, they sink below ground level so that, despite their extreme height at some points, in the building forecourt they generate a low, almost subterranean space. Where the thick walls of brise-soleil typically reach the ground or are supported on gigantic pilotis, here they stop short of the first floor or appear suspended above the ground or on slender posts. This tension in the role of the wall appears also in the ordering of the facades as frontal planes on the one hand and as exuberant sculptural form on the other.

The revealed sculptural play of overlapping volumes is unique to Le Corbusier's last works. Never before had he allowed such large organic shapes to appear on the exterior of a building as a challenge to the power of an interior grid. In this case, the box that canonically contains these shapes is the site itself—the cubic volume of space defined by the buildings on either side. In a departure from its early role as unifier of the plan, the ramp penetrates the visual center of the building from front to back along a primarily exterior route. The interior architectural promenade occurs along an alternate route, which descends among the pilotis and up the stair. A third, visual line of motion connects the layers of studios in an ascending spiral. Thus the building is understood as a complex combination of various paths that weave together the interior and exterior space.

Le Corbusier explained, in reference to the Center, that a difficult site generates a "hermetic solution giving pleasure to somebody who knows what underlies it." Perhaps he anticipated the criticism of his self-referential architectural dialogue and sculptural gymnastics as anti-contextual. What underlies his solution is a reexamination of his own vocabulary and lifelong urban vision. He called the building a gateway and imagined it as a popular route from old Harvard Yard to future university buildings beyond Prescott Street, through an elevated realm of gardens. He wanted

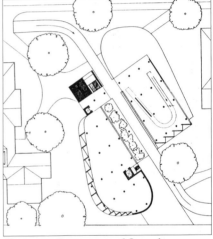

Carpenter Center, second floor plan

the summit of the ramp to be the Center's primary entrance, flanked by administrative offices and a gallery. The building seems, then, a diagram of the terraced dwellings and multitiered circulation routes he had always envisioned as the salubrious alternative to the existing city. The organic lungs of the studios with roof gardens rotate the building off the constricting grid of the street and Yard. The cubic box as man's orthogonal edifice stands at the building's center, oriented to the compass points. The ramp, half freeway, half path of the sun, rises and passes through.

Maison Currutchet 1949

Barrio el Bosque
La Plata

Le Corbusier and site
architect Amancio Williams

Buenos Aires 40km

VISITS: Private house visible from
street, in original form but
neglected condition.

LOCALE: La Plata, the capital of
the province of Buenos Aires, is a
small city about one hour from the
Capital Federal by car. It is a
planned town designed in the late
nineteenth century on a square grid
with intersecting diagonals. The
many parks and the grid define its
character.

DIRECTIONS: From Buenos Aires,
buses leave Plaza Constitucion
and trains depart Constitucion Station directly for La Plata. Once in
town, take one of the several buses
to Stadium of Estudiantes de La
Plata on street #1. The house is located across the boulevard from
the stadium, on a dead-end street.
In front of the house is a monolith
erected by the Society of Architects
of La Plata.

THIS SMALL RESIDENCE AND OFFICE FOR
the surgeon Currutchet fills a typical urban lot in a
South American setting. Le Corbusier visited Argen-
tina in 1929, delivering a series of lectures later
published as *Précisions,* but he never saw the particular site. The house is unique in its combination of
the purist aesthetic of Le Corbusier's Parisian town-
houses with elements of an emerging naturalism.

The architecture of the houses of the 1920s is
present in the placement of the free plan within the
expressed structure of horizontal slabs on slender
pilotis. The well-established elements of ramp,
curved bath enclosures, hearth, and stairwell are organized within a modulated column grid. The back
volume of the residence has a four-square plan in the
tradition of the Maison Cook "cubic house" (1925),
with the fireplace rather than the stair as the pivotal
element. The entire site is likewise divided into four
parts, with the office occupying the lower front quadrant. In response to the climate, the terrace of the
Parisian villas is reinterpreted as an open but shady
central court traversed by a ramp that recalls Villa
Savoye.

Not explicable in terms of his purist architecture
are the treatment of the facade and the extremely active appearance of the whole. For his tropical architecture, first at Villa Baizeau in Carthage (1929)

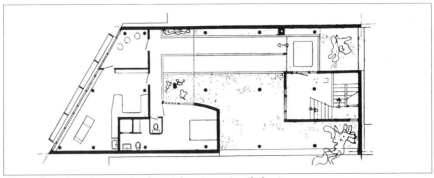

Currutchet, plan of mezzanine floor (above), section (below)

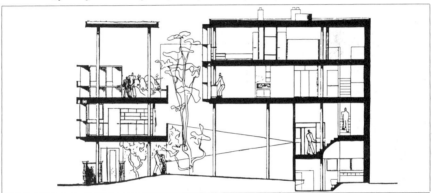

and then at the Ministry of Education in Rio (1938), Le Corbusier had developed a particular vocabulary of forms that included brise-soleil and a parasol roof on stilts to manipulate sun and breeze. In this house he adopted the thickened screen of the brise-soleil for climatic reasons but with formal consequences. Whereas the purist wall creates a painterly illusion of depth within a taut plane, the wall at La Plata manipulates actual depth using multiple layers of built form. The sequence of layers moves across the entire depth of the site, shifting from the angle of the city to the orthogonal of the yard while nevertheless maintaining its relation to the park across the street. It moves in three dimensions, up as well as back from the office brise-soleil to that of the house. This three-dimensional play involves a sculptural interpenetration of volumes as well as the sequence of flat planes. For example, the office slab intersects a rectangular volume defined by the pilotis that extend from the ground to the roof parasol.

The imposition of Le Corbusier's emerging sense of sculptural wall on the sense of the painterly plane has an unsettling if not surreal effect. The office brise-soleil is framed so that despite its obvious weight it appears to float in front of the glass wall and above the entrance. It also appears as if it were an immaterial projection of the rear brise-soleil onto the geometry of the street. The massive doorway is set in a wall that is basically imaginary, defined only by a mesh fence. A similar sensibility can be traced throughout the house.

In the process of opening up the early Parisian house to receive the park and climate, Le Corbusier introduced an intense, formal ambiguity in the conceptions of the wall and of space.

Brazilian Ministry of Education and Public Health

1938, 1943

(now called Palace of Culture or Ministry of Education and Culture)

Ruá da Imprensa 16
20030 Rio de Janeiro

Le Corbusier, consultant to Lúcio Costa, Oscar Niemeyer, Carlos Leo, Alfonso Eduardo Reidy, Jorge Moreira, and Ernani Vasconcellos.

VISITS: Open 9-6 Monday through Saturday year round. By special request, visitors may see the original offices of the Minister, which now house the Candido Portinari Museum. The fourth-floor library is open to the public. Direct further enquiries to the Fundaçao Nacional Pro-Memúria Library on the eighth floor.

LOCALE: The neighborhood of ministries is called Castelo, in reference to Castle Hill, which was removed in a wave of urban renewal starting in 1920. Despite their neoclassical facades, many of the surrounding ministry buildings date from the post-renewal period. Local points of interest include the ABI, Brazilian Press Building (1936), on the corner of Rua Araujo de Porto Alegre and Rua Mexico, by Marcelo and Milton Robert; the National Library (1910), built according to the design of General Francisco Marcelino Souza Aguiar, and the National Museum of Beaux-Arts (1908) by Adolfo Morales de los Rios, both on Avenida Rio Branca; the Municipal Theater (1906), across the street from the Library, on Praça Floriano, by Francisco Oliveira Passos; and the Academy of Letters (1978), Rua Pedro Lessa, designed by Mauricio and Marcos Roberto, which shows the continued importance of brise-soleil

THE COMMISSION OF THE MINISTRY OF Education coincided with both a government administration supportive of the arts and the emergence of a group of Brazilian architects in search of a modern national style. In 1936, at the request of the group's senior member, Lúcio Costa, Le Corbusier flew to Rio to act as consultant to the project. Although the European architect's thought pervades the project to such an extent that he receives credit for the design, in the course of developing his sketches the Brazilian team infused it with a new spirit.

Le Corbusier's most obvious contribution was the substitution of a glass-encased slab on pilotis for the traditionally neoclassical ministry buildings of Rio, which had solid, continuous street walls and shadowed interior courtyards. Into this context he inserted his tallest concrete frame to date: sixteen stories above ten-meter-high pilotis. The pilotis function according to principle here, allowing light and air to filter underneath the building and framing views of gardens designed by Roberto Burle Marx. The building highlights other typical attributes of Le Corbusier's concrete frame system, namely, the flat roof with gardens, non-bearing glass walls, and "free" interior plans. Today, the original layout is best demonstrated by the eighth floor, which has two-and-a-half-meter-high partitions instead of walls dividing the space. Also characteristic of Le Corbu-

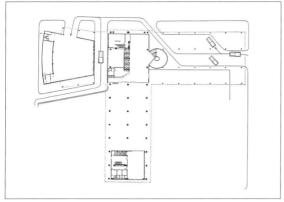

Brazilian Ministry, ground floor plan

in the architecture of subtropical Rio.

DIRECTIONS: From the popular beach areas, such as Ipanema, take any bus marked Castelo downtown to Avenida Presidente Antonio Carlos. It is easiest to get off at Praça dos Estados Unidos, cross to Rua Pedro Lessa, and walk west. The metro stop is Estaço Cinelandia, across from the National Library, two blocks west of the Ministry. From the beach by car (45 min.), follow signs to Centro along the *aterro* (Avenida Infante Dom Henrique), landscaped by Roberto Burle Marx, to Castelo and the Avenida Presidente Antonio Carlos. At its intersection with Avenida Nilo Pecanha is a municipal parking lot. The Ministry is three blocks south.

sier's thinking in this period is the definition of the function of the auditorium as a separate volume. Low, walled, and wedge-shaped, it stands in clear contrast to the tall frame of the slab.

The horizontal concrete panels for shade called brise-soleil, or sun-breakers, were a result of Le Corbusier's growing concern with architecture's relation to climate. In his earlier slabs he had experimented with hermetically sealed glass facades and mechanically processed interior climates. This first large-scale application of brise-soleil in combination with operable windows signaled a shift in his attitude toward the natural environment, a new willingness to work with its imperfections and variability. Although not mechanical, the brise-soleil were to be an exact technology. Le Corbusier's only criticism of the completed building was that the operable shutters were unscientific; whereupon Costa had them fixed to the optimal angle for the latitude.

In its development of Le Corbusier's sketches, the Brazilian team imbued recognizable purist elements of Le Corbusier's vocabulary with a "highly sensuous native expression which echoes in its exuberance the eigteenth-century Brazilian Baroque." The lobby sequence, from the curved information desk to the spiral stair, is an example of this sinuous interpretation of Corbusian form. Native materials, furnishings, murals, and sculptures work together to create a total Brazilian environment. The frescoes of *azulejos* (tiles) are by Candido Portinari; the roof sculptures are by Celso Antonio; and the figure of youth is by Bruno Giorgi. As Le Corbusier suggested, the solid walls and floors are clad in the native granite or in Portuguese-style faience tiles designed by Portinari. Furniture throughout is by Niemeyer, with rugs by Roberto Burle Marx. Le Corbusier shared the Brazilians' love of their native landscape and supported the synthetic presentation of architecture and art. In contrast to many countries with a legacy of Corbusian-style slabs of questionable merit, here his ideas found authentic expression in a culture he admired, and development through the work of its native architects.

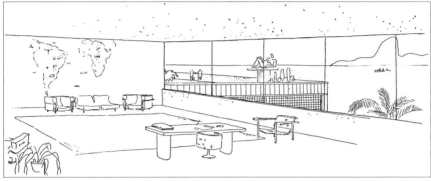

Minister's office, Le Corbusier's sketch

Tunisia

Villa Baizeau   1929

Iraq

Hussein Gymnasium   1980

Japan

National Museum   1959

USSR

Centrosoyus   1933

Villa Baizeau (Bézeult) 1929

Sainte Monique, Carthage

Le Corbusier and Pierre Jeanneret

VISITS: Private residence in poor repair but not altered.

LOCALE: Located next to the former Palace grounds of Carthage, in the suburb of Sainte Monique.

DIRECTIONS: Carthage is a northeastern suburb of Tunis. Take the TGM electric train from Place de l'Afrique station in Tunis, the La Goulette-La Marsa line.

LE CORBUSIER PUBLISHED TWO VERSIONS of Villa Baizeau in the first volume of his *Œuvre Complète*: a first, preferred scheme and a second one designed and eventually built according to the client's uncompromising demands. Impressed by the architect's contribution to the Weissenhof Exhibition in Stuttgart, the Tunisian industrialist M. Baizeau approached Le Corbusier to obtain general information about new construction methods and to commission a house for his family. Le Corbusier and Jeanneret designed the villa without visiting its site; instead, they depended on M. Baizeau's pictures and detailed descriptions of the site and its climate. Baizeau not only embodied the character of tropical Tunisia but also offered architectural solutions to its sun and to the hot wind from the south, known as the Sirocco.

Le Corbusier's first scheme addressed the problem of a tropical architecture in a variation on the Citrohan house he had built for the Weissenhof. It had a complex vertical section of three interlocking, double-height spaces for air circulation and a flat concrete roof raised on slender pilotis as an umbrella for shade. Baizeau rejected the scheme in part because its glass sheathing failed in his mind to satisfy particular problems of sun and wind. The same vertical section appeared in Le Corbusier's unbuilt apartments for M. Wanner but, along with the concrete parasol, emerged as an important feature only in his Indian architecture of the 1950s, particularly in Villa Shodhan.

After several attempts to revise the initial scheme, Le Corbusier and Jeanneret capitulated to Baizeau's increasingly specific demands for a house with terraces. They developed a version of the Maison Domino concrete frame in which each floor is a continuous concrete tray with turned-up edges carrying the

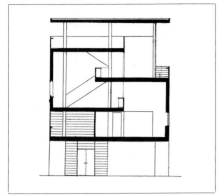

Section, first project, 1928; second floor

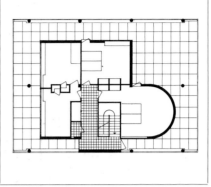

Second floor plan, as built

enclosed volumes of the house. The slabs are thus breezy balconies for the rooms recessed deep within and shade umbrellas for the floor below. The exposed frame of the villa was an alternative to the earlier purist houses, where the frame was suppressed within a tautly sheathed box. Although Le Corbusier projected an ambivalent attitude toward the house, he also recognized its clarity and included it as the third of his Four Compositions. There it appears as a diagram of various free plans sandwiched between layers of horizontal slabs.

The second scheme also had more distant ramifications for Le Corbusier's architecture. Tim Benton sees its perimeter of columns and square interior spaces as preparation for the next and penultimate purist house, Villa Savoye. An open building that draws the breeze deep into its center, Baizeau foreshadowed the tropical architecture Le Corbusier would design for Ahmedabad thirty years later. Seen at the time as an exemplar of universal, machine-age principles, the house also represents the beginning of a search that became paramount in his late work: the search for a way to deal with climate through architectonic form rather than technology.

Perspective from sea of first (unbuilt) scheme

Saddam Hussein Gymnasium 1980

Baghdad, Iraq

Le Corbusier with Georges Présenté

VISITS: Presently inaccessible because of Iran-Iraq War.

LOCALE: The gymnasium is across from the Baghdad Stadium, on the east side of the Tigris River.

THE ORGINAL PLANS FOR AN ATHLETIC complex in Baghdad featured a huge stadium for 100,000 spectators, a gymnasium for 3,500, playing fields for 3,000, a pool for 5,000, a restaurant, and a building for electronic displays of sound and light, which Le Corbusier added to the program. Work on the complex continued after Le Corbusier's death in 1965, until the Iraqi revolution of 1968. In 1973, George Présenté, Le Corbusier's engineer and initial contact with Iraq, received a contract to complete the one design fully developed by the architect, the gymnasium. The site of the gymnasium is not the original one, but rather a recently chosen location across the river from the original complex and opposite a stadium designed by F. K. D. Amarai, a Portuguese architect, in 1953.

The gymnasium belongs in spirit and form to Le Corbusier's group of unbuilt theater projects called *boites à miracles* (boxes of miracles), in reference to their simple shed volumes without windows, suited to the spectacles of theater. These boxes typically stand in relation to other proposed, open-air facilities for culture and recreation, as part of a public precinct. The hall in Baghdad houses an interior gymnasium framed on three sides by stands of seating called tribunes. The fourth wall is a 32x12m steel door that slides open along a concrete frame to reveal an adjacent playing field with stadium seating. Thus, the stage door transforms the scene, and the stage itself. When it is open, interior and exterior join as a single exhibition space surrounded by tribunes. When the door is closed, there are two spaces of extreme contrast: an open amphitheater and a dark, walled interior. Then the exterior door frame stands empty, like a minor proscenium. A theatrical concern with darkness and the intense contrast between light

and dark replace Le Corbusier's earlier enthusiasm for abundant light here as in many of his late works.

Building materials play an expressive role in relation to the gymnasium's box-like volumes. The curved profile of the shed (reminiscent of the stadium at Firminy) and the looping ramps exploit the plastic potential of concrete. Inside the building, the steel trusses are exposed. The steel door and frame are a simple but huge machine. Diverging from the primitivism of Le Corbusier's Indian concrete buildings, the gymnasium celebrates the power of modern engineering.

In contrast to the relative simplicity of the gymnasium shed, the circulation takes place along an elaborate system of ramps. The wide curve of the "grand ramp" ascends from the ground to a second level, where it divides in two, each branch leading to a secondary tribune. A third ramp, in a direction opposite to the first and coiled tightly around a pier, continues to the top level. As Suzanne Taj-Eldin has observed, the ramp, and the spiral ramp in particular, both originate in Mesopotamian architecture and so have special relevance to a building for Baghdad. Le Corbusier already acknowledged the origins of these forms in his first ramped project, the ziggurat of the Mundaneum (1929). The exposed circulation has importance not only as a sculptural ensemble at once biomorphic and culturally relevant, but also as a glorified system of movement for the spectator. From his first stadium projects of the 1930s, Le Corbusier was fascinated with the movement of great crowds of people in and out of an arena where "even 100,000 spectators participate in the games, where everything has self-control, style, and enthusiasm." The Saddam Hussein Gymnasium is the building that comes closest to realizing this early vision.

National Museum of Western Art 1959

7-7 Ueno Koen, Taito-ku,
Ueno
Tokyo
Tel. 828-5131

Le Corbusier with
Maekawa, Kunio and
Sakakura, Junzo
1979 Addition by
Maekawa, Kunio.

VISITS: Tues.-Sun. 9:30-5. Closed Tues. following a holiday and for New Year's holidays. Admission 250 yen.

LOCALE: Founded as one of Japan's first public gardens soon after the Meiji Restoration of 1878, Ueno Park contains Le Corbusier's Museum, a zoo famous for its pandas, the University of Fine Arts, the Shinobazu Pond, and the Tokyo Municipal Museum. The Municipal Museum and the nearby Tokyo Festival Hall are both the work of Maekawa, who worked in Le Corbusier's Paris studio before returning to Japan. Maekawa's addition to the museum, while architecturally distinguished, subverts the procession intended by Le Corbusier and contradicts any semblance of the original spiral. A lovely outing includes a visit to the sites of Ueno Park and lunch near Le Corbusier's museum, at Ueno Seiyoken, the restaurant that brought Western cuisine to Japan in the nineteenth century, or at a less expensive, yakitori shop. The best time to visit the park is in April, for the cherry blossoms.

DIRECTIONS: Ueno is in the northeastern section of central Tokyo. By metro it is within 30 min. of most anywhere in the metropolitan area. The easiest access is by the Yamanote or JNR lines to the Ueno stop. Hibiya and Ginza subway lines also have a Ueno stop with an exit directly to the park.

THE NATIONAL MUSEUM IS ONE OF THREE museums Le Corbusier built based on his idea for a Museum of Unlimited Growth (see the N. C. Mehta Museum at Ahmedabad for a discussion of the model). The building in Tokyo adheres to the basic organization of a "squared spiral" gallery on pilotis described in the model. An upper level of galleries wraps around a central court and penetrates it with balconies at several points. A secondary system of glass balconies within these galleries is actually an elaborate clerestory structure for lighting. (These clerestories contain artificial fluorescent lighting so ill-suited to the illumination of art that it renders some of the spiral gallery unusable. The split-level section they produce is also spatially awkward for the display of art.) Superimposed on the spiral, a "swastika," or pinwheel, pattern of circulation defines linear routes from central court to exit stairways. These stairs at the end of each pinwheel arm carry the sense of spin through to the rather static exterior of the box. To bring texture and scale to the intentionally faceless elevations, Le Corbusier used a well-detailed sheathing of small green pebbles set in concrete panels, which is common in the Japanese architecture of the period.

Of the three built spiral museums, the one in Tokyo most closely connects the spatial organization to its original programmatic content. Responding to the endless amounts of information available in machine-age culture, Le Corbusier proposed the establishment of a true museum that would "contain everything." The unlimited spiral form grew out of this true museum's need to constantly incorporate the artifacts of history as it occurs. In Tokyo the spiral was to present a factual account of the history of Western culture, although in limited form. The

Museum's collection of French impressionist paintings and Rodin sculptures originally belonged to M. Matsuka, a Japanese living in Paris at the time of World War II. Having confiscated the art during the war, the French government agreed to return it to Japan on the condition it be placed in a museum that, in Le Corbusier's words, "would acquaint the Japanese with the past, present, and future evolution of Western art in a scientific manner, beginning with Impressionism." For Le Corbusier, the era of Impressionism, as the "cradle of the new machinist civilization,"

belonged at the center of the spiral, as the Hall of the Nineteenth Century. He planned large photomurals for its walls that would demonstrate the communicative, artistic, and fact-finding power of the nineteenth-century tool, the camera. The murals were not executed, and Le Corbusier's unlikely scheme for a Museum of Unlimited Growth was never realized. The architectural quality of the building in Tokyo is dependent on the more traditional Corbusian elements of ramp ascending in a skylit court and a stair extending into nature.

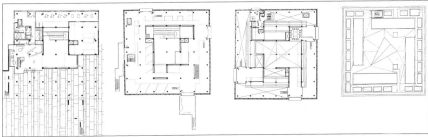

National Museum of Western Art, plans, floors 1-4

Centrosoyus (Tsentrosoiuz) Building 1933

Central Statistical Administration of the USSR Ulitsa Kirova, 39 Moscow

Le Corbusier and Pierre Jeanneret, with Soviet executive architect N. Kolli

VISITS: High security building off-limits to visitors. Though visible from the street, it is illegal to photograph it. Because the building is grim without the glow of the red stone in the daylight, the best time to visit is during the day in the springtime Those seen taking pictures (interior or exterior) are subject to police arrest.

LOCALE: The Centrosoyus is in a pleasant neighborhood of offices and residences developed at the turn of the century according to uniform zoning. On Ulitsa Kirova are important buildings by modern Soviet architects, including nos. 8/2 and no. 15 by Kuznetsov, no. 24 (Stroganov College, 1907) by F.O. Shektel, and no. 47 (Gostorg Building, 1927) by Barsch, Vegman, and Gaken. Other modernist buildings in Moscow include the Polytechnical Society Building (1904) by Kuznetsov, at 4 Ulitsa Griboedova; F. I. Afremov's Apartment House (1904), at 00 Shishkovskii, 19 Sadovaia-Spasskaia Ulitsa; the Narkomzen Building (1930) by A.V. Shchusev, at 1/11 Orlivkov pereulok; and the Naromfkin Housing by Ginzburg, which anticipates Le Corbusier's Unités, at 25 korpus B. Metro Krasnopresnenskaia-Barikadnaia, behind the U.S. Embassy.The best hotels to request from Intourist are the older grand European ones, including Hotel Bucharest and Hotel Metropol. Since good maps are scarce in Moscow, you should bring your own.

DIRECTIONS: From Red Square, either walk down Ulitsa Kirova to the ring road Bol. Sadovaia (25 min.) or take the subway (10 min.).

IN THE EMERGING SOVIET STATE, LE COR-busier found a receptive audience for his early critique of bourgeois capitalist culture and for his proposed architecture based on the potentials of industrialized production. During the 1920s, a dialogue grew between the Soviet architects and Le Corbusier. In the chaotic aftermath of the stock market crash, Le Corbusier found the capability for action provided by the Soviet authoritarian leadership increasingly appealing. At the same time, Soviet officaldom, through a process of three competitions, selected Le Corbusier as architect for the headquarters of the Central Union of Soviet Cooperatives.

In the design of this, his first major building, a vast complex of office space for 3,500, with recreation club, restaurant, and auditorium, Le Corbusier relied primarily on the principles of composition he had recently developed in the monumental League of Nations project. The building emerged from a series of schemes as an orthogonal frame about a central garden complex and auditorium. The elementarist definition of parts and the shifted axes connecting them both derive from the League. In particular, the auditorium and Secretariat of the unbuilt project appear as the auditorium and office slabs of the Moscow building.

Le Corbusier went beyond the League principles in his introduction of several new concepts relating to the wall and to circulation. He proposed to control the internal environment of the slabs using a two-part system: "exact respiration," which is a form of central air conditioning, and a "neutralizing wall." This wall calls for the continuous double-glazing of southern facades for the transmission of maximum daylight and a wide, hermetically sealed central cavity for the circulation of temperature-controlled air. The other facades contain windows within a sheathing of thick, pink tuffa stone from the Arctic region, chosen for its insulating capacity. This system thus determines the nature of the wall architecturally and metaphorically. The building surface becomes a taut glass and stone envelope, a biomechanical skin. As in each case where Le Corbusier intended to use this system, the clients balked at the cost of the power required to operate it. Incomplete, it proved inadequate to manage summer heat loads, requiring the installation of curtains between the layers of glass.

Le Corbusier imagined the users of this building as the "spectral Moscow crowd" and their needs as an issue of circulation. He posited the "obligatory classification of this crowd entering and exiting at the same time; need for a kind of forum at such hours for people whose overshoes and furs will be covered with snow.... Architecture is circulation." In order to create this architecture of circulation he lifted the entire building on pilotis. This act was the natural outgrowth of his Dom-ino structural frame system and his Five Points. It anticipated his development of a classless city on pilotis above a continuous garden called the Radiant City, which he first presented in his Response to Moscow (1929). Through the pilotis, the Centrosoyus "reveals itself entirely" to the moving eye and body. The pilotis create a vast internal field of columns below the separate office slabs. Le Corbusier described the role of this field in relation to the building complex: "It has been appropriate to set up such a classification in a building that knows two moments: the first, a period of disorderly flux on a horizontal ground plane vast as a lake, the second a period of stable, immobile work...[in] the offices, where each one is in his place and controllable." Thus the field of pilotis and ramps within it are the forms that accommodate the moments of flux. As in the building skin, there are biological overtones in the image of this internal realm of fluid circulation. Through this realm run two main routes, one up the curved ramps to the official quarters, the other along the linear ramps from the entrances to the auditorium; both are loosely defined and free-flowing compared to the rigid axial relations of the slabs above. While the huge slabs are impressive objects representing the social reality of the Soviet state, the columnar forum with its warped ground plane of ramps is the focus of the community and the place of great spatial invention.

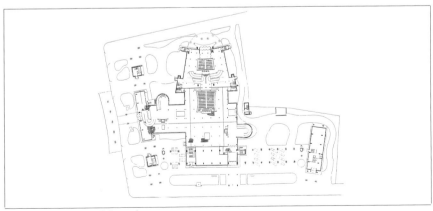

Centrosoyus, ground floor plan

AHMEDABAD, A THRIVING INDUSTRIAL and commercial center of two million people, is one of India's leading textile manufacturing centers. Although founded nearly a thousand years ago, there is little evidence of the city's past. Most remaining monuments are obscured by the growth of recent decades. But since Ahmedabad's golden age has been the twentieth century, its modern forms are interesting and impressive. The wealth created by industry has transformed the city into an important cultural and educational center. The patronage of the industrial elite is responsible not only for bringing both Le Corbusier and Louis Kahn to the city but for a flowering of the arts in general.

To see all of Ahmedabad takes about three days, preferably midweek. On the east side of the Sabarmati River are the old city and industrial districts. On the west bank are the more affluent residential neighborhoods, the University, and all of the buildings designed by Le Corbusier, except for Maison Sarabhai. You will probably want to stay on the west bank, where there are several good but expensive hotels. Because English is not widely spoken, you will want to get a map immediately. Besides the tourist office located near the Millowners Building on Sri R. C. Road, the best source for information is the School of Architecture at the University. Important sites include Louis Kahn's beautiful India Institute of Management; the Architecture School, Sangath Studio, and Tagore Theatre, designed by B. V. Doshi, who worked with both Kahn and Le Corbusier; the Sabarmati (Gandhi) Ashram by Charles Correa; Jama Masjid (Friday Mosque); and the remarkable Step Well of Dada Hari Ni Vav, in the industrial district.

Ahmedabad, Gujarat India

Bombay 491km, Delhi 939km

Millowners' Building	1954
Maison Sarabhai	1955
Villa Shodhan	1956
N. C. Mehta Museum	1958

DIRECTIONS: From Rajastan and Bombay there are both overnight trains and planes to Ahmedabad. The train station is east of the old city. Taxis and auto-rickshaws are recommended means of transportation throughout Ahmedabad, because distances are considerable.

Millowners' Association Building 1954

*Sri R. C. Road
Ahmedabad, Gujarat*

VISITS: Visitable during business hours.

DIRECTIONS: A possible itinerary for your trip to the Millowners Building begins at the western edge of the city, in the University area, with the Architecture School and Kahn's Institute, moves east to the Millowners, then ends a mile south at the Museum and Villa Shodhan. The Millowners Building is located on the west bank of the Sabarmati River, about 1/2km north of Nehru Bridge, off Sri R. C. Road.

THE MILLOWNERS' ASSOCIATION BUILDING has the feel of Le Corbusier's luxurious villas, both his houses in Ahmedabad and his Parisian residences of the 1920s. The Millowners are a group of Jain industrialists related by caste, religion, and blood and distinguished by their philanthropic and cultural concerns. They were Le Corbusier's patrons in Ahmedabad, commissioning houses, their association headquarters, and the museum. Le Corbusier understood that their headquarters was to be a meeting place for an intimate group of families of wealth and class, a private clubhouse with a certain symbolic and institutional role. He described it as a small palace and designed it according to his longstanding notions of *une maison-un palais,* or monumentalized house.

For the general scheme of the Millowners' Building, Le Corbusier returned to his early palatial houses in Paris. Like Villa Stein, it is a box with essentially blank side walls which act as a frame for the dialogue between front and back, street and garden, public and private, closed and open facades. As at Stein, through a series of straight and curving walls and implied planes, the interior space is expanded and compressed in relation to the facades and the regular column grid. These spaces and planes are experienced as part of a ceremonial procession that begins with the ramp and either moves across the building toward the views to the river or up the stairs to the curved assembly room within the double-height forum and then to the roof garden. This procession incorporates elements of early villas other than Garches: the main staircase at Maison Planex and the ramp at Villa Savoye, here externalized as a declamatory public route to the center of the building.

So that this "small palace" would reflect the Indian way of dwelling, Le Corbusier developed his preexisting vocabulary in terms of Indian climate and culture. As described in the Villa Shodhan entry, he recognized and explored the parallels between his parasol roof, entry court, and brise-soleil, and the forms of the Indian house. On the rear facade, the concrete brise-soleil is open and fragile, like an Indian wooden screen. It extends from roof to ground, replacing the typical Corbusian base of pilotis with a more continuous fabric. Through the brise-soleil, exterior space penetrates the interior plan and the columned halls take on the feel of traditional Indian courts and terraces.

As in the early villas, the particular incidents of plan contain architectural allusions, but ones relevant to India's cultural inheritance rather than a classical Western past. The side walls are made of the brick found in the Millowners' factories. Le Corbusier explained that he designed the rear screen to frame views of the textile workers washing clothes in the river amid cattle and herons, a reminder to the owners of the source of their wealth and of the cycles of nature that produce it. While these references identify the Millowners as wealthy, responsible businessmen, others are more fanciful in their allusions to royal life. William Curtis has connected the curved cocktail bar with a maharaja's pavilion and local industrial stacks, and the stair to the roof with a similar flight in the palace of Panch Mahal at Fathepur Sikri.

The assembly room is the most evocative room in the building, part tent, part organic form. Its biomorphic curves recall the shapes in Le Corbusier's late paintings and in the chapel at Ronchamp, with its set of natural and sacral allusions. It is lit through the clerestory and by reflections off the underside of the curved roof. On the roof terrace, this curve is revealed as parasol-shaped, like a crescent moon with a reflecting pool at its center. Intended as a setting for evening entertainment, the terrace forms suggest realms of both royal India and nature's enchantments. This building describes the world of its clients as Le Corbusier chose to see them, in relation to each other, to the community, and to both real and mythologized nature.

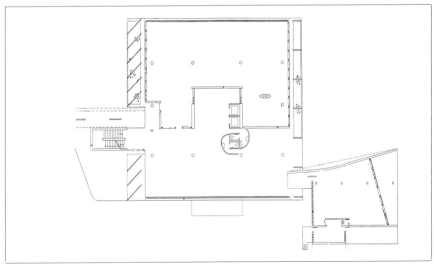

Millowners' Building, plan

Maison d'habitation de Mme Manorama Sarabhai 1955

Shahibag, Ahmedabad Gujarat

VISITS: Private residence. The house is located within the grounds of the Sarabhai family compound. Unscheduled visits not welcome.

LOCALE: See Ahmedabad. Shahibag is in the north part of town on the east side of the river, above Vadaj Low Level Bridge.

DIRECTIONS: For exact location, enquire at the Ahmedabad School of Architecture.

LE CORBUSIER'S TWO HOUSES IN INDIA ILLUStrate the two alternative strategies for dwelling proposed by the architect as early as 1923 in *Vers une architecture:* the Citrohan, a "masculine" cube, and the Monol, a "feminine" series of vaults. Villa Shodhan employs the box form of the Citrohan. By means of a series of parallel vaults, Maison Sarabhai reiterates the principles of the Monol type.

In many ways Sarabhai fulfills the potential Mediterranean character of the Maison Monol, previously limited in its execution by the demands of a northern climate. Like Maison de Weekend and Maisons Jaoul, both in Paris, the Indian house is built of parallel vaults combined on the interior to create rooms wider than a single bay. Deep edge beams spanning long distances allow for large openings in the walls beneath. The Indian house carries the sense of openness further than the northern examples: laterally, it joins together a long series of vaults; lengthwise, it extends them into the garden. Each vault ends in a verandah that is really a mediating room between house and nature. Several of the verandah walls are pivoted panels that, when open, make the house a channeled continuation of the garden space.

Maison Sarabhai blends in with its surroundings. The program, for a widow with two sons, called for an organization similar to Maisons Jaoul: a double-height block for the public rooms and the mother's suite, distinct from a low block for the sons' rooms. Unlike Jaoul, however, the design of the tall block disguises its mass. The roof is flat and covered with a lush garden. The plain fascia masking the vaults is the only separation between garden above and verandah below. Based on the vernacular structure of the Catalan, or cradle, vault, and placed in direct relation

Swimming pool

Interior vault

to a seemingly untouched landscape, Sarabhai suggests the first, Edenic house.

Given its Mediterranean tone, the question remains as to whether the house is appropriate to Indian culture in general and to its client in particular. Its vaults do recall the low, domed spaces in the Royal Apartments of the Red Fort at Delhi. The dual perception of the house as trabeated from the exterior, vaulted from within, is expressive of the

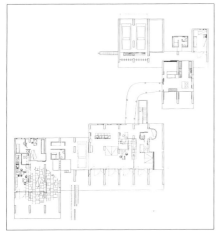

Maison Sarabhai, ground floor plan

private, interior life of the Indian home and the role of the woman in it. It was, in fact, Madame Sarabhai who requested that the vaults not be exposed on the facade, because she found them too industrial. Certainly, Le Corbusier's choice and development of the Monol type was a response to the local climate. The house is oriented to breeze and sun. The roof garden cools the spaces below. The permeability of the house allows it to adapt to the seasonal shift in prevalent wind direction. The most active features of the exterior—the scooped gutters, the sculptural spouts, and the water slide—celebrate monsoon rainwater while disposing of it. The shape of the slide recalls the azimuth triangle at the sacred astronomical site of Jantar Mantar near Delhi.

The building also reflects its owner's religion: the Sarabhai family are Jains, who value nature in its pure state and try to limit man's interference in it. The house, client, and culture are thus well matched. Le Corbusier found not only the proper climate but also the ideal inhabitant for his Edenic house.

Villa Shodhan
1956

Kharawala Road
Ahmedabad, Gujarat

VISITS: Private residence. If the groundskeeper is available, he will allow you to tour the outside briefly and from a distance.

LOCALE: See Millowners' Association Building. The villa is a mile from the Millowners Building on a suburban tract of land in the Ellisbridge district. Another mile or so south is Le Corbusier's museum.

DIRECTIONS: The villa is off the east side of Kharawala Road in the area of Mangaldas and N.C.C. Roads; since it is located behind other houses, it cannot be seen from the street. Because driveways are unmarked, it is likely you will explore quite a few before finding it.

IN THE *ŒUVRE COMPLÈTE* IT IS DESCRIBED as "Villa Savoye placed in a tropical setting"; in Le Corbusier's office it was known as the Arabian Nights. Together these epithets depict Le Corbusier's concerns in his first design for a millowner in Ahmedabad: the creation of a house equivalent in spirit to his purist villas but suited to a new climate and clientele. The original client, Surottam Hutheesing, was also a patron of the Millowners' Association Building. A wealthy, soon-to-wed bachelor, he required a house suited to various kinds of lavish entertaining. He sold the unbuilt plans to Shyamubhai Shodhan, another millowner, who had a family and a quieter lifestyle. Mr. Shodhan had the house erected on a different site with virtually no changes.

In form and organization, Shodhan is a descendant not just of Villa Savoye but also of many of the early villas. For example, Savoye is the source of the ramp ascending through the cubic volume, but the schemes for the tropical Villa Baizeau provided the parasol roof on slender columns, the complicated vertical section, and the open floors that, like horizontal trays, carry the enclosed volumes of the rooms. Within the typical Corbusian confines of a cube, the ramp and stairs divide the main house into quadrants. These quadrants are arranged according to purist principles of asymmetrical balance and counterpoint. The result is an interlocking composition of closed and open volumes focused about a double-height living room and three-story terrace.

In contrast to the fragile, floating quality of the early villas, Shodhan is robust and more grounded. Where a taut skin generally enveloped the purist boxes, here the composition of cubes is permeable and boldly sculptural. Le Corbusier's late interest in

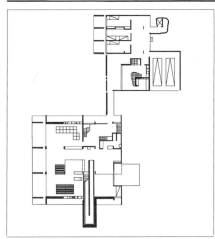

Villa Shodhan, ground floor plan

Mediterranean form and primitive technology coincided with the demands of India's tropical climate and local craftsmanship in their influence on the house's style. The surfaces are of rough, patched, now moldy concrete. The walls are screens of brise-soleil that are extremely open and extremely deep in order to both encourage breezes and provide shade.

Despite the abstraction of this concrete house, its forms resonate with those of the traditional Indian villa. Both employ an open and irregular grouping of rooms and the free, independent massing of porches. The parasol roof of Shodhan has precedents in Indian architecture as well as in Le Corbusier's tropical villa. The brise-soleil is recognizable as a large-scale variation of the Indian wooden screen. The double-height spaces behind the screen resemble the breezy, columned courts of the traditional Indian house. Doshi has described how Le Corbusier turned to Mogul miniatures of palaces as inspiration for the multilevel terraces and the individual sleeping balconies outside of each bedroom. As in Le Corbusier's purist villas, the architecture of Shodhan operates on at least two different levels, as an abstract, geometric composition and as an imaginative representation of class and culture.

N. C. Mehta Museum of Miniatures 1958

Bhagtacharya Road
Sanskar Kendra, Paldi
Ahmedabad, Gujarat
Tel. 78369

VISITS: Officially open 9-11 and 4-7 except Mondays, but call first.

LOCALE: See Ahmedabad. The museum is located about 3km southwest of the town center, across the plaza from the municipal theater. Nearby is the Ahmedabad Institute of Design, clearly derivative of Le Corbusier's architecture; its lush plants and small sculpture gardens make it especially pleasant to visit. The surrounding park also contains the Philatelic Museum.

DIRECTIONS: Take a taxi or auto-rickshaw to Bhagtacharya Road just west of the Sarder Bridge.

IN HIS 1925 BOOK *THE DECORATIVE ART OF Today,* Le Corbusier wrote, "Let us imagine a true museum, one that contains everything, one that could present a complete picture after the passage of time . . . . In order to flesh out our idea, let us put together a museum of our own day with objects of our own day; to begin: a plain jacket, a bowler hat, a well-made shoe . . . . Clearly this museum does not yet exist." In his critique, Le Corbusier upheld the status of the museum as a "sacred entity," but in the Encyclopedic tradition of the French Enlightenment he redefined its role from selective interpreter of history to inclusive catalogue. He observed the changes in this tradition brought about by the machine age: the new kinds of ethnographic facts, the new ways of gathering them, and a new, non-hierarchical assessment of their value. He wrote, "the fabulous development of the book, of print, and the classification of the whole of the most recent archeological era, have flooded our minds and overwhelmed us. We are in an entirely new situation. Everything is known to us."

Le Corbusier sought to design the architectural vessel appropriate to this new museum. He first proposed a three-dimensional spiral, or ziggurat, for the World Museum of his Mundaneum project (1929) and then a "squared spiral" on pilotis for his Museum of Modern Art project for Paris (1931) and his Museum of Unlimited Growth (Musée à croissance illimitée) (1939). The spiral had interested him from his earliest forest studies in La Chaux-de-Fonds as a pattern found in nature that describes organic growth according to an increasing series of proportions related to the golden mean. It thus reveals "a coherent system" within the wild variety of nature. Essential to the spiral is the order of its growth from a single point which becomes the center of an infinite pattern.

In the last decade of his life, Le Corbusier built three similar museums, in Ahmedabad, Chandigarh, and Tokyo, based on his youthful concept of the new museum and its spiral vessel. Since none is actually unlimited, Le Corbusier's attempt to give architectural expression to his ideas of history and information remains problematic. All three completed museums represent one yet focused inward on its own center. Each built museum has a central courtyard that is both entrance and exhibit hall, parallel bands of galleries about that center, a swastika pattern of passages, skylights that illuminate the interior independent of its facades, blank walls for facades, and a field of pilotis that provides passage to the entrance at the building's core. Each has some in-

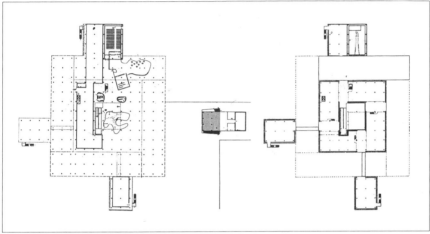

N. C. Mehta Museum, ground and first floor plans

stage in the development of the model Museum of Unlimited Growth. The construction of the model museum commenced with a single square court and was then to continue, as the museum collection grew, with a linear bay of standard elements wrapped around the central court. This process of growth generated "a building without a facade, one entered from below, in other words, from inside." In order to prevent the plan from becoming labyrinthine, Le Corbusier overlaid the spiral with the form of the "swastika." Each arm of the swastika defined a passage through the walls of the spiral that led back to the central court in one direction and to an exit at the building perimeter in the other. This pinwheel circulation also made the dual nature of the spiral clear as a form continually spinning outward

dication of the concept of expansion even if it is, as at Ahmedabad, only in the detailing of the brick joints.

As an insular, self-referential form with an abstract relation to the ground, the model museum was not only unlimited but also repeatable. Le Corbusier wrote in reference to the 1931 project, "It is built in a field of potatoes or beets. If the site is magnificent all the better. If it is ugly…, it doesn't matter." Lacking windows and terraces but low to the ground, the museum was to occupy its plot of land in a neutral fashion, without even the classical air of detachment that characterizes many of Le Corbusier's buildings, from Villa Savoye, the first box on stilts, to the Unités d'habitation. It thus lent itself to repetition on sites as diverse as Tokyo and Chandigarh.

Le Corbusier's original plan for the museum at Ahmedabad included wings for natural history, archeology, and anthropology, fulfilling his notion of the true and complete ethnographic collection. However, only the basic, squared spiral was completed. While adhering to the model configuration, the building manages to absorb a bit of the flavor of its native culture. From the outside it is a rather brutal box of local brick set on a rough concrete frame of pilotis. The concrete parasol roof lifted above the box is a form related to Indian native architecture which Le Corbusier used repeatedly in his Indian work. The central court is open to the sky, as appropriate to its tropical setting. The lighting of the galleries through courtyard windows and baffles below the parasol roof is primitive, but it leaves the roof surface free from skylights, for an elaborate terrace. In response to the climate, Le Corbusier envisioned many of the museum activities taking place in the evening on the roof terrace. There he placed forty-five water tanks each fifty meters square to cool the air and the galleries below and to hold flowering plants grown to enormous size with the help of a special fertilizer obtained through the Institut Pasteur. In contrast to the severity of this spiral, its roof was to be a Mogul garden with vines hanging down over the brick walls. Unfortunately, the magical flowers were never planted.

Chandigarh

Delhi 260km, Manali
313km, Simla 113km

Palace of Justice	1955
Secretariat	1958
Assembly Building	1961
Yacht Club	1964
Museum and Gallery	1964
College of Art	1965
College of Architecture	1965
Monument of the Open Hand	1955

LE CORBUSIER'S INVOLVEMENT IN THE design of a city after a lifetime of unrealized urban schemes came about through circumstance as well as through recognition of his ideas. The treaty that granted India her nationhood in 1947 also ceded the western part of Punjab, including the capital city of Lahore, to Pakistan. With the financial support of the central government at New Delhi, P. L. Varma, chief engineer of the Punjab, and P. N. Thapan, State Administrator, chose the site and name of the new capital of Indian Punjab. Chandigarh means "fortress of Chandi (the War Goddess)," a reference to a very old temple just north of the city erected to the goddess and her seven sisters. Albert Mayer, an American friend of Nehru's, was the planner for the new city. Charles Nowicki, a former collaborator of Le Corbusier's, was to be the architect, but he died in an airplane crash while the contract with Mayer was under dispute. Indian officials turned to Maxwell Fry and Jane Drew, British architects associated with the CIAM (International Congress of Modern Architecture), who in turn suggested Le Corbusier. Seduced by the scope of the project, Le Corbusier overcame his initial hesitancy regarding the low fee, long distance, and rushed schedule to accept the position as Architect Advisor, with the proviso that Pierre Jeanneret join him.

Although Mayer's original guidelines for the plan were to be followed, with a few key changes Le Corbusier was able to make it a clear reflection of his ideals as well. Mayer's concept of a zoned city was consonant with the principles of Le Corbusier's Radiant City as codified in the CIAM document, The Athens Charter. Le Corbusier accepted both the organization of a governmental head connected by an axial route to a commercial center and the separation of the industrial strip from the residential sectors by a

VISITS: Since 1984, the state of Punjab, of which Chandigarh is the capital (it is also the capital of Haryana), has been officially closed to foreigners due to Sikh unrest. It is forbidden to take photographs inside most government buildings in the city.

LOCALE: Since Chandigarh is a sprawling city, travel by auto-rickshaw is recommended to see it in a single day. If you have the time, take an itinerary on foot that starts at the capitol complex, including the rock garden and the yacht club, continues to the museum and the rose garden in Sector 16, and ends with the shopping center in Sector 17. The nicest hotel is the Oberoi Mount View (tel. 24729, 26021) near the museum. Hotel Aroma in Sector 22 (tel 23359) and the youth hostel just outside of town are good values. Monsoon season is July and August. Consequently, the landscape is at its most luxuriant in the fall, at its driest in the spring.

DIRECTIONS: Leaving from the New Delhi train station, the early morning Himalayan Queen, destination Kalka, arrives at Chandigarh before noon and returns to Delhi in the evening. Take a taxi to the city center. Buses, including luxury lines, leave from the Interstate Bus Terminal in Delhi, near Kashmir Gate, and take about five hours. Buses also run from Simla (5 hrs), Kulu (12 hrs), Manali (14 hrs), and Pathankot (7 hrs). There are daily flights from Delhi, Jammu, and Srinagar.

greenbelt. He straightened the curved roads defining the organically shaped sectors, thus reducing the garden-city quality of the plan, and he accepted Maxwell Fry's suggestion that the transverse axes bend slightly for variety and shade. The orthogonality and sheer dimension of Le Corbusier's major axes introduced a monumentality that refers more to the Western, colonialist planning of New Delhi than to any of the gridded precedents in Indian culture, such as Jaipur.

neret remained in India several years after Fry and Drew had left, supervising construction and leading a team of Indian designers in the continued development of Chandigarh.

Sector 1

The Secretariat, the Parliament, and the Court buildings are located within the capitol complex according to several sets of overlapping axes. The space of the complex is further defined through various manipulations in ground plane—

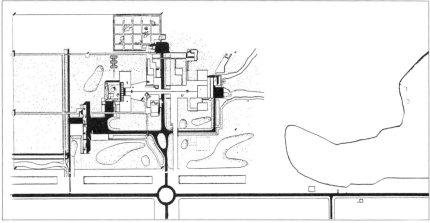

Site plan of capitol complex

Le Corbusier's vision for Chandigarh was also in tune with Nehru's. Both accepted the inevitable development in India of a machine culture. Rather than filling the current needs of an agricultural country still based on the bicycle, Le Corbusier scaled the axes of Chandigarh for cars and speed.

After laying down the general framework and principles he envisioned for Chandigarh, Le Corbusier withdrew from the planning process and devoted his efforts to the design of the capitol complex and several other small pieces of the town, including the art school, museum, and yacht club. Jeanneret, Fry, and Drew worked out the plan in detail and designed the bulk of the initial buildings. As official architect, Jean-

ditches, pools, and mounds—and through a group of monuments. Entrance to the complex from the city is along a pedestrian extension of the central boulevard. This axis was to have culminated in a sequence of courts reminiscent of Mogul gardens, and the Governour's Palace; however, Nehru decided it was an inappropriate symbol for the new democracy. Le Corbusier proposed in its place a Museum of Knowledge dedicated to advanced technological communications, but this, too, was not built. Until the spot has been filled, the plaza will remain significantly incomplete. On axis with the vacant site are a group of monuments, still incomplete: the Martyrs' Monument to the Punjab Partisans, a monument to the sun's course between the solstices, and the Tower of Shadow. A ramp from the tower leads to a mound inscribed with the sine curve of the daily solar cycle and then to the Trench of Consideration. To the right of the vacant site stands the Monument of the Open Hand. At the ends of the 450-meter cross-axis are the Palace of Justice on the east and the Assembly Building on the west. Behind the Assembly, the long Secretariat slab defines the edge of the complex. In order to assure the clarity of the conversation among his buildings and monuments, Le Corbusier sunk all the vehicular approaches five meters below the plaza (only later allowing the waste soil to be formed into mounds) and determined the locations to a fraction of the smallest modulor unit, believing his adjustments to be perceptible.

The planning of the capitol complex should be viewed against the background of both India's and Le Corbusier's past. The complex was for Le Corbusier the last of a series of un-built governmental palaces, such as the League of Nations, Palace of Nations, and Mundaneum. As in these earlier projects, the influences of the Greek acropolis, Baroque axes (especially the one from the Louvre to the Arc de Triomphe), and Beaux-Arts planning can be felt. Le Corbusier, like Nehru, appreciated the classical planning of New Delhi. If the Governour's Palace had been built at the north end of Sector 1, the analogy with the British colonial city would have been all the clearer. In designing the complex, Le Corbusier transformed his sources at their very roots, according to his modernist principles of balanced asymmetry and shifted axes. Norma Evenson has noted how the deliberate misalignments among the buildings create multiple perspectives "leading the eye to many points of view without tension being broken."

Commercial center (Sector 17)

Critics seem to agree that nothing can convey the vastness of the site or the quality of Le Corbusier's imprint on it. Some feel the buildings are simply too small and distant to create a sense of place. Others describe the how the reflecting pools and the mounds of soil, like foothills to the Himalayas, at once compress distance within the complex and link the buildings to the horizon. Le Corbusier explained his composition in terms of the flat, overpowering site that stretched out before the Himalayas: "It was a matter of occupying a plain...; the geometrical event was, in truth, a sculpture of the intellect..., the battle of space fought with the mind."

Residential Sectors

In order to function as a self-contained community, each residential sector includes a community center, schools, and a small bazaar along a central street. Accepting the Indian status quo, the housing is divided according to social class, with the highest caste occupying the sites that are largest and closest to the capitol complex. Depending on its caste, a sector has between 5,000 and 20,000 inhabitants. Drew, Fry, and Jean-neret defined guidelines for thirteen classes of housing to be designed by them, the city architects, and private developers. By and large, the guidelines replaced the traditional Indian court house on narrow streets with a row-house arrangement on wider routes. They vary in strictness, ranging from "frame control," where the developer has design freedom within a deep white frame he must literally build around the house, to regulations of height and materials only. Because Sector 22 has been privately developed, it is more varied, more dense, and, consequently, more urban than the other neighborhoods. Although the team designed a decent dwelling for the pariah, not enough of them have been built to house the population. Consequently, there has emerged a second Chandigarh of residential shanties just beyond the city limits and commercial sheds on empty lots in the planned sectors. The city government is attempting to find a place for these people within the parameters of the original plan.

Sector 17

The commercial center of the town, Sector 17 was intended as an Indian crossroads marketplace, or *chowk*. Around an open piazza are office buildings with ground floors devoted to commercial use. They are unified by a continuous arcade of seventeen-foot bays with second-story verandahs. Pierre Jeanneret, Satynam and Namita Singh, and others designed the larger civic buildings, including the town hall and banks, using variations on the standard facade screen. The uniformity and scale of the verandah, and the vast size of the piazza are at odds with the traditional *chowk,* which is characterized by a dense intermingling of functions and narrow, hence shaded passages.

Roads

In addition to its system of sectors, the major feature of Chandigarh is its system of circulation. Since the 1920s, when Le Corbusier, among others, envisioned multilayered circulation systems, the separation of pedestrian from vehicular traffic had become a truism of modern planning. Le Corbusier first developed for Bogota, Colombia, the seven ways, or 7v (*voies*), he used in Chandigarh. They are: v1, the intercity thoroughfare; v2, the city's monumental axis and cross-axis; v3, the primary grid dividing the sectors; v4, the main division of the sectors along the shopping street; v5, the residential streets within the sectors; v6, the ways to the dwellings; and v7, the pedestrian garden paths that allow children to go to school without crossing a street.

Chandigarh is a new city designed for a machine-age future in a nonindustrial culture. Considering his gradual loss of faith in Western industrial nations and the increasing primitivism of his European work, it is oddly appropriate that Le Corbusier found himself in the midst of this technological dilemma. In the capitol complex, his solution was to use reinforced concrete according to the ability of his workforce and to forge a spiritual bond with the landscape. In India, he wrote, "man is face to face with nature…with her violence also." To the extent that he involved himself in the design of the city, he accepted the necessity for low-rise buildings but rigidly adhered to patterns of circulation and functional separation inappropriate to the Indian present. Today Chandigarh is acknowledged throughout India to be a pleasant place to live, with high standards of public utilities and services but without the richness and texture of the traditional Indian buildings that Le Corbusier himself observed and appreciated.

Palace of Justice (High Court) 1956

Sector 1
Chandigarh

VISITS: Visitable without supervision. Ask to see tapestries in the courtrooms, designed by Le Corbusier and executed in Kashmir.

LOCALE: See Chandigarh.

DIRECTIONS: See Chandigarh.

THE PALACE OF JUSTICE DEPARTS FROM traditional courthouse architecture in the organization of its parts. The courtrooms are boxes between pylons fronting directly and individually onto the plaza. To the right of the entrance is a two-story-high block of eight courtrooms unified by a continuous brise-soleil. To the left of the entrance is the High Court. The entrance is an open portico among the fully revealed pylons; it has no connection with the courtroom interiors. The ceremonial ramp at the back of the portico leads only to the offices on the upper floors. Movement on the upper floors is along an open-air corridor at the rear of the building, screened by brise-soleil. The unity of the building arises not from an internal, hierarchical system of lobbies and corridors related to the seats of justice, but from the activity of the citizens as they move from plaza to

Ground floor plan

courtroom to portico. Although some critics find problematic the use of vaults on the underside of a canopy that is really post and beam construction, Curtis has observed that the vaulted forms relate to the basilica of the ancient Roman court as well as to the seventeenth-century Red Fort of Delhi. Thus Le Corbusier inserted the courtroom into a classical framework.

Palace of Justice, Le Corbusier's sketches

The modest brick buildings stepping back behind the Palace proper are additional courtrooms designed by Le Corbusier when, early in the courthouse's history, it became evident that its facilities were inadequate. Their cellular arrangement allows for future expansion without further disturbance of the foreground building.

Le Corbusier conceived the independent parts of the Palace in terms of the natural forces of climate as well as the mechanisms of justice. The canopy of vaults is an umbrella for sun and monsoon rain. The space between the roofs allows cooling air currents to circulate. The wall of the courtrooms is a 4'-7" deep screen of brise-soleil that shades the glass behind it from heat and glare.

These features are more monumental expressions of architecture's relation to climate than tools that successfully cope with the extremes of heat and rain that occur in Chandigarh. For example, a low porch has been added to the facade because the great canopy does not cast its shadow far enough to cover the plaza activity generated by the courts.

Interior ramp

Secretariat 1958

Sector 1
Chandigarh

VISITS: Visitable during working hours. Entrance is to the left of the building's center. No cameras allowed inside. Roof accessible from 10-12. Although the building remains unaltered, it has not weathered well, especially the concrete, which is flaked and moldy in patches.

LOCALE: See Chandigarh.

DIRECTIONS: See Chandigarh.

THE 254-METER-LONG SECRETARIAT CONsists of six eight-story blocks connected by expansion joints and a continuous screen of brise-soleil. Together they house the various ministries of the Punjab and Haryana states. Originally, Le Corbusier proposed a tower for the Secretariat in the mode of his Algiers office project of 1942, but he capitulated to the demands of officials and designed a horizontal slab that in essence turns the Algiers project on its side.

As a wall that selectively reveals the order of the office blocks behind, the brise-soleil assumes an expressive role in the definition of a unified Secretariat. In terms of utility, it is the shading device of a three-part system Le Corbusier used throughout India in place of the traditional window. The other parts are the *ondulatoire*, or fixed glazing, which admits light, and the *aerateur*, a hinged metal panel, which opens for ventilation, in front of fixed copper mosquito netting. The brise-soleil of the Secretariat has 63 bays about 4 meters wide filled with 2,000 screen units. The breaks in the pattern correspond not to structural definitions but to function and spatial organization. For example, the colossal bays of blocks 5 and 6 mark the entrance for officials. The double-height ministers' chambers in block 4 have a three-dimensionally activated screen of corresponding double units, with symbolic inserts in the shape of a bull's horn or sky-scoop.

The ramp towers project the inner life of the building even beyond its perimeter. Although there is an orderly system of access via a central corridor flanked with elevators and stairs, Le Corbusier favored the ramp as the celebratory promenade to and from the workplace, in accordance with the solar

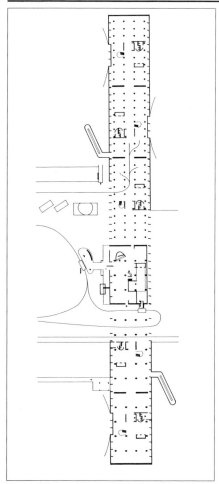

Ground floor plan

Main facade

The Secretariat has an ambiguous role in the capitol complex; it acts as both an edge, or backdrop wall, to the space and a building within it. Its main approach is not across the plaza surface but along a sunken, utilitarian roadway ending in a forecourt which is also a parking lot. Because of the excavated court, the lower perimeter of the building is varied and ambiguous, with pilotis hidden behind the plaza level. As Paul Rudolph has observed, the slab is conceived in dimensions other than those of a flat surface. Approaching the capitol complex from the town, the Secretariat is the first building in view, "sitting at a right angle to the mountains, rising from the plain. In every way it opposes the mountains; the angled stairway, the ramp on the roof..., all of these angles are obviously and carefully conceived to oppose the receding angles of the land masses." It is wall-like yet an enormous object with a fixed outline, designed in relation to a vast landscape.

cycle, and so articulated it as a curved figure at an angle to the rectilinear slab.

Assembly Building (Parliament) 1961

Sector 1
Chandigarh

VISITS: Severely restricted visits allowed when accompanied by security guard. Request permission in the main lobby. Cameras not allowed.

LOCALE: See Chandigarh.

DIRECTIONS: See Chandigarh.

AS IN THE PALACE OF JUSTICE AND THE Secretariat, the inspiration for the forms of the Assembly Building came both from the Indian climate and from Le Corbusier's conceptualization of the function and organization of a government assembly. In plan, a U-shaped office block and a front portico together form the perimeter of a hypostyle concourse within which stand the hyperbolic volume of the General Assembly (Upper Chamber) and the cube of the Governour's Council (Lower Chamber). The two volumes rise through the building and emerge on the roof as strong geometric solids, a slant-topped cone and a pyramid, connected by a delicate service bridge. Le Corbusier conceived of the concourse as a forum, "a great space for favorable encounters among law-givers." As he said of the forum of the earlier Centrosoyus building in Moscow, "architecture is circulation." The fluid space and the complex of ramps invite movement, activity, and communication. There are no stairs. The slender columns, high ceiling painted black, and clerestory lighting all add to the expansive, dimensionless feeling of the space. Within this seemingly free space, the paths of circulation are rigidly divided among parliament members, visitors, and the press, with the most splendid procession reserved for government officials.

In the architecture of the forum, Le Corbusier reversed the traditional relation between circulation and the assembly rooms. Rather than the culmination of a linear corridor, the General Assembly is a circular solid asymmetrically disposed within the space of the forum. Visually, it "invites circumambulation, like a stupa." As Colin Rowe has remarked, this plan reverses the centralized organization of neoclassical architecture in general and the Altes Museum by Schinkel in particular.

The freed figure of the General Assembly is the focus of much of the cosmological symbolism of the building. It is a vessel of both government and light, of both earthly and cosmic law. On the one hand, its shape and thin-shell concrete structure, less than 150mm thick, connect it to the cooling towers of Ahmedabad, symbols of India's emerging modernity; on the other hand, it recalls the eighteenth-century astronomical instruments of Jantar Mantar in Delhi. Le Corbusier equipped its top with a "veritable laboratory of machinery emitting natural and artificial light," including some for a "solar festival once a year to remind men they are children of the sun." On this day, the opening of Parliament, Le Corbusier imagined that the representatives and governor would pass through the great pivoting door to the General Assembly. A light from the oculus would strike a column next to the speaker's rostrum, which is dedicated to the first Indian ruler, Asoka. As in the cult of the French sun-king, solar, quasi-religious symbolism is given an overt political role.

After several rounds of calculations, Le Corbusier abandoned the attempt to adjust the skylight for the solar ritual of Asoka's Column. He also acknowledged the other acoustic and illumination problems inherent in the curved concrete shape. Despite the tiered system of sound-absorbent panels, the room is still too vibrant for speakers to be understood without microphones.

Le Corbusier's cosmology also appears on the great door's enamel panels. Most simply interpreted, the exterior depicts the big and small arcs of the sun and the sine curve of the solar cycle above a landscape with animals of the countryside; the interior's more mysterious configuration includes

natural forms Le Corbusier admired, such as pine cones and spiral shells, and the head of a bull, which some associate with the minotaur and the solar myth of vernal rebirth.

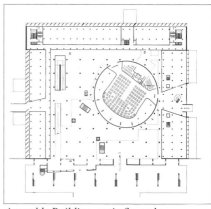

Assembly Building, main floor plan

Besides the intense sun, the monsoon rain plays a profound role in the architecture of the capitol complex. The portico and roof of the Parliament create both "a veritable cathedral for shade" and huge channels for rainwater. Le Corbusier equipped the roof with two gutters the size of canals, which he called the "two rivers," in reference to the two rivers of Chandigarh. They direct the rainwater to scuppers, basins, and, finally, the pools around the building. In these pools, Le Corbusier celebrates water's property of reflection. In the manner of Indian palatial architecture, from the Taj Mahal to Diwan-I-Khas, he used the pools to transform the flat ground into an illusory plane, like a horizon, between the building and the deep space of its reflected image. As he noted, the pool "squares the building." In other words, the rough concrete Assembly and its incorporeal reflection together describe an almost perfect cube. The complete image of the cube appears with the monsoon rains that fill the pools, and alters as the waters evaporate.

The Yacht Club (Lake Club) 1964

Sector 1
Chandigarh

VISITS: Clearly visible from edge of lake.

LOCALE: See Chandigarh.

DIRECTIONS: The club is on the southwest edge of Sukhna Lake, less than a mile east of the capitol complex.

LE CORBUSIER DID NOT WANT BUILDINGS erected north of the city sectors, because they would obstruct the view of the mountains. When officials pressured him into placing the club on the lake, he sunk it three meters below road level and placed a simple concrete colonnade along the lakeshore. The plan has similarities to his early, purist compositions, with curved walls reminiscent of Roman fragments disposed within a regular column grid. The grid is classically rendered as a portico on the edge of an artificial lake, recalling both Western works, such as Hadrian's Villa, and Indian palatial architecture, such as the fifteenth-century Sarkej Pavilion near Ahmedabad.

At the insistence of P. L. Varma, chief engineer of Punjab, in 1955 a river was dammed to create the huge Sukhna Lake. The lake provides water, keeps down the dust, and even mitigates the extremes of the local climate. Le Corbusier designed a gateway to the landing stages and a memorial stone commemorating the dam's construction.

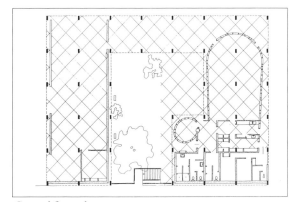

Ground floor plan

Museum and Art Gallery 1964

Jan Marg, Sector 10
Chandigarh

VISITS: Open daily except Mondays.

LOCALE: The Museum is located on the Jan Marg, to the side of the Leisure Valley. It is part of an educational-cultural complex that includes the College of Arts. Chandigarh's best hotel, the Oberoi Mount View, is nearby.

DIRECTIONS: Take an auto-rickshaw or one of the many bus routes to Sector 10.

THE MUSEUM AT CHANDIGARH ADHERES to Le Corbusier's model for a Museum of Unlimited Growth in its arrangement of galleries around a central courtyard that extends the height of the building (see the N. C. Mehta Museum at Ahmedabad for discussion of the model). For this particular courtyard, Le Corbusier devised a processional ramp to the upper-level galleries and a differentiated group of pilotis—some lozenge-shaped, others rectangular—that create rhythm without destroying the continuity of the grid.

One notable departure from the model is the design of the lecture hall. The stone hall is placed up against the museum in tense opposition to the sedate brick perimeter and in conflict with the principle of unlimited growth. It is an independent, angular box with a front portico that recalls the small walled theater, or *boite à miracles* (box of miracles) found in many of Le Corbusier's projects for cultural complexes.

Whereas the solid walls and roof of the hall make it a room of theatrical darkness, an ordered system of linear diffusers makes the museum a vessel for light. The diffuse, calm quality of light in the museum is particularly apparent in relation to the bright colors of the walls—black, white, red, and yellow. On top of the museum, an elaborate superstructure with clerestory openings, gutters, and sculptural spouts controls water as well as sunlight.

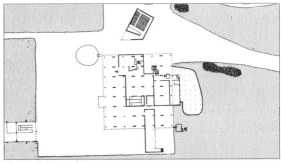

Ground floor plan

College of Art, Punjab University 1965

College of Architecture, Punjab University 1965

Sector 10
Chandigarh

THE BUILDINGS OF THESE TWO COLLEGES are quite similar in design and organization. In both colleges, the individual studio unit with a curved concrete roof and clerestory lighting is based on Le Corbusier's 1929 unbuilt studio for himself. Like Le Corbusier's personal project, these are modest masonry structures, low to the ground, with a vernacular Mediterranean quality. The shape of the roof at Chandigarh is the result of calculations of local sun angles. The simple side walls of local brick have vertical slots for ventilation and concrete waterspouts for drainage.

The organization of the independent cells around a central courtyard recalls Le Corbusier's early plans for an art school at La Chaux-de-Fonds (1910) as well as the Carthusian Monastery at Ema, which he thought the perfect model for a balanced community. The front block, shielded by brise-soleil, contains the administrative offices.

VISITS: Check with administrative offices of schools.

LOCALE: Both schools are located in Chandigarh's Leisure Valley, a cultural and recreational complex set in greenery. Although Le Corbusier conceived of extensive entertainment facilities in the Valley, featuring an open-air theater, today its buildings are primarily educational, including Punjab University, designed primarily by Jeanneret, and the Art Museum by Le Corbusier.

DIRECTIONS: Take a local bus or auto-rickshaw along the Jan Marg toward Sector 10. The entrances are off the parking lot side of the Leisure Valley.

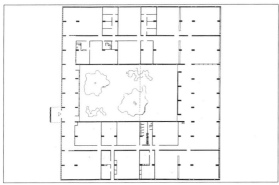

Ground floor plan

Monument of the Open Hand
1955, 1986

Sector 1
Chandigarh

VISITS: Accessible open-air sculpture.

LOCALE: See Chandigarh.

DIRECTIONS: See Chandigarh.

THE SYMBOL OF THE OPEN HAND HAD AP-
peared in Le Corbusier's artwork and writings long
before he designed the monument for Chandigarh.
Mary Sekler has carefully traced it to a series of
drawings in the early 1940s in which an open hand
somewhat resembling a cockle shell floats above the
horizon and echoes the shape of the human figures in
the foreground. She has also connected it to images
of tree branches and thus to Le Corbusier's analogy
among plant growth, man, and a healthy society, in
the tradition of John Ruskin. Le Corbusier's "Poem
to the Right Angle" (194753), after describing the
relation of a hand to the physical and spiritual world,
concludes with the lines, "With a full hand I have
received/ With a full hand I give."

Some have criticized Le Corbusier's choice of a
personal symbol for a monument in Chandigarh, but
others, including Indian officials and Le Corbusier
himself, thought its sentiment of reciprocal giving
consonant with the life of the new nation. Le Corbusier wrote, "this sign of the Open Hand, a sign of
peace and of reconciliation, must arise at Chandigarh.... This sign of the Open Hand, to receive the
created riches, to distribute [them] to the peoples of
the world should be the sign of the epoch.... " According to P. L. Varma, head engineer of Chandigarh, Indian philosophy is "the philosophy of the Open
Hand..., faith born of the surrender of the will to the
Ultimate Source of Knowledge, service without
reward."

At Chandigarh, the hand rises from the Ditch of
Consideration, an amphitheater for public debate dug
from the earth, so that those gazing up at it see only
its form outlined against the sky. Its shape simultaneously opens up to the landscape and draws the

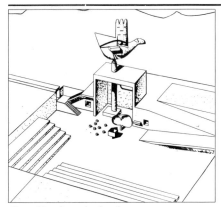

Open Hand, study sketch

sky into its palm. The outline also suggests a bird, perhaps a tree. The enameled metal hand turns on ball bearings according to the direction of the wind, "not to show the incertitude of ideas, but to indicate symbolically the direction of the wind (that is, the state of affairs)." In all these features—movement, siting, and silhouette—the Open Hand suggests a reciprocity between the will of man and the forces of nature.

Glossary

aedicule: A framed opening. Originally composed of columns supporting an entablature and pediment.

aerateur: Wall opening with operable hinged door and fixed mosquito netting intended as ventilation. One part of a three-part system developed by Le Corbusier to replace the traditional window, the other two parts being a brise-soleil for shade and *ondulatoire* for light.

Athens Charter: Document of urbanism developed by CIAM (International Congress of Modern Architecture) in 1933. Published by Le Corbusier in 1943.

azulejos: Brightly colored glazed tiles of Spanish-Moslem origin.

balustrade: Railing supported by posts, urns, or miniature pillars.

béton brut ("rough concrete"): Exposed concrete left with the imprint of the form work, usually deliberately.

bloc à redents: Linear block of apartments with setbacks developed by Le Corbusier for his Contemporary City (1922). Their stepping profile is reminiscent of French baroque palaces. The blocks possess collective services for recreation and domestic care.

brise-soleil: Sun-break made of concrete, often a non-structural gridded screen or system of balconies. One part of a three-part system Le Corbusier intended as a replacement for the standard window. The other two parts are the *ondulatoire* for light and the *aerateur* for ventilation.

Catalan vault: Brick vault without true formwork. Associated with the vernacular architecture of the Catalonian region.

cella: The walled enclosure of a Greek or Roman temple.

clerestory: Upper level windows in a wall that rises above adjoining roofs.

dry assembly: The assembly of prefabricated parts on a construction site without mortar.

entablature: Horizontal members supported by columns. Major constituent parts are the architrave, cornice, and frieze.

fascia: A plain horizontal surface. Originally the overlapping planes of an architrave.

Fibonacci series: The unending sequence 1,1,2,3,5,8... where each term equals the sum of its two predecessors.

Five Points of Modern Architecture: Le Corbusier's formulation of architectural principles derived from the potentials of the concrete frame. They are the pilotis beneath the house, the roof garden on top, the free plan inside the house, the free facades outside, and strip windows.

Four Compositions: Le Corbusier's categories of spatial organization derived in part from the Five Points and Maison Dom-ino. Each Composition refers to one of his house designs of the 1920s. They are: (1) Maisons La Roche-Jeanneret, picturesque and animated but depending on classical hierarchy to discipline it, (2) Villa Stein, a prismatic volume, (3) Villa Baizeau, a practical combination of an exposed Dom-ino frame and the free plan, (4) Villa Savoye, an interior with the qualities of (1) and (2) within the envelope of (3).

free facade (or plan): In both cases, the wall is free of structural constaints and supports no weight other than its own.

golden section (also called golden mean): A ratio between two portions of a line or between the two dimensions of a rectangle, in which the lesser of the two is to the greater as the greater is to the sum of both. $A:B = B:A + B$. It is approximately equal to .616.

hipped roof: A roof that slopes inwards on all four sides.

hôtel: French town house.

immeuble villa **(villa apartment):** A perimeter apartment block from Le Corbusier's Contemporary City in which each dwelling is a maisonnette, a two story apartment with adjoining garden. The organization of each apartment derives from the Maison Citrohan. The block has an interior shared garden and collective housekeeping services and facilities.

lamella: A vertical fin used as a sun-break on a building facade. Usually made of concrete.

loggia: Roofed porch, gallery, or balcony arcaded on one or more sides.

Maison Citrohan: One of Le Corbusier's prototypical dwellings intended for mass production. There are several versions of this house, some with pilotis. All of them are free-standing rectangular (double square) boxes with larger industrial sash windows at the front and primarily blank side walls. The plan is organized around a double-height salon with sleeping balcony.

Maison Dom-ino: Le Corbusier's formulation of the reinforced concrete frame, characterized by its smooth slabs without expressed beams and straight columns without capitals. The columns are set in from the edge of the slab. Bay and cantilever widths are determined by rules of quadrature and the golden section.

Maison Monol: One of Le Corbusier's prototypical dwellings intended for mass production. It is a vaulted linear volume of concrete that can stand independently or as a part of a series of attached units.

Modulor: Le Corbusier's system of proportion and measure based on the golden section as it applies to the human figure. First applied in his post World War II work.

mullion: Veritical member between the panes of a window.

objet-type: Anonymous object evolved through mass production to a perfected standard.

odeion: Small Greek roofed theater.

ondulatoire: Fixed glazing with mullions. One part of a three-part system developed by Le Corbusier to replace the traditional window in his late architecture. The other parts are brise-soleil for shade and *aerateur* for ventilation.

orthogonal: Pertaining to right angles and/or perpendicular lines.

pan de verre: Le Corbusier's version of the glass curtain wall.

pergola: An arbor of trellis work supported by columns. A colonnade in the form of an arbor.

piano nobile: The raised public floor with reception rooms of an Italian palazzo.

piloti(s): Le Corbusier's term for ground-level columns that support a building raised above them. The extension of piles (in French *pilots*) above the ground for the purpose of supporting a raised building so that the ground level is left open.

post and lintel: Construction system of vertical posts spanned by horizontal lintels.

primitivism: The attitude that primitive or crude qualities of form and technology have current value.

Purism: Artistic movement defined in 1916 in reaction to Cubism, with the intent of restoring the integrity of the object to still life painting. In mature form its spatial structure resembled that of synthetic cubism. Generalized as a cultural aesthetic, it called for the evolution and refinement of type objects to a perfected standard.

taylorization: The scientific study and management of industrial production in order to increase efficiency; named after F. W. Taylor an American engineer who was its exponent.

trabeation: Post and lintel construction.

tracés régulateurs (**regulating lines**): Le Corbusier's first proportioning system of angled lines based on quadrature and the properties of the golden section.

Unité d'habitation: A housing type proposed by Le Corbusier in the form of a free standing slab on pilotis. Apartments were arranged along corridors called interior streets.

Ville Contemporaine: Contemporary City for Three Million Inhabitants, Le Corbusiers's first city plan on a virgin site, exhibited in 1922. It has a center of office towers in a park surrounded by residential and cultural districts. Industrial zones stand beyond a green belt with accompanying residential garden communities.

Ville Radieuse: Radiant City, Le Corbusier's second ideal city plan, first proposed in 1930. It contains parallel bands zoned for business, residences, recreation, and industry arranged along a central linear circulation spine.

ziggurat: Stepped pyramid.

Notes

Introduction

Hellman, Geoffrey "From Within to Without," *New Yorker April 26, 1947.*

Le Corbusier, *Modulor, de Francia, Peter and Bostock, Anna, trans. (Cambridge: Harvard, 1980) 31.*

Maison Planex

Benton, Tim, *Les Villas de Le Corbusier and Pierre Jeanneret 1920–1930* (Paris: Editions Sers and the Fondation Le Corbusier, 1984), 129-61.

Von Moos, Stanislaus *Le Corbusier: Elements of a Synthesis* (Cambridge: MIT Press, 1982), 93.

Le Corbusier and Pierre Jeanneret, *Œuvre Complète*, (Zurich: Les Editions d'Architecture, Artemis) vol. 1.

Asile Flottant

Taylor, Brian Brace, *Le Corbusier, La Cité de Refuge* (Paris, 1980).

Serenyi, Peter in Serenyi, ed., *Le Corbusier in Perspective* (Englewood Cliffs: Prentice Hall, 1975) 112-3.

Von Moos, *Elements,* 154-7.

Tafuri, Manfredo and Dal Co, Francesco, *Modern Architecture* (New York: Harry N. Abrams, 1979) 142.

Curtis, William J.R. *Le Corbusier: Ideas and Forms* (New York: Rizzoli, 1986) 98-104.

Œuvre Complète, vol. 2.

Atelier Ozenfant

Jencks, Charles, *Le Corbusier and the Tragic View of Architecture* (Cambridge: Harvard University Press, 1973) 50, 59.

Banham, Reyner, *Theory and Design in the First Machine Age* (London: The Architectural Press, 1960) 217-18.

Benton, *Villas,* 36-7.

Pavillon Suisse

Œuvre Complète, vol. 3.

Curtis, *Ideas and Forms,* 104-9.

Moore, Richard, "Alchemical and Mythical Themes in the Poem of the Right Angle 1947–65" in Frampton, Kenneth, ed., *Oppositions 19/20* (Cambridge: MIT Press, 1980).

Maitland, Barry "The Grid" in Frampton, Kenneth, ed., *Oppositions 15/16* (Cambridge: MIT Press, 1978).

Maisons La Roche et Jeanneret

Walden, Russell in Walden, ed., *The Open Hand: Essays on Le Corbusier* (Cambridge: MIT Press, 1977).

Etlin, Richard "A Paradoxical Avant-Garde, Le Corbusier's Villas of the 1920s," in *Architectural Review,* January, 1987.

Gidieon, Sigfried in Serenyi, *Perspective,* 33-5.

Œuvre Complète, vol. 2.

Porte Molitor

Maitland, "The Grid," 107-9.

Yosizaka, Takamasa, "Le Corbusier's Apartment House at Porte Molitor," *GA (Global Architecture) 18* (Tokyo: ADA Edita)

Maisons Lipchitz and Ternisien

Benton, *Villas,* 85-97.

Maison Cook

Œuvre Complète, vol. 1, 130.

Maitland, "The Grid," 101-7, 111-12.

Etlin, "A Paradoxical Avant-Garde,".

Eisenman, Peter, "Aspects of Modernism: Maison Dom-ino and the Self-Referential Sign," *Oppositions 15/16,* 121-8.

Maisons Jaoul

Stirling, James in Serenyi, *Perspective,* "Garches to Jaoul: Le Corbusier as Domestic Architect in 1927 and 1953," 55.

Le Corbusier, *Towards a New Architecture,* trans. Frederick Etchells (New York: Holt, Rinehart and Winston, 1960) 177–79.

Gorlin, Alex "The Ghost in the Machine: Surrealism in the Work of Le Corbusier, *Perspecta 20*, 1984.

Blake, Peter, *The Master Builders*, (New York: W.W. Norton, 1963) 89.

Œuvre Complète, vol. 2, 59.

Le Petit Cabanon
Conversation with Francesco Passante

Le Corbusier, *Towards* 193.

Le Corbusier, *The City of Tomorrow and Its Planning* trans. Frederick Etchells (Cambridge: MIT Press, 1971) 24, 29.

Grave of Le Corbusier
Curtis, *Ideas and Forms*, 223.

Quartier Moderne Frugès
Taylor, Brian Brace in Walden *The Open Hand*, 162–186.

Boudon, Philippe *Lived-In Architecture: Le Corbusier's Pessac Revisited* (Cambridge: MIT Press, 1979)

Rasmussen in Serenyi, *Perspective*, 90.

Jencks, *Tragic View*, 74.

Villa le Sextant
Œuvre Complète, vol. 3, 135–7

Frampton, Kenneth, *Modern Architecture 1851–1945*, (New York: Rizzoli, 1983) 427.

Unité d'habitation Nantes-Rezé
Architectural Review, vol. 3 Nov. 1955 327.

Colquhoun, *Modern Architecture*, 39.

Le Corbusier, *My Work*, trans. James C. Palmes (London: Architectural Press, 1960) 272.

Villa Fallet
Sekler, Mary in Walden, *The Open Hand*.

Gubler, Jacques in Russell, Frank, ed., *Art Nouveau Architecture*, (New York: Arch Cape Press, 1986).

Villa Stotzer
Baker, Geoffrey, *Le Corbusier: an Analysis of Form*, (Berkshire: Van Nostrand Reinhold Co. Ltd. 1984) 35–7.

Petit, Jean, ed., *Le Corbusier lui-même (Geneva: Rousseau, 1970) 216.*

Gubler in Russell, *Art Nouveau*.

Villa Père-Jeanneret
Turner, Paul Venable *The Education of Le Corbusier (New York: Garland, 1977).*

Von Moos, *Elements*, 17, 28.

Villa Favre-Jacot
Von Moos, *Elements*, 17.

Cinéma Scala
Banham, *Machine Age*, 260.

Jencks, *Tragic View of Architecture*, 40.

Villa Schwob
Sekler in Walden 51.

Von Moos, *Elements*, 34–5.

La Petite Maison
Le Corbusier, *Une Petite Maison* (Zurich: Editions d'Architecture Artemis, 1981).

Immeuble Clarté
Taylor, Brian Brace, "The City of Refuge: Laboratory or Prototype" paper delivered Le Corbusier Symposium

Von Moos, *Elements*, 90, 152.

Centre Le Corbusier
Crosset, Pierre-Alain, "Conversation with Heidi Weber," *Rassegna 3*, 1979

Maison Guiette
Le Corbusier, *Towards*, 223.

Weissenhof Houses
Benevolo, Leonardo, *History of Modern Architecture*, vol. 2, trans. H. J. Landry (Cambridge: MIT Press, 1971) 51–53.

Le Corbusier, "The Significance of the Garden City" Hubert, Christian, trans., *Oppositions 15/16*, 202.

Berlin Unité
Pawley, Martin *Le Corbusier*, (New York: George Braziller, 1970).

Pavillon de l'Esprit Nouveau
Vidler, Anthony, "The Idea of Unity and Le Corbusier's Urban Form," *Architects Year Book 15, 1968.*

Fishman, Robert *Urban Utopias in the Twentieth Century: Ebenezer Howard, Frank Lloyd Wright and Le Corbusier,* (Cambridge: MIT Press, 1982) 194.

Le Corbusier, *City of Tomorrow.*

Le Corbusier, *The Decorative Art of Today,* Dynnett, James, trans. (Cambridge: MIT Press, 1986) xiv-xix.

Von Moos, *Elements, 148.*

United Nations Headquarters
Œuvre Complète, vol. 4.

Goldberger, Paul *The City Observed, New York: A Guide to the Architecture of Manhattan,* (New York :Vintage Books, 1979) 132.

Von Moos, *Elements, 248.*

Carpenter Center
Sekler, Edouard and William Curtis, *Le Corbusier at Work: The Genesis of the Carpenter Center for the Visual Arts,* (Cambridge: Harvard, 1978).

Curtis, *Ideas and Forms,* 234-8.

Brazillian Ministry of Education
Goodwin, Philip *Brazil Builds (New York: Museum of Modern Art, 1943).*

Frampton, *Modern Architecture,* 254.

Villa Baizeau
Benton, Tim "The Client's Pencil," *Rassegna 3.*

Sadam Hussein Gymnasium
Taj-Eldin, Suzanne, "A Box of Miracles" *Architectural Review,* January, 1987.

Œuvre Complète, vol. 90–3

Centrosoyus
Cohen, Jean-Louis, "Le Corbusier and the Mystique of the USSR," trans. Sartarelli, *Oppositions 23.*

Frampton in *The Le Corbusier Archive, vol. 14.*

National Museum of Western Art
Le Corbusier, *Decorative Art,* 1.

Millowners' Association Building
Von Moos, *Elements,* 97, 103.

Curtis, *Ideas and Forms,* 201.

Maison Mme Manorama Sarabhai
Serenyi in *Le Corbusier Archive , vol. 26.*

Curtis, *Ideas and Forms,* 210.

Von Moos, *Elements,* 96.

Villa Shodhan
Doshi, Balkrishna, "Sarabhai House, Shodhan House" *Global Architecture 32, 1974.*

Serenyi in *Le Corbusier Archive , vol. 26.*

N. C. Mehta Museum
Le Corbusier, *Decorative Art,* 16, 22.

Von Moos, *Elements,* 100

Curtis, *Ideas and Forms,* 203.

Chandigargh and its Buildings
Evenson, Norma, *Chandigarh,* (Berkeley; University of California Press, 1966).

Evenson, Norma, *The Machine and the Grand Design,* (New York: George Braziller, 1969).

Von Moos, Sarin, Drew and Fry in Walden, *The Open Hand .*

Curtis, *Ideas and Forms,* 189-201.

Scully, Vincent *Modern Architecture (New York: George Braziller, 1986) 144-51.*

PHOTO CREDITS

All photos by the author except:

La Fondation Le Corbuiser: 49,59,63, 70,101,102,114,124,131,141,146,147, 160,173,174,175. Drawings: 16, 17, 19, 22,64,79,98,125,127,132,135,142, 145,177.

La Bibliothèque de La Chaux-de-Fonds: 26,28,89,113,117.

Alan Plattus 130; Harvard University 136; D. Speranza and M. Casella 138; Elizabeth Harris 140; Francesco Passante 39,40; Swiss National Tourist Office 120; Caroline Hancock 129; Carol Willis 148,150; Marl Dulaney Glen and James Wallace: 154,158,163,165,167,168,169,170,171; Liz Moule and Stefanos Polyzoides: 157; Peter Serenyi: 156,160.

Maps

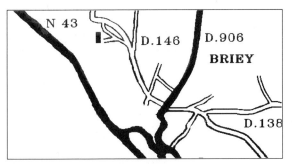

Briey-en-Forêt
Unité d'habitation

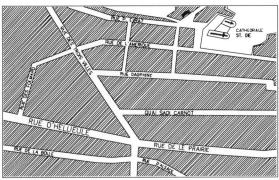

St-Dié
Manufacture Duval

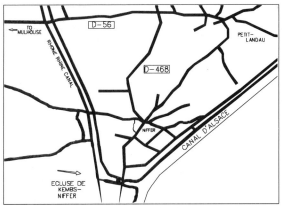

Kembs-Niffer
Écluse de Kembs-Niffer

Firminy-Vert

Marseille
Unité d'habitation

Le Pradet
Villa de Mandrot

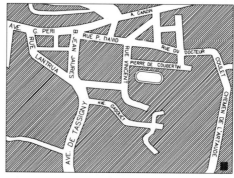

Roquebrune-Cap-Martin
Le Petit Cabanon

Grave of Le Corbusier

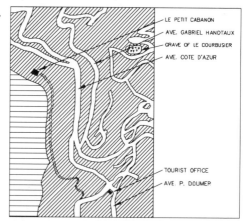

La Palmyre
Villa le Sextant

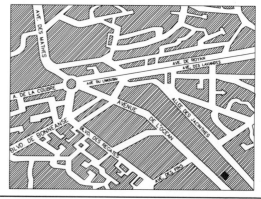

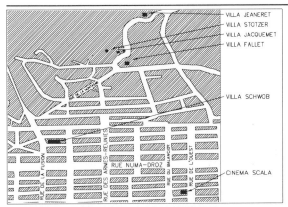

Chaux-de-Fonds
Villa Jeanneret
Villa Stotzer
Villa Jacquemet
Villa Schwob
Cinema Scala

Le Locle
Villa Favre-Jacot

Vevey
La Petite Maison

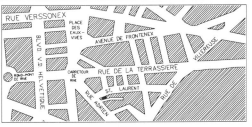

Geneva
Immeuble Clarté

Zurich
Centre Le Corbusier

Antwerp
Maison Guiette

Berlin
Unité d'habitation

Rio de Janeiro
Brazilian Ministry

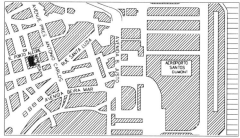

Tokyo
National Museum of
Western Art

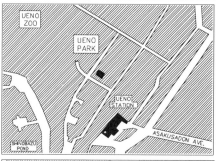

Moscow
Centrosoyus

Ahmedabad
Millowners' Building
Villa Shodhan
N.C. Mehat Museum

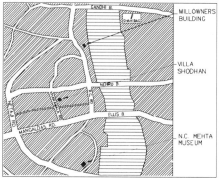

Index

Deborah Gans, an architect in New York City, has taught at the Institute for Architecture and Urban Studies, Parsons School of Design, and the Pratt Institute. She has a degree in Art History from Harvard University and a Masters of Architecture from Princeton University.